MW01596815

The Genus Bazzania In Central And South America

• ANNALES CRYPTOGAMICI et PHYTOPATHOLOGICI •

Volume III

BAZZANIA

ANNALES CRYPTOGAMICI

et PHYTOPATHOLOGICI

(incorporating Annales Bryologici)

edited by

FRANS VERDOORN, Ph.D.

*Managing Editor of Chronica Botanica 'A New Series of Plant Science
Books', etc. Bibliographer Arnold Arboretum of Harvard University,
Bot Adviser, Board for the Nith Indies, Hon Sec, Bot Section,
Intern Union of Biological Sciences, etc*

> *Wij en konnen den Heer en maker van het geheel
> Al met meer verheerlijken, als dat wij in alle zaken,
> hoe klein die ook in onse bloote oogen mogen zijn, als
> zi maar leven en wasdom hebben ontfangen, zijn al
> tuijth it en volmaaktheit, met de uiterste verwondering
> sien uit steken*
>
> *Antoni van Leeuwenhoek*

1946

WALTHAM, MASS., U.S.A.

Published by the Chronica Botanica Company

The GENUS BAZZANIA
in
Central and South America

by

MARGARET FULFORD, Ph.D.

Assistant Professor of Botany, University of Cincinnati,
Curator of Hepatics, Sullivant Moss Society

1946

WALTHAM, MASS., U.S.A.

Published by the Chronica Botanica Company

First published MCMXLVI
By the Chronica Botanica Company
of Waltham, Mass, U. S. A.

New York, N. Y.: G. E. Stechert and Co.,
31 East 10th Street.

San Francisco, Cal.: J. W. Stacey, Inc.,
236-238 Flood Building.

Ottawa, Ont.: Thorburn and Abbott, Ltd.,
115, Sparks Street.

Mexico, D. F.: Libreria Cervantes,
Calle de 57 No 1, Despacho 3; Ap. 2302.

Bogota and Medellin: Libreria Central

Lima: Libreria Internacional del Perú

Santiago de Chile: Libreria Zamorano y Caperan

Rio de Janeiro: Livraria Kosmos,
Rua do Rosario, 135-137; Caixa Postal 3481

Sao Paulo: Livraria Kosmos,
Rua Marconi 91.

Buenos Aires: Acme Agency,
Bartolomé Mitre 552.

London, W. 1: Wm. Dawson and Sons, Ltd.,
43, Weymouth Street.

London, W. C. 1: H. K. Lewis and Co., Ltd.,
136, Gower Street.

Groningen: N. V. Erven P. Noordhoff

Uppsala: Lundequistska Bokh.

Paris VI: Librairie H. Le Soudier,
174, Bvd. St. Germain

Torino: Rosenberg & Sellier,
Via Andrea Doria 14.

Moscow: Mezhdunarodnaja Kniga,
Kuznetski Most 18.

Calcutta, Bombay and Madras: Macmillan and Co., Ltd.

Johannesburg: Central News Agency, Ltd.,
P. O. Box 1033.

Sydney: Angus and Robertson, Ltd.,
89 Castlereagh Street.

Melbourne C. 1.: N. H. Seward, Pty., Ltd.,
457 Bourke Street.

Made and printed in the U. S. A.

PREFACE

The study of Central and South American Hepaticae has been under way for about two hundred years and yet there is probably no other group of plants in that area in which the species are so little known or in which the taxonomy is in a worse state of confusion. This has not come about through any lack of interest in the plants in the field, for there is a long record of accumulated collections, but rather, it is due to the almost complete absence of critical revisions and monographs, without which an orderly taxonomy in any group is impossible. In addition to the usual accumulation of new species over this long period, there has also been an unfortunate rapid and voluminous production of "new species" by a few authors, among them STEPHANI, who described more than 1300 new species of hepaticae from tropical America alone.

Monographic work is tedious and difficult because much of the original material and the obscure older literature is scarcely obtainable, yet the results reveal that the hepatics present as many and at least as varied problems of speciation, variability, distribution, and ecology as are to be found in other groups.

This work is humbly offered as the result of a taxonomic study of one of the larger American genera. The conclusions do not always agree with those of the earlier workers but it is sincerely hoped that those who use this volume will find the interpretations of the groups and species judicious and the text adequate.

• *Annales Cryptogamici et Phytopathologici*, a new serial of which the present volume forms the third part, consists of memoirs (each forming a separate volume) devoted to general and systematic cryptogamy and to phytopathology. — It continues *Annales Bryologici* — Vol. 1, GARRETT's *Root Disease Fungi* was published in 1944, Vol 2, HORSFALL's *Fungicides and their Action* in 1945. Vol 4, CHESTER's *Cereal Rusts as Exemplified by the Leaf Rust of Wheat* and Vol. 5, COPELAND's *Genera Filicum* are in press. — One or two volumes will be published every year at prices ranging from about $4.00 to $6.00.

• *Annales Bryologici*, a journal devoted to the study of mosses and hepatics, of which we published (in the beginning in cooperation with Messrs. Nijhoff) 12 volumes and 4 supplementary volumes, between 1927 and 1939 is now being continued by the *Annales Cryptogamici et Phytopathologici*. Complete sets and single volumes of *Annales Bryologici* are still available at $4.00 a volume.

• The bryological exsiccati formerly issued by DR FRANS VERDOORN: *Bryophyta Arduennae Exsiccata* (dec 1-5, 1927/29), *Hepaticae Selectae et Criticae* (11 series, 1930/39) and *Musci Selecti et Critici* (7 series, 1934/40) have all been sold out.

• *The Chronica Botanica Co.* also publishes "A New Series of Plant Science Books" and "CHRONICA BOTANICA, an international Collection of Studies in the Method, Philosophy, and History of Biology and Agriculture". — A catalogue with full information about these publications will be sent on request

ACKNOWLEDGMENTS

The writer wishes to express her appreciation to all those persons and institutions who have assisted in any way with the accomplishment of this monograph Plants from many herbaria have been studied, and the location of the individual specimens has been designated by the symbols enumerated as follows: (B) Botanical Garden and Museum, Berlin; (C) Field Museum, Chicago, (F) the herbarium of the writer; (G) herbarium of the University of Geneva (material from the STEPHANI Collection), (H) Cryptogamic Herbarium of Harvard University (material from the SCHIFFNER, STEPHANI and TAYLOR Collections), (L) Rijksherbarium of Leiden, (NY) herbarium of the New York Botanical Garden (including material from the MITTEN Collection); (P) the private herbarium of the late F M PAGAN, Puerto Rico; (S) Botanical Garden, Goteberg, Sweden; (V) Natural History Museum, Vienna; (W) United States National Herbarium (including the collections of P. STANDLEY); (Y) herbarium of Yale University (including the private collection of A. W. EVANS)

I also wish to acknowledge the generous cooperation of the Lloyd Library of Cincinnati in the loan of much valuable literature; the assistance and kindness of Dr. D H. LINDER and associates of the Farlow Herbarium during visits there, and the generosity of the New York Botanical Garden in providing facilities for research and several Research Scholarships at various times. Here Miss ROSALIE WEIKERT has been a valuable assistant in the care and handling of the plant material and Mrs LAZELLA SCHWARTEN much aid in the Library.

To Dr. A. W. EVANS of Yale University, for his kind cooperation, for his helpful suggestions and criticisms, and for reading much of the manuscript, the writer is deeply grateful.

The author of this volume and the editor of the *Annales Cryptogamici et Phytopathologici* would like to acknowledge their obligation to the University of Cincinnati, which kindly awarded them a subsidy towards the cost of the illustrations.

to

ALEXANDER W. EVANS

CONTENTS

INTRODUCTION AND HISTORY

The genus *Bazzania* was first proposed by S. F. GRAY (1821, 704 as *Bazzanius*), when he recorded *B. trilobata*, formerly a part of the old genus *Jungermannia*, from England. Ten years later DUMORTIER (1831, 68) proposed the name *Pleuroschisma*, and soon after this, NEES VON ESENBECK (1833a, 96) introduced the name *Herpetium* for *Jungermannia trilobata* and allies; in the year 1845 NEES VON ESENBECK, LINDENBERG and GOTTSCHE (1844-47, 214) adopted the name *Mastigobryum* for the group. They divided the genus into three sections: *A.* Folia integra, including species with entire leaves; *B.* Folia bifida, including species with two-toothed leaves; and *C.* Folia tridenticulata, including species with three-toothed leaves. LINDENBERG and GOTTSCHE (1851) followed this same classification in a monograph of the genus, which at that time included 68 species. Later, STEPHANI (1886, 244), in a synopsis of the genus, classified the species under eleven sections, *Integrifolia, Bidentata, Inaequilatera, Connata, Vittata, Parvistipula, Serrulata, Appendiculata, Fissistipula, Cordistipula* and *Grandistipula*. SCHIFFNER (1893, 101) described the genus under *Bazzania* and transferred the sections which STEPHANI had made for *Mastigobryum* to this genus. Fifteen years later STEPHANI published his monograph of the genus *Mastigobryum* (1908, 413) in which he rearranged his former classification within the genus, raising three of his earlier sections to subgeneric rank and adding a fourth under which he included seven of the remaining sections. The Section *Connata* was here divided and included as subdivisions of the Sections *Grandistipula* and *Serrulata*. His revised classification follows:

> *A.*   *Integrifolia*
> *B.*   *Bidentata*
> *C.*   *Tridentata*
>   *1.*   *Parvistipula*
>   *2*   *Grandistipula*
>   *α connata*
>   *β libera*
>   *3.*   *Serrulata*
>   *α connata*
>   *β libera*
>   *4.*   *Appendiculata*
>   *5.*   *Fissistipula*
>   *6.*   *Cordistipula*
>   *7.*   *Vittata*
> *D*   *Inaequilatera*

A study of the American species (and 122 type specimens have been examined), indicates that in so far as the American species are concerned, the groupings of species which STEPHANI made were sometimes incorrectly assembled, and what is more important, were, in the case of several of the groups, purely artificial segregations based on characteristics so variable that one species might be included in several sections. For this reason it seems advisable to revise the classification to more nearly conform with the natural groups within the genus. One of STEPHANI's subgenera and several of his sections have been discarded and one of his older sections revived. The reasons for these changes together with the characteristics of the subgenera and sections are discussed in the following.

Integrifolia — a subgenus in which the species have leaves which are *not* three-toothed or two-toothed, although the margins may be entire, serrulate or even dentate. Neither of the American species included here by STEPHANI actually belongs here, for both of them possess some leaves with three teeth more or less well developed; and in addition, one of the species, *M. Schwaneckianum,* has the underleaf connate with one leaf. There are no representatives of this subgenus in America, and it may be that an examination of the foreign species of this group will show that they also, should be included in the sections of the Subgenus *Tridentata.*

Bidentata — a subgenus made up of species in which the leaves are bidentate. This is a natural group of species which can be easily distinguished from those of the other subgenera. The individual species show a closer relationship to one another than to any of the species within the other groupings.

Tridentata — a subgenus made up of species in which the leaves are three-toothed (sometimes only faintly so). The vast majority of the American species belong to this group. STEPHANI's classification includes the following seven sections:

1. *Parvistipula* — made up of species with small underleaves. The American species which he included here are, for the most part, small, depauperate plants of species included in the following section. Only one, *M. tricuspidatum,* is a distinct species. The section has no distinctive characteristics except size of underleaves, and this character alone is untrustworthy as a basis for segregation of a section.

2. *Grandistipula* — made up of species having leaves without a vitta or conspicuous auricles or appendages, and the teeth with entire margins. Two subdivisions are included by STEPHANI, *libera,* in which the underleaves are free from the leaves, and *connata,* in which the underleaves are connate with the leaves to a greater or lesser degree. The members of the *connata* group show a closer relationship to the members of the next section than to the *libera* group, and have been transferred. The members of the *libera* group, form a natural, closely related unit.

3. *Serrulata* — a section characterized by having the leaf margins more or less serrulate or spinose in the apical part. This section likewise is made up of two groups, *libera* and *connata*. The serrulate character is present to some degree throughout the group, but it is very variable and it is not always so distinctive as one might wish. All of the American species of this section also have the underleaves connate with one or both leaves; and at least some of the species of the *libera* group are actually connate It is my opinion that the species having the underleaves connate with one or both leaves form a closely related developmental group, and should be recognized as such, as STEPHANI did in his earlier classification (1886, 245) Since the serrulate condition of the leaf margins seems usually to be associated with the connate condition of the underleaves, but since not all of the species with connate underleaves have conspicuously serrulate leaf margins it seems wise to redefine the group and to discard the Section *Serrulata* in favor of the Section *Connata* in order to avoid confusion.

   This Section would then include all connate species in the Subgenus (and also *M. Schwaneckianum* from the Subgenus *Integrifolia*). The species of the *libera* group — if the leaves and underleaves actually are free, a point which should be carefully investigated for all of the species in question — belong in other already established groups.

4. *Appendiculata* — made up of species in which the ventral bases of the leaves are auriculate or appendiculate. This is a very distinct and natural segregation in which the characteristic tendencies of the group are exhibited in varying degrees by the members.

5. *Fissistipula* — including species in which the leaves are not serrulate along the apical margin, and are without ventral appendages. The underleaves are deeply incised or long-toothed. The group appears to be natural and distinct. It is not represented in the Americas.

6. *Cordistipula* — including species with more or less cordate underleaves. The group is wholly artificial, since for the most part, it is made up of robust plants of species also included under the *Grandistipula* section, or rather slender plants of species belonging to the *Appendiculata* section. The Section has been discarded and the species for the most part reduced to synonymy in other sections.

7. *Vittata* — made up of species in which the leaves all have conspicuous vittas. This seems to be a natural assemblage of closely related species easily distinguished from those of the other sections.

Inaequilatera — the species of this subgenus have already been transferred to the genus *Acromastigum* (EVANS, 1934).

As here revised, the organization of the genus *Bazzania*, based on a study of the American species, includes the following subdivisions:

Bidentatae
Tridentatae
    Grandistipulae
    Connatae
    Appendiculatae
    Fissistipulae
    Vittatae

Of the 444 species recognized in STEPHANI's Monograph (1908-09; 1924), 115 species are reported from the Americas. Since that time other species have been added. Of the 122 species and varieties studied, 71 were reduced to synonomy, and one was transferred to another genus; 22 species and varieties were not available.

The species of North America north of Mexico have already been treated in detail (FULFORD, 1936), so are not again included in this paper, since the southern boundary of the United States appears to mark the geographic boundary of the species of temperate North America on the south, and the tropical and subtropical species on the north.

CHARACTERS OF THE GENUS BAZZANIA

Bazzania

Bazzania S. F. Gray, Nat Arr Br. Pl. 1: 704. 1821 (as *Bazzanius*).
Pleuroschisma Dumort., Syll. Jungerm. 68. 1831.
Herpetium Nees, Nat. eur. Leberm. 1 96. 1833.
Herpetium, sect *Mastigobryum* Nees, Nat. eur Leberm. 3· 43 1838.
Mastigobryum Nees, Lindenb. & Gottsche, Syn. Hep. 214. 1845.

Plants in large tufts or depressed mats, bright green to olive-green, golden yellow, reddish or brown; stems filiform to robust, the vegetative branches of two sorts, leafy and flagelliform; the leafy branches from the ventral half of lateral segments, very rarely ventral, forming apparent dichotomies, the angle more or less constant for a species, in most cases less than 90 degrees, the incomplete leaf undivided, acute; cells of the leafy axis showing little differentiation internally, mostly thick-walled, the cortical layer similar to those of the medulla but of shorter cells, sometimes deeply pigmented with brown; the flagelliform branches intercalary, arising mostly singly in the axils of underleaves, long, filiform, often branched, their branches intercalary, both lateral and ventral: rhizoids colorless, arising from the leaves of the flagelliform branches, the lower portions of the female bracts, and in some cases from the underleaves: the leaves incubous, alternate (rarely opposite), obliquely inserted, the line of insertion straight to strongly curved in its upper half, distant to imbricated, plane to deflexed, unsymmetrical, ovate to lanceolate, the dorsal base often strongly convex to cordate, the ventral base frequently more or less auricled, the apex in most species truncate, two- to three-toothed (in some four-toothed), in a few undivided; leaf margins in most cases entire, sometimes serrate to spinose-dentate, sometimes ciliate or appendiculate at the ventral base; the leaf cells quadrate to hexagonal in outline and more or less uniform except at the base where they are larger, or differentiated, with 6 to 12 series through the center of the leaf much enlarged, often of a different content, forming a vitta; the trigones very small to large and well developed, often coalescing; the cell lumina rounded, or angular-rounded to stellate; the cuticle smooth to verruculose: the underleaves distant to imbricated, quadrate, elongate or ovate, sometimes cordate at the base, the line of attachment transverse, slightly oblique, or recurved, sometimes connate with leaves on one or both sides, the apex truncate, rounded-entire to two- to four-toothed or lobed, or variously incised, the margins entire, crenulate, spinose-dentate to ciliate; the cells usually similar to those of the apical region of the leaf, all alike or those of the margin hyaline: dioicous, the male and female branches intercalary, in the axils of the underleaves; the male branches few to several on a stem, catkin-like, the bracteoles slightly smaller than the bracts, the bracts in five or more series, ovate, concave to subcomplicate-convolute; the apices truncate, bilobed to bispinose, rarely denticulate to entire; antheridia solitary or in pairs: female branches solitary, few to several on a stem; the bracts and bracteoles scarcely differentiated, in four or more series, closely imbricated, the innermost series largest, orbicular-ovate to ovate-lanceolate, the apex at least somewhat lobed, often two-, three-, or four-divided, the margins crenulate to laciniate-ciliate, the cells all alike or differentiated: the perianth to 6 mm. long, ovoid-cylindrical, terete below, becoming three-keeled in the upper part, contracted at the mouth, of one layer of cells above, one to several layers below, the mouth of three ciliate to dentate lobes, usually contracted · the capsule oblong-ovoid, the wall usually of five layers of cells, the outermost layer with brown thickenings appearing as knots along the vertical walls, the innermost layer with brown thickenings arranged as half-rings or bars on the inner tangential walls; the capsule stalk with a cortical layer of 16 large cells and a medulla of many smaller cells; the spores small, brown; elaters long, slender, bispiral; vegetative reproduction by means of vegetative shoots from the cells of ordinary, as well as caducous leaves and underleaves.

The plants of the West Indies, Mexico, Central America and South America give evidence of the same wide range of variation within a species as was pointed out (FULFORD, 1936) for the species of the United States and Canada.

As in the case of the latter, these modifications seem to be of two sorts: the simpler, and by far the more common type, include those "temporary modifications" which have to do with the adaptations which occur in the individual plant in response to the conditions of the environment, and have been enumerated and discussed by BUCH (1928; 1929) in his studies of *Scapania* and *Lophozia;* the other sort seem to be, in part at least, hereditary and perhaps might be referred to as the various biotypic or genotypic expressions of the comprehensive Linnaean species. These "temporary modifications" include such characteristics as the variation in the amount of thickening in the secondary membranes, the degree of pigmentation of the cell membrane, the length of the internodes on the stem, and the size of the underleaves. Without doubt all of the characters listed above are influenced by the heredity of the species in question, but within limits, they may be strongly modified by environmental factors, particularly by the substrate, moisture, humidity, and the intensity of light.

The writer has attempted to classify the species of *Bazzania* from the Americas with these concepts in mind. In many instances the results do not agree with those of earlier writers, particularly those of STEPHANI, but a study of all of the type material available has indicated that there are several instances in which he overlooked some of the most outstanding characteristics of the plant when making his classification. No doubt other workers will likewise find inconsistencies and errors of judgment incorporated here. However, we like to agree with SPRUCE (1890, 116) when he states that, "in a genus where the numerous species are separated by such minute characters, two equally conscientious observers will often differ as to which are species and which are varieties".

DESCRIPTION OF THE SPECIES

The arrangement of the species follows in a general way that of STEPHANI in the *Species Hepaticarum* (1908-09; 1924) and the unpublished *Icones*, and in part both his subgeneric and sectional names, with feminine endings have been used. As has already been noted, p. 2, in some instances the characteristics of a species were not the same as the characteristics of the subdivision under which STEPHANI placed it, so that a transfer to a more suitable group has been necessary; other changes were necessary because certain of the sections, the *Parvistipula* and *Cordistipula* were purely artificial segregations based on extremely variable characters; while still other changes have resulted from an attempt to bring together the members of a closely related unit.

All of the American species of the genus *Bazzania* belong to two subgenera*, the *Bidentatae* and the *Tridentatae*. The latter group is further subdivided into the sections *Grandistipulae*, *Connatae*, *Appendiculatae*, and *Vittatae*.

Key to the Subgenera

Leaves predominantly two-toothed . . . . Bidentatae (p 8)
Leaves three-toothed, occasionally only faintly so . Tridentatae (p 37)

---

*The American species which STEPHANI included in his Subgenus *Integrifolia* actually belong to the Subgenus *Tridentatae*, see p. 2, *M. diversicuspe* is a member of the section *Grandistipulae*, p. 38, and *M. Schwaneckianum* a member of the *Connatae*, p. 103

SUBGENUS BIDENTATAE

Leaves predominantly bidentate, rarely tridentate or acute; underleaves attached in a straight line, not cordate at the base.

The species form a well defined subgenus, all of them possessing the characters listed above. The American members are apparently restricted to the tropics and subtropics, for there are no records for any of the species in the temperate zones. The leaves of *B. ambigua* of Canada and the northern United States are often two-toothed but most of the plants have some three-toothed leaves, for the species is definitely a member of the subgenus *Tridentatae*, closely allied to *B. tricrenata* and *B. denudata*. Of the seven species found in tropical America, *B. bidens*, *B. cuneistipula*, and *B gracilis* are widespread in distribution, while the others seem to be restricted locally: *B. phyllobola* to northern South America, *B. Herminieri* to Guadeloupe, *B. platystipula* to Jamaica and Puerto Rico, and *B. roraimensis* to British Guiana.

Key to the Species

I. Stems coarse thread-like to delicate filiform, slender.
  2. Plants forming mats of very slender, dark brown, filiform stems, often without leaves.
    3. Leaves vittate, caducous   . 7 **B. gracilis** (p 30)
    3. Leaves without a vitta, persistent (rarely absent), often reduced and inconspicuous, forms of . .   . 2 **B. phyllobola** (p 11)
  2. Plants forming mats of coarser, green to brown stems, at least some leaves usually present, deflexed.
    3 Leaves in part caducous.
      4. Leaves with a vitta, the cell walls thin, the trigones small; underleaves small, distant .   . 7 **B gracilis** (p 30)
      4. Leaves without a well differentiated vitta, the cell walls thin, the trigones very large, with convex sides, underleaves large, approximate to imbricated . .   5 **B. platystipula** (p 25)
    3 Leaves persistent
      4 Underleaves large, approximate to imbricated; cells of the leaves with thin walls and large, rounded trigones,
                                   5. **B. platystipula** (p. 25)
      4. Underleaves small, distant.
        5 Underleaves orbicular, entire or nearly so; trigones of the leaves large, rounded .   . 6 **B. roraimensis** (p 27)
        5 Underleaves trapezoidal to subquadrate, two- to four-lobed at the apex   . . . . 4. **B. cuneistipula** (p. 19)
1 Stems not filiform, larger, the leaves spreading.
  2. Plants with leaves narrow-elongate to elongate-ovate.
    3 Margins of the teeth entire; underleaves subquadrate, the apical margins often faintly two- to four-lobed . 1. **B. bidens** (p. 9)
    3. Margins of the teeth usually crenulate; underleaves with the margins variously and deeply incised, toothed, and lobed,
                                2. B. phyllobola (p. 11)

2. Plants with leaves unsymmetrically ovate
    3   Leaves with a vitta of larger, thin-walled cells with conspicuous trigones, the teeth large
    4. Teeth equal, the cells thin-walled, trigones small,
                                                7. **B. gracilis** (p 30)
    4   Teeth unequal, the acroscopic tooth larger, the cell walls thin, the trigones large . . . . . . 3 **B. Herminieri** (p. 15)
3. Leaf cells not differentiated, the teeth short, subequal; under-leaves trapezoidal to subquadrate, usually lobed at the apex,
                                                4. **B cuneistipula** (p 19)

1. **Bazzania bidens** (Nees) Trevis. Mem. Ist. Lomb. 13: 415. 1877.
Jungermannia tridens? Montagne, Ann Sci Nat. Bot. II. 3: 216. 1835, not Nees
Herpetium stoloniferum var *bidens* Nees in Montagne, Ann. Sci Nat. Bot. II. 14: 333. 1840
Mastigobryum bidens Gottsche & Lindenberg, in G. L. & N., Syn. Hep. 228. 1845.

Plants in mats, depressed to ascending, mostly large, yellow-green to brownish, becoming deeply pigmented with brown in the older portions: stems slender to robust, to 5 cm. or more in length, with leaves to 3 5 mm. broad; in longitudinal section the cells elongate, the medullary to 0.17 mm., the cortical shorter, both averaging 24μ in diameter, the vertical walls uniformly thickened and containing frequent pits, the end walls thin; lateral branches frequent, mostly 5 mm. apart, diverging at a wide angle; flagelli-form branches numerous, long; rhizoids colorless, from the bases of the leaves of the flagelliform branches · the leaf insertion curved in its upper part; leaves distant to subimbricated, long, linear lanceolate, plane or only a little deflexed, 1.5 mm. - 2 mm long, 0.3 mm. - 0.5 mm. broad at the base, little narrowed to the trans-versely truncate, bidentate apex; the dorsal margin convex from a straight base, the ventral margin straight to slightly concave, the base scarcely dilated, the apex two-toothed, the teeth very large, acute, mostly six to eight cells long and three to six cells wide, often divergent, the sinus deep, acute, the margins entire; leaf cells thin-walled, the trigones large, with bulging sides, mostly coalesced, the cell lumina angular-rounded, the cuticle faintly verruculose; cells of the apical portion 32μ × 32μ, of the interior larger, and of the basal portion 42μ - 64μ × 32μ, a vitta not differentiated: under-leaves small, distant, subquadrate, a little wider than the stem, attached in a straight line, 0.35 mm. - 0 40 mm. long × 0.31 mm - 0.35 mm. wide, the lateral margins nearly straight, entire, the apex undulate, variously toothed or lobed, the cells as in the apical por-tion of the leaf · leaves of the flagelliform branches scale-like, ovate, acute to bifid · male branches frequent, several on a stem; the bracts concave, ovate, bifid, crenulate, the cells to 48μ long × 24μ wide, the bracteoles similar, smaller; antheridia in pairs. female branches solitary, several on a stem (very poorly preserved) ; bracts of the intermediate series divided to one-third into usually three laciniae, the margins serrate to laciniate: sporophyte not seen.

HABITAT: Over rocks, logs, and on trunks of living trees.
The distinguishing characteristics of the species are its rather robust habit, the yellow-brown color, and the plane, long, linear-

Fig 1. — *Bazzania bidens* (Nees) Trevis. — 1. Portion of a stem, ventral
view, × 12. 2. Underleaves, × 30   3 A cell from the apical portion of a
leaf, × 400   4. Portion of a stem and leaves, dorsal view, × 40   5. Leaves,
× 25. 6 A tooth of a leaf, × 200   7 Cells from the dorsal margin of a leaf
near the base, × 200. 8. Cells of the basal portion of a leaf, × 200 9. Underleaf, × 60. 10. Portion of a transverse section of a stem, × 310. 11 Female
bracts of an intermediate series, (immature) × 30. Nos. 1-3 drawn from the
type material from French Guiana; 4-11 from material collected by EVANS
in Puerto Rico

lanceolate, strongly bidentate leaves which are usually approximate. The plants are often quite brittle. (FIGURE 1, nos. 1-11).

While there is considerable variation in the size of the plants and the size of the trigones of the leaves, the leaves are always narrow, elongate, and the trigones always large with convex sides (see FIG. 1, nos. 1, 3, 5 and 6)

The female branches were poorly developed and in a poor state of preservation in all the examples available. The bracts of the intermediate series are broadly ovate and are to one-third divided into two or three laciniae (FIG. 1, no. 11). The lateral margins are serrate, dentate or laciniate. This agrees in general with STEPHANI's figure in the *Icones, Mastigobryum* no. 25. He shows the bracts of the innermost series as being two-thirds divided into two, dentate-ciliate laciniae. Unfortunately, bracts of this series were too poorly developed for comparison.

SPRUCE (1885, 371) described and later distributed in the *Hepaticae Spruceana*, plants from Brasil as *B. bidens*, which are of an entirely different habit from those of the type collected by LEPRIEUR in French Guiana. SPRUCE's plants represent a large form of *B. gracilis* and are discussed further under that species.

DISTRIBUTION. D o m i n i c a . without locality, Elliott, cited by Stephani (1908, 440). — G u a d e l o u p e without locality, l'Herminier, cited by Stephani (1908, 440); without locality, Duss, cited by Stephani (1908, 440). Duss 1096 (NY) should be referred to *B. Herminieri*. — M a r t i n i q u e : without locality, Husnot, Pl. Antilles, 241b (H,G) Some of the packets also contain a little *B. longistipula* (NY). — P u e r t o R i c o . without locality, Schwanecke (G); without locality, Sintenis 37, cited by Stephani (1888a, 279); El Yunque, Luquillo Mountains, Evans 51 (Y, NY); Sierra de Naguabo, Shafer 3750 (NY); El Yunque, Pagán 494 (NY). — F r e n c h G u i a n a : without locality, Leprieur, the type (G); without locality, Hb Hooker (NY). — P e r u : without locality, Lechler (G). — G u i a n a : without locality, Montagne (NY).

The specimens from Brasil distributed by SPRUCE in *Hepaticae Spruceana:* Amaz. et And. as *B. bidens* are *B. gracilis*.

REFERENCES. Lindenberg and Gottsche (1851, 87, pl. 15), Hampe and Gottsche (1852, 346); Husnot (1875, 3); Spruce (1885, 371), Stephani (1888a, 279; 1908, 439, Icones, Mastigobryum no 25), Bescherelle (1893, 186); Pagán (1939, 38).

2. **Bazzania phyllobola** Spruce, Trans. & Proc. Bot. Soc. [Edinburgh] 15 · 372. 1885.

Mastigobryum phyllobolum Stephani, Spec. Hep 3. 439 1908.
Bazzania bidens var *dissodonta* Spruce, op. cit p. 371.
Bazzania dissodonta Spruce ms.
Mastigobryum dissodontum Stephani, Trans. Linnean Soc. Bot. II. 6 98. 1901-05.

Plants slender, brownish green to deep reddish brown in the older portions: stems to 6 cm. long, with leaves to 3 mm. broad, depressed to ascending: stem cells in longitudinal section elongate, to 0.17 mm. long, the cortical shorter, both averaging 15μ in diameter, the vertical walls uniformly thickened and containing frequent pits, the end walls thin; lateral branches frequent, 5 mm.

or more apart, diverging at a wide angle; flagelliform branches frequent, long; rhizoids colorless, scarce, on the bases of leaves of the flagelliform branches · leaf insertion little curved in its upper part; the leaves approximate to subimbricated on well developed plants, deflexed when dry, unsymmetrical, elongate-ovate, ascendent, 0.75 mm. - 1.5 mm. long, 0.5 mm. broad at the base, narrowed a little to the transversely truncate, bidentate apex; the dorsal margin arched from a scarcely rounded base, covering approximately one-half the stem, the ventral margin nearly straight, the base scarcely dilated, the apex two-toothed, the teeth large, acute, six to eight cells long, five to seven cells broad, the sinus deep, acute, the margins crenulate, serrate or even shortly denticulate; leaf cells thin-walled, the cell lumina rounded, the trigones small, conspicuous, rarely coalesced, the cuticle verruculose; the cells of the apical region mostly $20\mu \times 20\mu$, those of the base 36μ - $40\mu \times 24\mu$, a vitta not differentiated: underleaves distant to approximate, more or less quadrate in outline, attached in a straight line, little broader than the stem, mostly 0.26 mm. - 0.32 mm. long and broad, the apex irregularly divided into irregular, long or short, blunt to acute teeth, the lateral margins entire, or variously toothed, the cells mostly as in the apical part of the leaf; leaves of the flagelliform branches scale-like, ovate, acute to shortly bifid · female branches frequent, solitary, one to several on a stem; the bracts and bracteoles similar, the outer series small, ovate, one-third divided into two blunt teeth, the lateral margins serrate; the intermediate and innermost series (immature) ovate, to one-half or more divided into two or three long, slender, laciniae, one or two cells broad, twelve or more cells long, the lateral margins serrate to ciliate · perianth (immature) mouth densely long-ciliate: male bracts and sporophytes not seen.

HABITAT · On tree bases, forests in the mountains.

The distinguishing characteristics of the species are its greenish brown to reddish stems, the deeply two-toothed leaves, the crenulate to denticulate margins of the teeth, or long, reddish stems with smaller, scattered, acute, two- or three-toothed leaves of various sizes; the strongly and irregularly toothed underleaves (sometimes entire on filiform stems); and the female bracts divided in the upper part into long, slender, ciliate laciniae. (FIG. 2, nos. 1-19).

FIG 2. — *Bazzania phyllobola* Spruce — 1, 2, 3 Portions of stems, ventral view, × 30 4. A cell from the apical portion of a leaf, × 400. 5. A lacinia from a female bract of the innermost series, × 100. 6. Cells of a lacinia of this series, × 310. 7. Cells from a portion of the mouth of the perianth, × 310 8. Outermost female bract, × 30. 9 Portion of a stem, ventral view, × 30. 10 Dorsal side of stem to show leaf attachment, × 30 11 A cell from the apical region of a leaf, × 400. 12 Apical tooth of a leaf, × 310. 13. Cells from the dorsal margin of a leaf, × 310 14 Cells from the base of a leaf, × 310. 15. Cells from the apical portion of an underleaf, × 310 16 Female bracts of an intermediate series, × 30 17. Female bracts (immature) of the innermost series, × 30. 18 A lacinia from a bract of this series, × 100. 19. Portion of the perianth mouth (immature), × 100. Nos. 1-8 drawn from a portion of the type material; 9-19 drawn from the material of *B. dissodonta* Spruce ms. collected by SPRUCE on Mt. Guayrapurina.

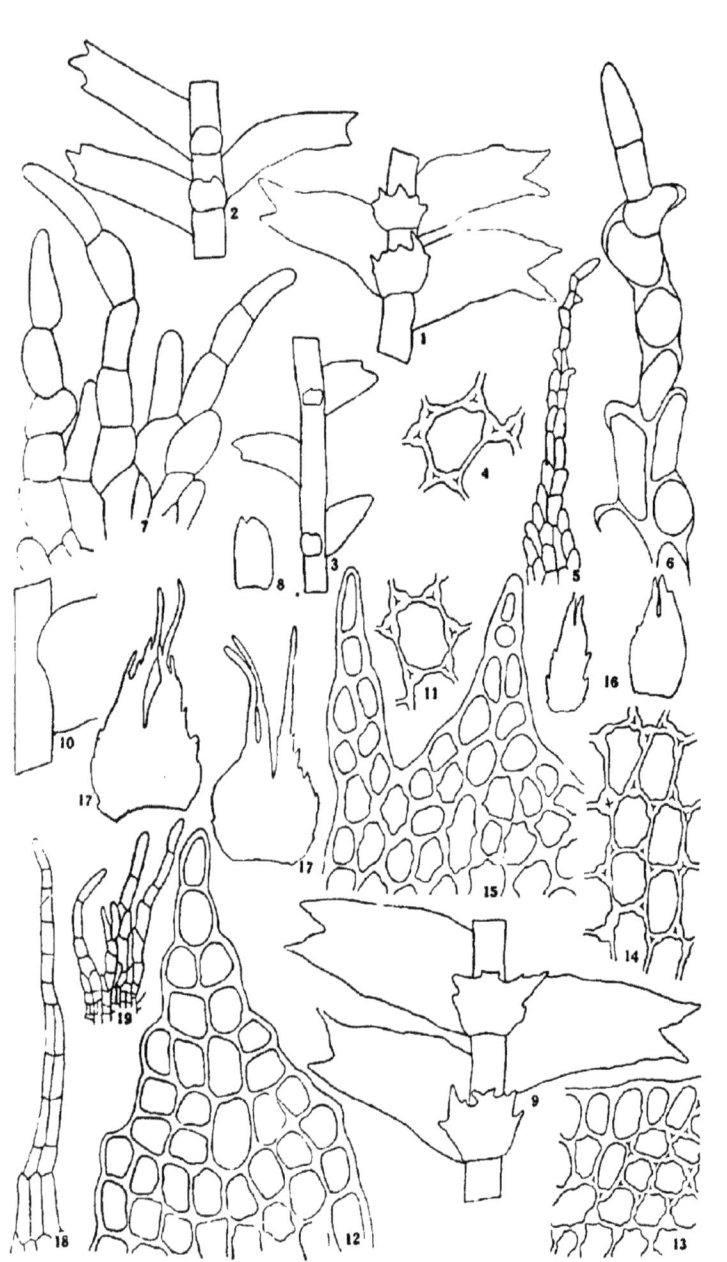

The original material of *B. phyllobola* distributed by SPRUCE is made up mostly of very long, red brown stems with distant leaves (FIG. 2, nos. 1-4), some of which may have been caducous, because stems without leaves except at the tips occasionally occur. The leaves are mostly linear, shortly bilobed or acute, and usually small. On a few of the stems occasional leaves are well developed and identical with those of *B. bidens* var *dissodonta* in shape, cell structure, and configuration of the apical margin (compare FIG. 2, nos. 1 and 9). The underleaves, for the most part, are very small and entire or faintly toothed or lobed on the apical margin, but all gradations up to the large, toothed sort, characteristic of *B bidens* var. *dissodonta* can be found with little difficulty on stems where the leaves are more or less well developed. Flagelliform branches are produced in abundance and very often become leafy In addition, the main stems with well developed leaves may become smaller, the leaves lose their characteristic shape and become linear-bifid or acute, and the underleaves become entire or nearly so, so that the stems assume a flagelliform appearance. Many of the plants, even those with few leaves, had produced several female branches. The archegonia were unfertilized and the bracts had not matured The intermediate and innermost bracts are ovate, divided into long, slender, ciliate laciniae, and are identical with those of *B. bidens* var. *dissodonta* (compare FIG. 2, nos 5-8 with nos 16-19). They are in agreement with those of STEPHANI's *Icones, Mastigobryum* nos. 28 and 33 According to the labels, SPRUCE collected both his *B. phyllobola* and *B. bidens* var. *dissodonta* in the Peruvian Andes on Mt. Guayrapurina

B. bidens var. *dissodonta* (FIG. 2, nos. 9-19) represents the more typical, normally developed aspect of the species Here the plants are large, conspicuously leafy, greenish brown instead of red-brown, and only rarely do leafy stems become flagelliform in appearance. The leaves are unsymmetrically ovate, well developed, and deeply two-toothed. The teeth are large, more or less spreading, and the margins are characteristically crenulate or even denticulate. Three-toothed leaves are occasionally present. The leaf cells do not differ from those of the leaves of *B. phyllobola* The enlarged cells of the interior suggest a vitta, although they are not particularly conspicuous.

The underleaves are very characteristic. They are broader than the stem, irregularly and deeply toothed and lobed, and tend to be quadrate in outline.

The female branches, which are numerous, possess bracts (immature), which are ovate in outline and to one-half divided into long, ciliate laciniae. A few of the plants in the mat are smaller, with more distant leaves and are more nearly like the original material of *B. phyllobola*. The perianth mouth is long ciliate.

The species, when well developed, is similar in many ways to *B. bidens* but can readily be distinguished from it because of the crenulate to denticulate margins of the teeth of the leaves, and the variously incised and toothed underleaves. The female bracts of the two species are very similar. The small forms of the species are similar to *B. gracilis* but can usually be distinguished by the absence of a well defined vitta in the small leaves.

DISTRIBUTION. B r i t i s h G u i a n a : without locality, McConnell & Quelch as *M. dissodontum*, cited by Stephani (1901-05, 98). — B r a s i l : without locality, Ule (H); Santos, Horeau, cited by Stephani (1908, 439). — C o l o m b i a , cited by Stephani (1901-05, 98). — P e r u Mt Campana, Spruce as *B bidens* var. *dissodonta*, cited by Spruce (1885, 371), Mt Guayrapurina, Spruce as *B. dissodonta*, Hepat. Spruc. (NY); Mt. Guayrapurina, Spruce, the type, Hepat. Spruc (NY)

The plants collected by STANDLEY 48091 in Costa Rica (Herzog 1938, 19) are *B. gracilis*.

REFERENCES: Herzog (1938, 19); Stephani (1886, 134, 1901-05, 98; *Icones, Mastigobryum* nos 28, 33).

3   Bazzania Herminieri (Steph.) comb nov.

Mastigobryum Herminieri Gottsche in HUSNOT, Rev. Bryol. 2. 3 1875. (nomen nudum), in STEPHANI, Hedwigia 25: 8. pl. 4. fig. 3-6. 1886.

Plants growing in depressed to ascending mats, mostly large, dark brown in the older portions, light yellow-green to brown at the growing tips: stems slender to robust, to 10 cm. or more long, with leaves 2 mm. - 2.5 mm. wide, mostly ascending to erect; in longitudinal section the cells elongate, the medullary cells averaging 0.18 mm long, the vertical walls uniformly thickened and containing frequent pits, the end walls thin, the cortical cells shorter, the walls thicker, deeply pigmented with brown, both averaging 18μ in diameter: lateral branches infrequent, diverging at a wide angle; flagelliform branches frequent, long; the line of leaf-insertion curved in its upper half; the leaves imbricated, plane to convex, often becoming strongly deflexed on drying, — so that dried stems appear to be laterally compressed, —-unsymmetrically ovate, more or less falcate, to 1 mm. long, 0.6 mm. - .72 mm. wide at the base, narrowing to 0.3 mm. at the bidentate apex: the dorsal margin strongly convex from a curved base, the ventral margin straight to concave, the apex two-toothed, the acroscopic tooth the larger, acute, mostly eight to ten cells broad at the base, six to twelve cells long, widely spreading, the sinuses lunulate to deep and acute, the margins entire, somewhat undulate; leaf-cells of two sorts, those of the marginal and apical portions more or less isodiametric, averaging 18μ, the trigones large with bulging sides, often becoming coalesced, the cell cavity angular-rounded; those of the median and basal portions of the leaf elongate, forming a distinct vitta near the base, averaging 50μ long $\times$ 25μ wide: the cuticle verruculose: underleaves attached in a straight line, distant, becoming subimbricated near the growing point, subquadrate, as broad or broader than the stem, 0.32 mm. - 0.4 mm. wide, 0.24 mm. - 0.54 mm. long, the apex faintly to deeply two- to four-lobed, the lobes rounded-entire, the sinuses mostly narrow-acute, the lateral margins straight to convex, undulate: leaves of the flagelliform branches scale-like, convex, to 0.18 mm. long, ovate, the apex obtuse to bidentate: male branches usually several on a stem; the bracteoles small, rectangular in outline, somewhat convex from below, 0.4 mm. -

0.45 mm. long × 0.24 mm. - 0.3 mm. wide, the lateral margins straight, entire, the apex faintly to strongly two- to four-lobed, with shallow, acute sinuses; the bracts larger, broadly quadrate-orbicular, strongly convex from below, averaging 0.56 mm. long, to 0.7 mm. wide, the lateral margins bulging, entire to crenulate, the apex with two to four short teeth and lunulate to acute sinuses; the cells of the apical portion with large, confluent trigones, the cell-lumina stellate, those near the base rectangular, thick-walled, the trigones not conspicuous; antheridia usually in pairs: female branches frequent, solitary, one to several on a stem; the outer-most bracts averaging 0.48 mm. long × 0.32 mm. broad, the margins entire, the apex mostly two-lobed, the cells elongate except at the margin, thick-walled; the intermediate bracts larger, mostly 0.72 mm. long × 0.5 mm. wide, the upper third divided into three or four narrow, mostly blunt, entire laciniae, the lateral margins entire to obscurely dentate, the cells elongate, $30\mu \times 12\mu$ in the upper portion, $45\mu \times 18\mu$ near the base, thick-walled, often irregularly so, the trigones large: perianth to 6 mm. long, ovoid-cylindrical, contracted at the mouth, of one layer of cells throughout, at the mouth divided into numerous, unequal, mostly narrow, short to long-pointed laciniae, the margins entire to serrate, the cells 20μ - 36μ long, mostly 15μ wide, the walls thick, cells of the basal portion mostly $65\mu \times 18\mu$, the walls unevenly thickened: sporophyte not seen.

HABITAT: "Abundant on rocks", HUSNOT, Pl. de Antilles; on rocks, tree bases and stones.

The distinguishing characteristics of the plant are its medium size, the elongate, vittate leaves which tend to be slightly falcate and which are mostly unequally two-toothed at the apex; the thin cell walls and conspicuous, often confluent trigones; and the quadrate mostly four-lobed underleaves. (FIG. 3, nos. 1-20).

The leaf apex is quite variable. It is usually unequally two-toothed, with the acroscopic tooth the larger, but in some of the leaves the teeth tend to become equal or to disappear completely.

The vitta is well defined. It consists of five or six rows of cells running through the middle of the leaf from the base half-way to the apex. It is more or less sharply distinct from the cells of the ventral margin because of the difference in the size of the two, but the distinction between it and the cells of the dorsal margin is less

FIG. 3 — *Bazzania Herminieri* (Steph.) Fulford. — 1. Portion of stem, dorsal view, × 30 2. Portion of stem, ventral view, × 12. 3. Leaf, × 30. 4. Underleaves, × 30. 5. Cells from the apical portion of an underleaf, × 260. 6. Apical tooth of leaf, × 260. 7. Cells from dorsal margin of leaf, × 260. 8. Cells from the ventral margin of leaf, × 260. 9. Cells from the base (vitta) of a leaf, × 260. 10. Portion of a longitudinal section of a stem, × 260. 11 Portion of a cross-section of stem, × 260. 12. Female bract of the outermost series, × 30. 13. Female bracts of intermediate series, × 30. 14. Female bract of the innermost series, × 100. 15. Apical tooth of bract, × 100. 16 Portion of mouth of perianth, × 30. 17. Portion of mouth of perianth, × 100. 18. Cell from near the base of perianth, × 260. 19. Male bracteole, × 30 20. Male bracts, × 30. Nos. 1-9, 11-13, 19, and 20 drawn from material of Husnot, Pl. Antilles, no. 211; nos. 10, 14-18 drawn from material collected by l'HERMINIER, in the Herbarium of GOTTSCHE.

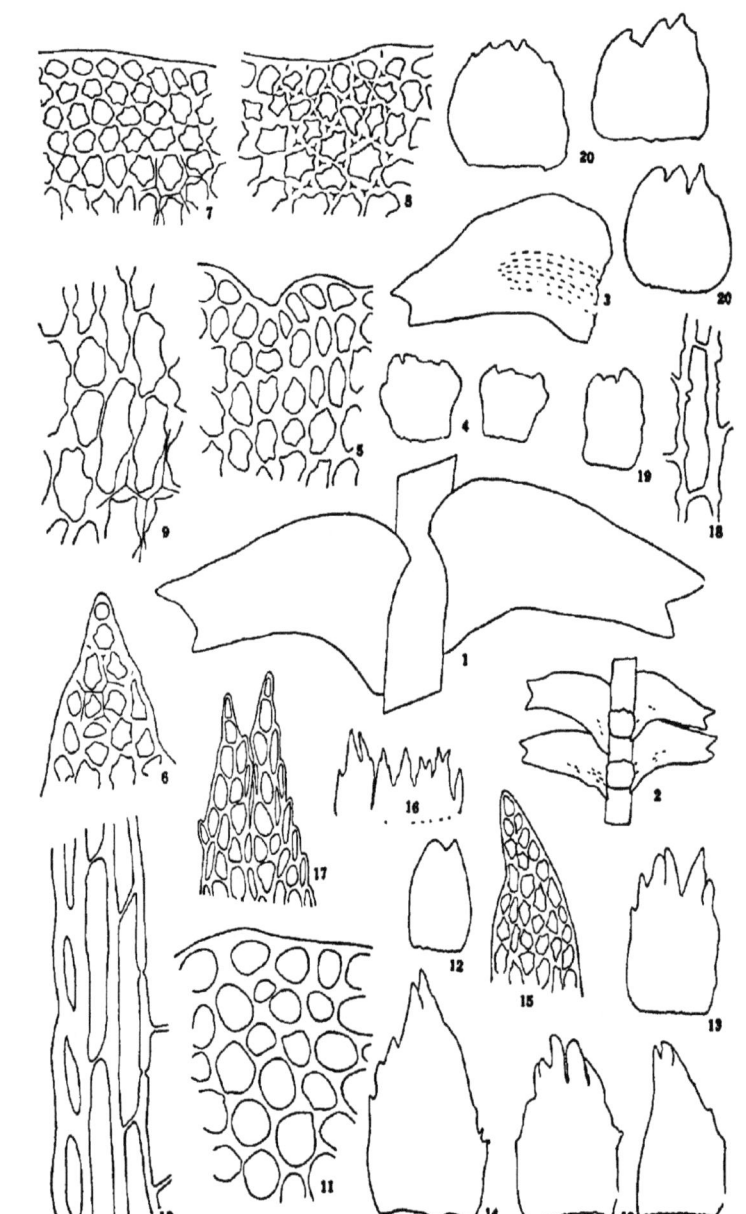

pronounced because of a more gradual transition (FIG. 3, nos. 2, 3, 7-9).

The underleaves are quadrate, a little broader than the stem, and lobed along both the lateral and apical margins in well developed plants (FIG. 3, nos. 2 and 4). Many variations in size and form occur. In some, the lateral margins tend to become straight and entire, and the lobing of the apices less distinct. Quite often in some of the less well developed forms the underleaves are much broader at the apex than at the base and cannot readily be distinguished from those of *B. cuneistipula.*

The thickness of the walls of the stem cells varies with the age of the plant, as does the degree of brown pigmentation. The size of the trigones and the thickness of the cell-walls in both leaves and bracts also show a direct correlation with age and exposure. The deposit is often very irregular on the inner walls of the cells of the female bracts and the perianth (FIG. 3, no. 18).

Plants collected by DUSS, no. 1096, among mosses and Sphagnum, in Guadeloupe, vary considerably in appearance from the usual forms. They grew erect in compact tufts. For the most part, the stems are more slender than in plants from other habitats, and the leaves, while well developed, are distant or only approximate.

GOTTSCHE designated several forms in the material from Guadeloupe. The forma *latior* G. with shorter leaves is less well developed than the type, and has the vitta not so conspicuous as in the larger plants. The forma *applanata* G. is of the usual size, with plane, spreading leaves which are unequally bidentate and have conspicuous vittae. The variety *brevifolia* G. is a depauperate stem with the leaves very distant. All of them could no doubt be duplicated in any large collection of the species.

The plants are somewhat similar to those of *B. bidens* and *B. phyllobola.* The large, plane, elongate leaves with large equal teeth of *B. bidens*, and the large crenulate teeth and the conspicuously incised and toothed underleaves of *B phyllobola* will readily identify those species. The female bracts of the three species are also distinctive.

DISTRIBUTION. Guadeloupe: Soufrière, l'Herminier, distributed in Husnot, Pl. Antilles, 211, the type (H, Y, NY); plants of the same collection from the Herbarium of GOTTSCHE 23, 36 (NY); plants of the same collection as var *brevifolia* G., forma *applanata* G., and forma *latior* G. (H); Soufrière, Duss 1034, 1077 and 1096 as *M. tenerum* (NY), nos. 62, 98, 102, 122, 302, 309, 310, 321, 328 (H). — Martinique: Mt. Pelée, Duss 348 as *M. variabile* (NY).

REFERENCES: Bescherelle (1893, 186); Stephani (1903, 22; 1909, 437; *Icones, Mastigobryum* no. 31)

4. **Bazzania cuneistipula** (Gottsche & Lindenb.) Trevis. Mem. Ist. Lomb. 13· 414. 1877.

Mastigobryum cuneistipulum Gottsche & Lindenberg, in G. L & N , Syn. Hep. 225 1845
Mastigobryum tenerum Gottsche & Lindenberg, loc cit
Bazzania tenera Trevis loc cit
Mastigobryum variabile Hampe & Gottsche, Linnaea 25 348 1852
Mastigobryum brevifolium Gottsche, Ann Sci Nat. Bot. V 1. 141. 1864
Mastigobryum corticola Stephani, Spec Hep 3 467 1908

Plants scattered or growing in depressed mats, small, dull gray-ish green to yellow-brown stems slender, to 5 cm. or more in length, with leaves mostly 1 mm. - 1 5 mm wide, prostrate to scarcely ascending; in cross-section the cells averaging 18μ in diameter, the walls thickened, the pits numerous; lateral branches frequent, 3 mm. or more apart, diverging at a wide angle; ventral branches abundant, long, often branched, flagelliform, sometimes becoming leafy; rhizoids colorless, abundant on the leaves of the flagelliform branches the line of leaf insertion a little curved in its upper half; the leaves distant to subimbricated, ascending, plane to more or less convex, becoming deflexed or wrapped around the stem when dry, unsymmetrically ovate, mostly 0 7 mm - 1 mm. long, 0 4 mm - 0 5 mm wide at the base, narrowing to the biden-tate apex; the dorsal margin convex from a straight or rounded base, extending over one-third of the stem, the ventral margin nearly straight, the apex normally two-toothed, the teeth mostly subequal, two to five cells long, spreading, the sinus broad, lunulate to acute; the leaf cells thin-walled, the trigones conspicuous, often confluent, the cell lumina angular-rounded, the cuticle verruculose; cells of the apical portion and dorsal base 18μ - 27μ in diameter, those of the median portion larger, those of the base to 36μ × 20μ, a vitta not differentiated. underleaves distant, attached in a straight line, squarrose, as broad or broader than the stem, sub-quadrate, truncate-trapezoidal to quadrate-orbicular, 0.24 mm - 0.36 mm long and wide, often narrowing a little to the base, the lateral margins straight to slightly undulate, the apex mostly four-lobed, the lobes broad, rounded, the sinuses shallow, narrow, acute to rounded, the cells as in the apical portion of the leaf· leaves of the flagelliform branches scale-like, appressed, ovate, mostly 0 12 mm long, the apex rounded, acute to bidentate· female branches frequent, one to several on a stem, the bracts and bracteoles similar; the outermost series small, rectangular in outline, usually shortly two-lobed, the margins entire; the intermediate series ovate, averaging 0 64 mm. - 72 mm long, 0 4 mm. broad at the base, approximately one-fourth divided into usually two, sometimes three, narrow, entire, blunt to acute teeth, the lateral margins crenulate, often undulate, the cells elongate, those of the apical portion averaging 25μ long × 15μ wide, of the basal portion 54μ × 18μ, the walls mostly uniformly thickened, trigones not con-spicuous; the innermost series (not mature) ovate, to 0.96 mm long, the upper fourth divided into two or three, mostly entire laciniae, the lateral margins crenulate to dentate, the cells elongate, more or less uniform throughout, in the median portion averaging 72μ × 18μ, the walls rather thin, the trigones indistinct· the perianth (immature) mouth divided into numerous laciniae, often ciliate · male branches and sporophytes not seen.

HABITAT: On trees and logs in woods.

The distinguishing characteristics of the plant are its small size, the shortly bidentate leaves with mostly lunulate sinuses and large thin-walled cells with conspicuous trigones; and the trapezoidal to round-quadrate underleaves with mostly four-lobed apices. (FIGS. 4, nos. 1-18; 5, nos. 1-14).

While most of the underleaves of the type material show the straight lateral margins and the cuneate tendency as shown in FIG 4, no 9, others show no decrease in width from the apex to the base (FIG 4, no. 2), and in some instances the margins are convex or bulging and to a slight degree undulate. The underleaves on the plants examined, in no case exhibited so marked a difference in width between apex and base, as is indicated by the figures in the *Species Hepaticarum* (LINDENBERG and GOTTSCHE, 1851, pl. 13). The apices instead of being usually more or less deeply bifid, as they have indicated, are only slightly depressed, or more often, nearly straight or inconspicuously four-lobed. The same variations are even more pronounced on the less well developed parts of a plant.

The degree of brown pigmentation and the thickness of the cell walls vary with the age and habit of the plant. This is noticeable in both the leaves and in the stem. Stem sections from near the growing tip showed only one layer (cortical) of cells with extremely thick, light brown walls, and a medulla of many thin-walled cells, while sections from much older parts of the stem showed a much wider border of thick-walled cells strongly pigmented, and only a few thin-walled cells. In older leaves the cuticle is strongly verruculose. Those plants from the mountains are usually brown except at the growing tips.

The leaves are prevailingly two-toothed at the apices, but very often show modifications as indicated in FIG. 4, no. 4. There is much variation even in the two-toothed condition. In some, the apex is narrow and the sinus narrow and deep, in others the apex is broad, the teeth are broad and short, and the sinus is lunulate. The teeth are long or short, rounded to acute, and equal to strikingly unequal. The leaves are mostly broader and shorter than LINDENBERG and GOTTSCHE have indicated (1851, pl. 13, fig. 4).

FIG. 4 — *Bazzania cuneistipula* (Gottsche & Lindenb.) Trevis. — 1. Portion of a stem, dorsal view, × 30 2 Portion of a stem, ventral view, × 30. 3 Leaf, × 30 4. Variations in leaf apices, × 30. 5. Cells from the apical portion of a leaf, × 260. 6. Cells from the dorsal margin of a leaf, × 260. 7. Cells from the ventral margin of a leaf, × 260. 8 Cells from the basal portion of a leaf, × 260 9. Underleaves, × 30. 10. Cells of the upper part of an underleaf, × 260 11 Portion of a cross-section of a stem, × 260. 12 Female bract of the outer series, × 30. 13 Female bracts of an intermediate series, × 30 14 Upper part of a female bract of the intermediate series, × 260. 15 Female bracts of the innermost series, × 30 16. Outline of a portion of the mouth of a perianth, × 30. 17 Portion of perianth mouth, × 260 18 A cell from the base of a bract showing irregular thickenings of the wall, × 260. Nos. 1-18 drawn from a portion of the type material.

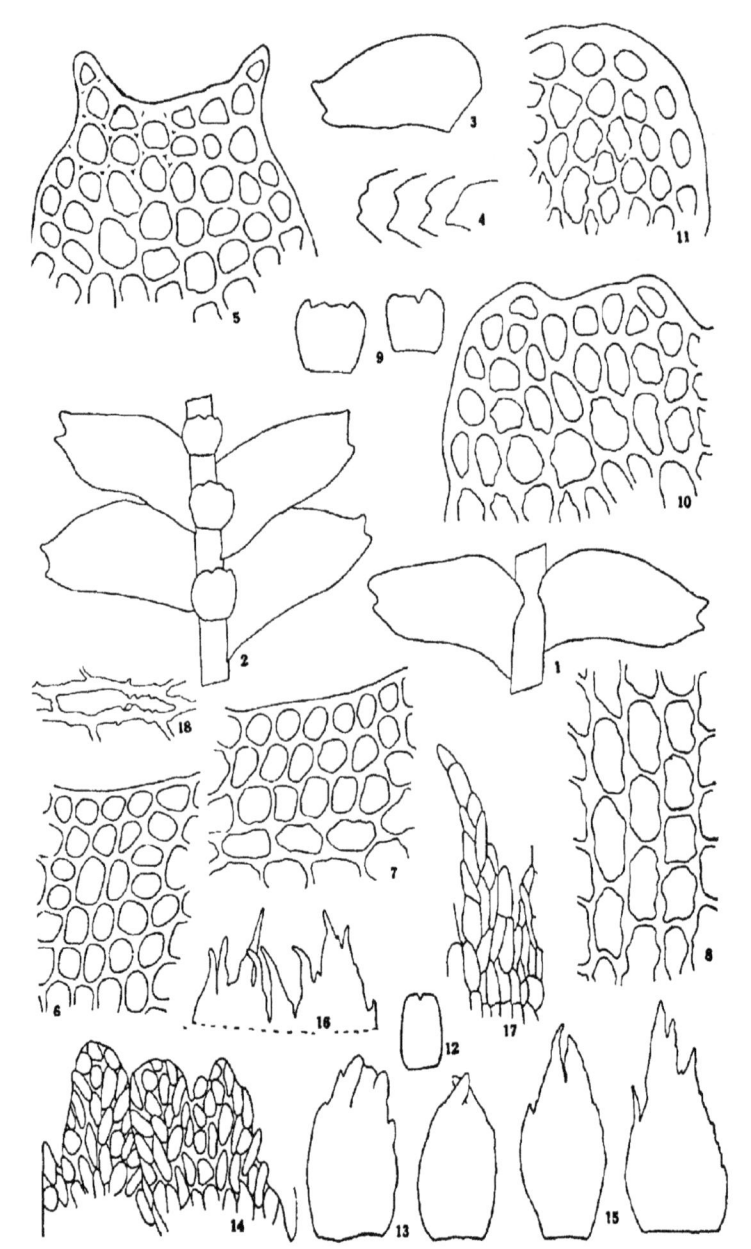

Most of the cells of the bracts show a uniformity in the thickness of the cell walls, but often (in older bracts), the walls of many of the basal cells show wart-like lumps of thickening irregularly scattered over the inner surfaces (FIG. 4, no. 18). The number, size, and shape of these thickenings vary in different cells. The same condition has been observed in the cells of the female bracts and perianths, and even the stems of many of the species of the West Indies. EVANS (1933, 74) has described the same condition in the cells of the perianth of *B. loricata* from Sumatra.

The species is quite similar in many ways to the more northern *B. ambigua* of the northwestern United States and Canada, which often has many bidentate leaves, and underleaves with mostly straight sides. The two species are approximately the same size and the same color, and have the same prostrate to ascending habit of growth. However, the leaves of *B. cuneistipula* are larger, and are composed of larger cells. They also have a greater number of enlarged cells in the basal portion. The two are further distinguished by differences in the female bracts and in the perianths.

Some of the plants from Jamaica show certain characteristics which do not occur in plants of the type collection. They are mostly yellow-brown, smaller, and have a coarse filiform appearance. The leaves are strongly deflexed, much more so than in the type, and curve around the stem when dry. The underleaves vary from trapezoidal to quadrate-orbicular.

Few comments concerning the size and habit of *M. tenerum* can be made from the type[1] since so little material has been available for study. Most of the other specimens also are either very meager or in a poor state of preservation. The plants of the type material of *M. variabile* are a little larger and slightly more compact than the plants of *M. tenerum*. The angle of divergence of the branches, the flagelliform branches, the rhizoid production on the underleaves, and the divergence and shape of the underleaves are identical (compare FIG. 5, nos. 1-4 and nos. 10-14). The cell walls are a little thinner but this difference is neither uniform nor constant. *M. varibile* is so similar to the parts of the plants of *M. cuneistipulum* with quadrate-orbicular underleaves that I have concluded that they belong to one species. Based on the available material,

[1] The portion of the type material available for study consists of one branched stem approximately 1.5 cm. long.

FIG. 5. — *Bazzania cuneistipula* (Gottsche & Lindenb) Trevis. — 1 Portion of a plant, ventral view, × 30. 2. Leaf, × 30 3. Cells from the apical portion of a leaf, × 260. 4 A cell from the apical portion of a leaf, × 350. 5. Portion of a plant, ventral view, × 30. 6. Apices of leaves, × 30. 7. A cell from the apical portion of a leaf, × 400. 8. Portion of a plant, ventral view, × 30. 9. A cell from the apical portion of a leaf, × 400. 10. Portion of a plant, dorsal view, × 30 11. Portion of a plant, ventral view, × 30. 12 Portion of a ventral leafy branch, × 30. 13. Cells from the apical portion of a leaf, × 260. 14 A cell from the apical region of a leaf, × 350 Nos. 1-4 drawn from a portion of the type of *M. variabile*, from Puerto Rico; 5-7 from the type of *M. brevifolium*, from Colombia; 8-9 from the type of *M. corticola*, from Brazil; 10-14 from the type of *M. tenerum* from St. Kitts

except for the trapezoidal outline of many of the underleaves of many of the plants of *M. cuneistipulum*, the two seem to be identical. Additional collections from all types of habitats will no doubt add to our knowledge of the variability of the species. None of the plants of *M. tenerum* or *M. variabile* had sexual branches. According to HAMPE and GOTTSCHE (1852, 348), the female bracts of *M. variabile* are ovate, with the apices bifid to bidentate, and the lateral margins are dentate to long ciliate. This agrees with the female bracts of *M. cuneistipulum*. The female bracts of *M. tenerum* were not described.

M. brevifolium G. from Colombia is another species with characteristics similar to those mentioned above. The type consists of a portion of a plant 1 cm. long, very poorly developed. The leaves at the growing point of the stem tend to be small and juvenile, and none of them are well developed. GOTTSCHE (1864, 141) has already mentioned the similarity to *B. longistipula* (*M. elegantulum*), and also to *M cuneistipulum*, and since most of the leaves are bidentate one suspects that the species does not belong to the *Tridentatae group*. STEPHANI's figure (in the *Tridentatae* Subgenus, in the *Icones, Mastigobryum* no 153) shows the leaves to be two- or three-toothed, and the margins of the teeth serrate. He also describes the species in two places in the *Species Hepaticarum* (3 · 467 and 517). These descriptions agree in most of their details, but in the earlier one he describes the leaves as tridentate (often bidentate), while in the later one he describes them as bidentate (rarely tridentate) The portion of the type from the STEPHANI Herbarium in Geneva consists of stems with most of the leaves bidentate (see FIG. 5, nos. 5 and 6). The margins of the teeth are entire. The species is another example of *B. cuneistipula*.

M. corticola, collected in Brazil by WEINIO, should also be included here. The leaves are two-toothed, the cells are thin-walled but have conspicuous trigones, and the underleaves are subquadrate with convex sides (see FIG. 5, nos. 8-9).

The species is readily distinguished from *B. bidens* and *B. phyllobola* because of their large, spreading leaves with large teeth, and from *B. Herminieri* because of its ovate, vittate leaves with large unequal teeth.

DISTRIBUTION: C u b a . without locality, Wright, Hep. Cub (H). — G u a d e l o u p e . without locality, l'Herminier (H) The specimen cited by Stephani (1903, 41) from Guadeloupe, collected by Duss, should be referred to *B. Herminieri* — J a m a i c a . without locality, Hb Hooker, the type (V); without locality, Hart, cited by Boswell (1887, 50), New Haven Gap, Underwood 911, 1024, 1054 (Y, NY); slopes of Sir John, E G Britton 1193 (Y); near Cinchona, Bower, cited by Pearson (1931, 96); without locality, Borgensen, Jansen, Harris, cited by Stephani (1908, 438). — M a r t i n i q u e : Mt. Pelée, Duss 638 (H) — P u e r t o R i c o without locality, Schwanecke, the type of *M. variabile* (B), Sierra de Naguabo 690-1035 m., Shafer, a, e, 3712 (NY) — S t. K i t t s : Mt. Misery, Breutel, the type of *M. tenerum* (V). — T r i n i d a d : without locality, Cruger, cited by Stephani (1908, 438). — B r a z i l : Lafayette, Weinio, the type of *M corticola* (H). — C o l o m b i a . Mt Quindio, Triana and Planchon, the type of *M brevifolium* (G).

REFERENCES: Boswell (1887, 50); Gottsche (1864, 141), Jack and Stephani (1892, 13), Lindenberg and Gottsche (1851, 70, 71 pl. 13); Pagán (1939, 39); Pearson (1931, 96); Stephani (1888a, 279; 1903, 23; 1908-09, 437, 438, 467, 517; *Icones, Mastigobryum* nos. 27, 35, 36, 153, 155).

5. **Bazzania platystipula** Fulford, Bryol. 44: 145-146. Fig. 1-11. 1941.

Plants growing in depressed mats or scattered among other bryophytes, light green becoming yellow-brown in the older portions; the stems slender, often coarse thread-like, to 5 cm. long, with leaves to 2 mm. broad, prostrate; stem cells in longitudinal section elongate, the medullary cells averaging 0.17 mm. long, the cortical cells shorter, deeply pigmented, both averaging 22μ in diameter, the end walls thin, the vertical walls uniformly thickened and containing frequent pits; lateral branches frequent, mostly 5 mm. apart, diverging at a wide angle; flagelliform branches numerous, long; rhizoids present on the leaves of the flagelliform branches: the line of leaf insertion curved in its upper part; the leaves approximate to densely imbricated, ascendent, nearly plane, becoming strongly deflexed when dry, unsymmetrically ovate, 0.7 mm. - 1.2 mm. long, 0.5 mm. broad at the base, narrowed to the obliquely truncate, bidentate apex; the dorsal margin arched from a curved base, covering one-half the stem, the ventral margin straight, the base scarcely dilated, the apex two-toothed, the teeth acute to acuminate, two to four cells high, two to three cells broad at the base, the sinuses lunulate to acute, the margins entire; leaf cells large, thin-walled, the cell lumina angular-rounded, the trigones large, with convex sides, sometimes becoming confluent, the cuticle smooth to faintly verruculose; cells of the apical portion and dorsal base 24μ - 32μ in diameter, of the median portion larger, and of the base 46μ - $50\mu \times 32\mu$, not forming a vitta · underleaves approximate to imbricated, subquadrate in outline, broader than the stem, the line of attachment straight, to 0.65 mm. long and broad, the lateral margins a little convex from a straight base, the apex undulate to deeply four-lobed, the cells as in the apical portion of the leaf: leaves of the flagelliform branches scale-like, ovate, acute to shortly bidentate female branches solitary, one to several on a stem, the bracts and bracteoles similar, ovate, the outermost series small, entire to shortly bidentate, the intermediate series larger, to one-third divided into usually three laciniae, the lateral margins ciliate to dentate, the innermost series (immature) to one-third divided into three laciniae, the lateral margins usually long ciliate and serrate to dentate the perianth (immature) mouth short ciliate. male branches and sporophytes not seen.

HABITAT: On tree bases and logs, in mats or scattered among other bryophytes.

The distinguishing characteristics of the species are its small size, the greenish or yellowish brown color; the ascendent, shortly bidentate leaves, with large, thin-walled cells and large, rounded trigones with convex sides; and the approximate to imbricated, subquadrate underleaves with undulate to four-lobed apices. (FIG. 6. nos 1-11)

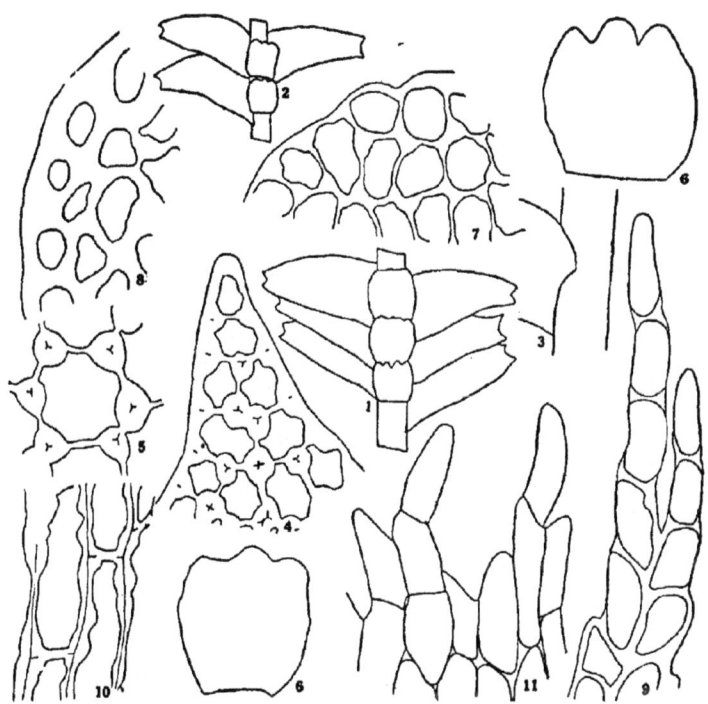

FIG 6. — *Bazzania platystipula* Fulford — 1, 2. Portion of a plant, ventral view, × 15. 3. Portion of a stem and leaf, dorsal view, × 30. 4 A tooth of a leaf, × 310 5. A cell from the apical portion of a leaf, × 400. 6. Underleaves, × 30. 7 Portion of the apical margin of an underleaf, × 310. 8 Portion of a transverse section of a stem, × 310. 9. Cells of one of the laciniae of an innermost female bract, × 310. 10 Cells from the lower portion of the same bract, × 400. 11. Cells from the mouth of the perianth, × 310 Nos 1-11 drawn from the type material.

The plants are slender, coarsely to finely filiform and form depressed mats on the bases of trees or logs. They vary in color from light green at the growing tips to yellow-brown below, sometimes becoming very dark. The leaves are imbricated, ascendent, deflexed or even curled around the stem when dry, and are bidentate with conspicuous, acute teeth. Some of the leaves on a few of the stems appeared to be caducous but the underleaves were persistent.

The underleaves are large, conspicuously broader than the stem in robust plants (see FIG. 6, no. 1), where they are imbricated. On the less well developed stems they are not quite so broad, but nevertheless are large, and are usually approximate. The lateral margins are convex, entire, and the apices are undulate to two- to four-lobed (see FIG. 6, nos 1, 2, 6).

The cells of both the leaves and underleaves are very large (see FIG. 6, nos. 4, 5, 7), and have thin walls. The trigones are large and have convex sides so that they appear to be rounded. They form one of the conspicuous characteristics of the species

The female branches were poorly developed and in a very poor state of preservation. The intermediate and innermost series are to one-third divided into usually three laciniae (see FIG 6, no. 9), and the lateral margins are variously incised, serrate, dentate and ciliate The perianths were not developed except for the cells of the mouth. This appears to be short ciliate (see FIG. 6, no 11).

The species is similar in several respects to *B. roraimensis*, the description of which follows It can be separated from the other *Bidentatae* of similar size and habit because of its large underleaves, and the large, thin-walled cells with very large, rounded trigones.

DISTRIBUTION Jamaica John Crow Peak, 5500-5800 ft., Underwood 692, the type (NY, Y), Blue Mountain Peak, Patterson 23 (F) — Puerto Rico Luquillo Mountains, E G Britton (NY)

6. Bazzania roraimensis (Steph.) comb. nov.

Mastigobryum roraimense Stephani, Trans Linnean Soc. Bot. II. 6: 97. 1901-05.

Plants in mats, green to golden brown, becoming darker in the older parts, stems slender to filiform, to 4 cm. in length, with leaves to 1 5 mm. broad, prostrate· lateral branches frequent, 5 mm. or more apart, diverging at a wide angle, sometimes becoming flagelliform; ventral branches flagelliform, numerous, long; rhizoids frequent, from the bases of the leaves of the flagelliform branches: the line of leaf insertion curved in its upper part: leaves approximate to imbricated, plane, becoming strongly deflexed when dry, ascendent, unsymmetrically narrow-ovate to oblong, 0.6 mm. - 0.8 mm. long, mostly 0.42 mm. broad at the base, narrowed to 0.15 mm. at the shortly bidentate apex; the dorsal margin arched from a straight base, covering less than one-half the stem, the ventral margin straight, the base not dilated, the apex two-toothed, the teeth sharp, two to four cells high, two to four cells broad at the base, the sinuses lunulate, the margins entire; the leaf cells thin-

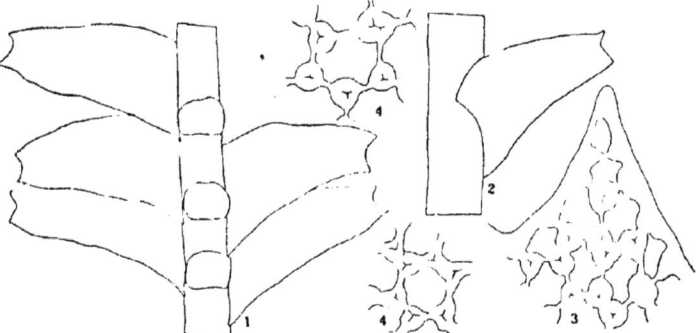

FIG 7. — *Bazzania roraimensis* (Steph) Fulford — 1. Portion of a plant,
ventral view, × 30   2 Portion of a stem with leaf, dorsal view, × 30   3 A
tooth of a leaf, × 310   4 Cells from the apical portion of a leaf, × 400   Nos.
1-4 drawn from a portion of the type material.

walled, the cell lumina angular-rounded to stellate, the trigones conspicuous, large, often becoming confluent, the cuticle faintly verruculose; cells of the apical region and dorsal base 20μ - 24μ in diameter, those of the median portion larger, those of the base to $50\mu \times 20\mu$, a vitta not differentiated: underleaves distant, rounded in outline, not as broad as the stem, attached in a straight line, the margins entire, the apex sometimes undulate, the cells of the interior mostly 20μ in diameter, thin-walled and with conspicuous trigones, the marginal row thick-walled: leaves of the flagelliform branches scale-like, ovate, acute to shortly bidentate: male branches catkin-like, solitary, one to several on a stem, the bracteoles similar to the bracts, smaller, the bracts ovate, bidentate, the antheridia occurring singly· female branches and perianths not seen. (FIG. 7, nos. 1-4).

HABITAT: Not given

The portion of the type material in the STEPHANI Herbarium at Harvard does not agree in all of its characteristics with STEPHANI's original description, or his figures in the *Icones, Mastigobryum* no 34. His description and drawings were no doubt made from robust, well developed plants, while the plants in the Harvard collection are small and slender (see FIG. 7, nos. 1-4), with long internodes The chief difference is in the underleaves. STEPHANI's figures (*Icones, Mastigobryum* no. 34), and description show them as being broader than the stem, subquadrate in outline, and usually two- to four-lobed at the apex while the underleaves of the Harvard plants are small, scarcely broader than the stem, orbicular in outline, and entire or only faintly lobed along the apical margin. Unfortunately, it was not possible to obtain additional material so that a more complete examination could be made at this time

The plants (based on the Harvard material) are readily distinguished from the other members of the *Bidentatae* by their brown color, the filiform stems with persistent leaves, the large cells with thin walls and very large trigones which soon become confluent, and the small, distant, orbicular underleaves which are usually entire.

The species is similar to *B. platystipula* except for the size of the underleaves and the length of the internodes. Since, however, *B. roraimensis*, according to STEPHANI, does become more robust and the underleaves larger and more densely imbricated than the plants figured here, it may be that *B. platystipula* and *B. roraimensis* as described here, are different expressions of one species.

Additional collections from Jamaica and British Guiana will no doubt furnish the necessary information but until further evidence should confirm this it seems best to consider the two as distinct. *B. roraimensis* can readily be separated from the small forms of *B. cuneistipula* because of its small, usually entire, orbicular underleaves, and its large cells with thin walls and large trigones.

DISTRIBUTION B r i t i s h G u i a n a : summit of Mt. Roraima, McConnell and Quelch 523, the type (H).

REFERENCES: Stephani (1908, 436; *Icones, Mastigobryum* no 34).

7. **Bazzania gracilis** (Hampe & Gottsche) Stephani, Hedwigia 27: 279. 1888.

Mastigobryum gracile Hampe & Gottsche, Linnaea 25: 346 1852
Mastigobryum cuneifolium Gottsche, in Duss, Fl Crypt Antilles Fr Hep 23 1903 (nomen nudum)
Mastigobryum parvum Stephani, Spec. Hep 3· 438 1908
Bazzania bidens var *vittata* Spruce, Trans & Proc Bot Soc [Edinburgh] 15 371 1885
Bazzania trichodes Spruce ms Hepat Spruc
Mastigobryum trichoideum Stephani, Spec Hep 3 532 1909
Bazzania bidens Spruce, Trans & Proc Bot Soc [Edinburgh] 15 371. 1885
Not *M. bidens* Gottsche & Lindenberg
Bazzania bidens var Spruce ms. Hepat Spruc

Plants scattered or growing in depressed mats, the slender forms yellow-brown to red-brown, larger plants yellow-green to olive-green; stems slender to filiform, prostrate to ascending near the growing tip, to 5 cm. long, with leaves 1.5 mm. - 2 mm. wide, leaves often becoming scale-like, on many of the stems caducous; stem cells in longitudinal section elongate, the medullary cells averaging 0.16 mm. long, the cortical cells shorter, both about 14μ in diameter, the end walls thin, the vertical walls irregularly thickened and containing pits; lateral branches frequent, 3 mm. - 10 mm. apart, diverging at a very wide angle; flagelliform branches numerous, very long, often branched· the line of leaf insertion curved in the upper part; leaves distant to subimbricated, ascendent, nearly plane, becoming convex on drying, unsymmetrically ovate, becoming nearly symmetrical in the smaller forms; in the normal condition averaging 0.65 mm. - 0.85 mm. long × 0.4 mm. wide at the base, narrowing to the apex, often much smaller and scale-like, averaging 0.5 mm. or less long and 0.3 mm. wide at the base; the dorsal base straight to somewhat rounded, the dorsal margin convex in the typical forms, both the dorsal and ventral margins slightly convex in the reduced forms, the apex irregularly two-toothed becoming mostly acute in the smaller leaves; the teeth two to three cells long, acute, the acroscopic tooth often the longer, the sinus broad, lunulate to acute; the leaf cells thin-walled, the trigones small, conspicuous, often confluent, the cell lumina angular-rounded, the cuticle smooth to faintly verruculose; cells of

FIG 8 — *Bazzania gracilis* (Hampe & Gottsche) Steph. — 1 Portion of a stem of a small form, dorsal view, × 30. 2 Portion of a stem, ventral view, small form, × 30. 2a Portion of a stem of large form, ventral view, × 30 3 Portion of stem with leaves much reduced, dorsal view, × 30 4. Portion of stem of another large form, ventral view, × 30 5 Leaves of the small form, × 30. 6 Tip of leaf of small form, × 260. 7. Cells from the dorsal margin of leaf of small form, × 260 8 Basal cells of leaf (vitta) of small form, × 260. 9. Underleaf of the small form, × 30. 10 Cells from underleaf of a small form, × 260. 11 Portion of a cross section of stem, × 260. 12 Portion of a longitudinal section of a stem, × 260 13. Male bracteole, × 30. 14 Male bracts, × 30. 15. Tip of male bract, × 260. 16 Female bract of outer series, × 30. 17. Female bracts of intermediate series (not mature), × 30. 18. Female bract of innermost series (not mature), × 30. 19. Portion of perianth mouth (not mature), × 30. 20. Portion of perianth mouth, × 260. Nos 1, 2, 2a, 5-12 drawn from a portion of the type material; 3, 13-15 from plants collected in Puerto Rico by EVANS, 57; 4, 16-20 from plants collected by UNDERWOOD, no. 659, in Jamaica.

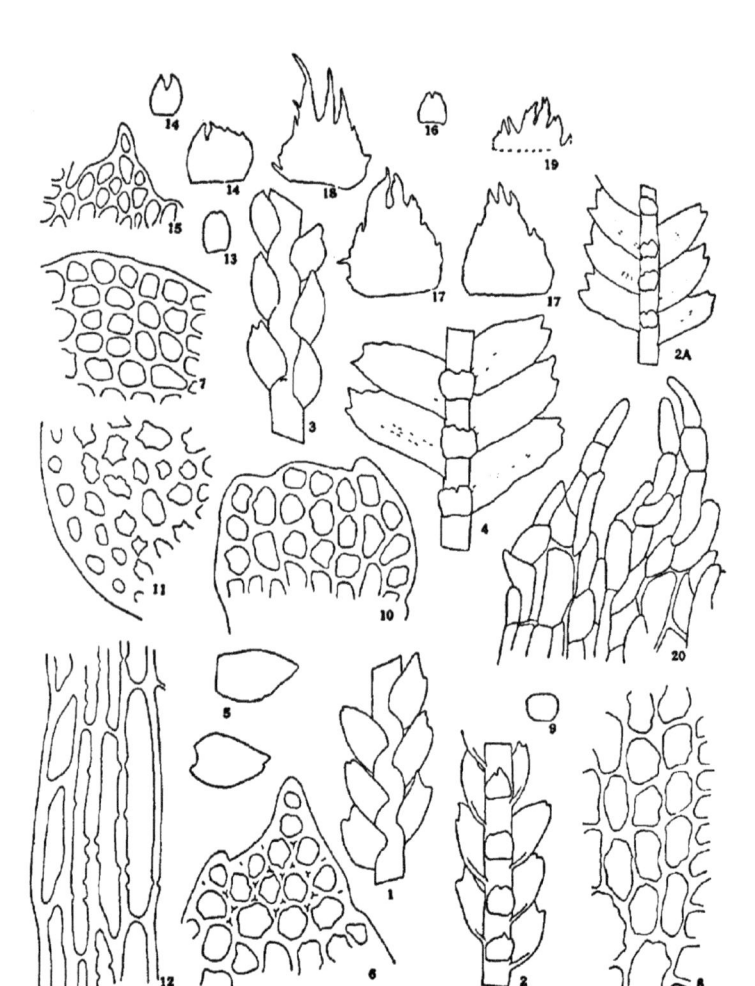

the apical portion and dorsal base 16μ - 20μ in diameter, the cells of the basal portion mostly $40\mu \times 15\mu$, forming a narrow but usually distinct vitta: underleaves small, distant, often as broad as the stem, attached in a straight line, on well developed stems often squarrose, quadrate to quadrate-orbicular, mostly 0.2 mm. - 0.32 mm long $\times$ 0.2 mm. - 0.3 mm. wide, much smaller in reduced forms, the lateral margins slightly convex, the apex entire, straight to rounded, or shortly one- to four-toothed or -lobed, the cells as in the apical portion of the leaf; leaves of the flagelliform branches scale-like, to 0.08 mm. long, ovate, entire to bidentate· male branches frequent, usually several on a stem; the bracteoles small, oval, mostly 0.16 mm $\times$ 0.08 mm., entire to bifid; the bracts larger, ovate, bifid, emarginate to crenulate, the cells of the apical portion averaging $27\mu \times 16\mu$, the cell walls thin, the trigones distinct along the margins· female branches occasional, usually several on a stem   bracteoles and bracts similar, those of the outermost series small, quadrate, averaging 0 25 mm. $\times$ 0 08 mm., entire to bidentate; those of the intermediate series (not mature) ovate, the upper third or fourth divided into usually three, entire or dentate laciniae, the lateral margins often dentate; the innermost series (not mature), broadly ovate, the upper part divided into three laciniae, the margins dentate to ciliate, the cells all of one kind, elongate, mostly $45\mu \times 18\mu$, thin-walled: perianth (not mature) mouth divided into numerous long laciniae similar to those of the innermost bracts.

HABITAT: In depressed mats or scattered among mosses, tree bases, logs, and over rocks and soil.

The species is easily distinguished from the other *Bidentatae* by its mostly slender or filiform appearance, and by the leaves which are small, often scale-like throughout much of the plant, two-toothed, with thin-walled cells, conspicuous trigones and a distinct vitta   They are usually caducous.   The small form appears as interwoven mats of brown hairs or threads while the larger forms have light green leaves.   (FIGS. 8, nos. 1-20; 9, nos. 1-5).

B. gracilis shows the usual wide series of variations from the large, green plants with persistent, well developed leaves and underleaves, to the filiform, red-brown stems usually without leaves except at the apices of the stems.   A stem may produce normal, spreading leaves for a distance and then, through a gradual decrease in size, the small scale-leaves which are appressed, or it may produce only one kind.   In the dry condition the branches with the small leaves appear similar to the flagelliform branches and only by a careful examination can they be distinguished. In the original description of the type material collected by SCHWANECKE, HAMPE and GOTTSCHE mention a variation β *trichodes*, which is depauperate, with the leaves squamiform except on shoots which tend to become erect, where they show a tendency to be large and spreading in the upper part of the stem.   This description obviously has reference to plants in which most of the leaves are reduced, especially in the older portions of the plant.

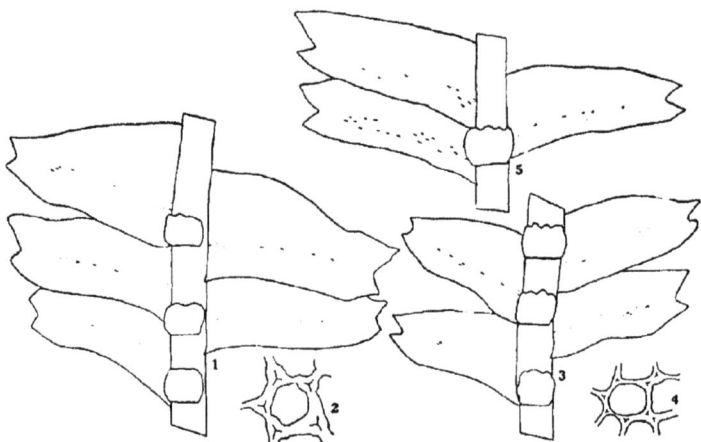

FIG. 9. — *Bazzania gracilis* (Hampe & Gottsche) Steph — 1. Portion of a plant, ventral view, × 30 2. A cell from the apical portion of a leaf, × 400 3 Portion of a plant, ventral view, × 30 4 A cell from the apical portion of a leaf, × 400 5. Portion of a plant, ventral view, × 30 Nos 1-2 drawn from a portion of the type of *M parvum*, 3-4 from a portion of the type of *B. trichodes* Spruce (NY), 5 from a portion of *B. bidens* Spruce (NY)

The authors further state that the variation should not receive the dignity of a varietal rank. The cause of the alternating change in the kind of leaves produced is not known. It occurs in plants growing in a number of situations but is most conspicuous in the plants of higher elevations; it may be due to the same influences which frequently cause the flagelliform branches to develop ordinary leaves

An interesting modification of the usual condition of the walls of the stem cells is often present. The thickenings of the vertical walls of the cells of the medulla, instead of being uniform, as is the usual condition, are very irregular, and in many of the cells small lumps of thickening protrude as warts into the cell-lumina as indicated in FIG. 8, no. 12. This same condition of irregular thickenings on the inner walls of the cells is present in the basal cells of the inner series of the female bracts and in the perianths of many of the West Indian species.

Plants collected by UNDERWOOD in Jamaica were principally of the well developed type (FIG. 8, no. 4), described by HAMPE and GOTTSCHE (1852, 346) as the typical form The stems are mostly 3 cm. - 4 cm. long and with leaves mostly 1 mm. wide. The leaves are very often caducous and stems without leaves throughout much of their length are not uncommon. This caducous habit seems to be best developed in the normal type of leaf for in stems or parts of stems with reduced or scale-like leaves, rarely do they become detached. Furthermore, only rarely does one find this habit present in the underleaves, so that stems without leaves but with the underleaves persisting are not uncommon.

The leaves are slightly ascendent, and this character becomes more strongly developed in the smaller forms (FIG. 8, nos. 1-4). They average 0.65 mm. - 0.85 mm. in length and 0.4 mm. in width and are unsymmetrically ovate. The dorsal margin is conspicuously arched from a straight to slightly rounded base; the ventral margin is straight to a little concave The apex is more or less transversely truncate and bidentate. The teeth show a high degree of variability in size. In most of the well developed leaves the teeth are mostly equal, two to three cells high, deltoid and acute, and separated by a lunulate sinus; in the less well developed forms all variations are found from the sort just described, through the unequally two-toothed forms with a lunulate to deep and acute sinus, to finally, the sharply acute, scale-leaves of the filiform branches.

The cells of the normal leaves are similar to those of the reduced forms shown in FIG. 8, nos. 6-8, except that there are a greater number of elongated cells in the basal region. These extend toward the middle of the leaf in one to three rows and form a fairly distinct vitta.

The underleaves, FIG. 8, nos. 2 and 9, are small, quadrate, and appressed on the filiform stems but tend to become larger, FIG. 8, nos. 2a and 4, on the robust plants. Here they tend to be elongate-subquadrate, squarrose, and are approximately as broad as the stem. The lateral margins are mostly straight or only slightly bulging, usually mostly entire, and the apex is emarginate to two- to four-crenate or -lobed.

The male branches were numerous on the plants collected by EVANS in the Luquillo Mountains, Puerto Rico. They were produced on the normal stems as well as on the stems with reduced leaves.

The type collection contains plants of two sorts; larger plants as indicated in FIG 8, no 2a, with comparatively large leaves which are spreading, often caducous and have a more or less distinct vitta, and smaller plants with small, scale-like, persistent leaves which are appressed The portion of the type material in the Farlow Herbarium (from the Hb. of JACK) is made up almost entirely of this smaller form, which HAMPE and GOTTSCHE distinguish as β trichodes.

The small red-brown variation seems to be more abundant in the West Indies than the large, leafy one, while in Central and South America the leafy variation is more often collected.

The plants from Martinique distributed under the manuscript name *M. cuneifolium* Gottsche, and listed by DUSS, are typical of the species *M parvum* collected by GLAZIOU in Rio de Janeiro is another example of the larger plants with caducous leaves (see FIG 9, nos. 1-2).

The plants described by SPRUCE from Mt. Chimborazo under *B. bidens* var. *vittata* which were distributed by him as *B. trichodes* and later described by STEPHANI as *M. trichoideum* also belong to *B. gracilis*. The plants are very similar to the larger plants from the West Indies except that they are not so strongly pigmented, the cell walls are not quite so thick, and trigones are not so large (FIG. 9, nos. 3, 4). Some of the leaves are caducous. *B. bidens* of SPRUCE from Rio Negro and Uaupés and his *B. bidens* var., "foliis brevioribus" from Manáos and San Carlos have the characteristics of his *B. trichodes* — leaf shape, cell pattern, underleaves, etc., except that the plants are more robust, with the leaves more densely imbricated and larger (see FIG. 9, no 5). The underleaves are also larger but show the characteristic shape with the four-lobed apices. The leaves were not caducous on the plants examined. SPRUCE seems to have misinterpreted the species *B. bidens*, for he states that the figures of *M. bidens* in LINDENBERG and GOTTSCHE, *Species Hepaticarum*, show the leaves a little longer than in his own specimens (which he considered *typical*), and that the form with long leaves was also collected in Guadeloupe by HUSNOT. I have examined the type of *Herpetium stoloniferum* var. *bidens* Mont. collected by LEPRIEUR in French Guiana and also the HUSNOT specimen and find no close similarity between them and SPRUCE's plants. *B. bidens* can always be readily distinguished because of its long, more or less linear leaves. The cells are all very large and the trigones very large and often confluent. A vitta is not differentiated.

DISTRIBUTION. J a m a i c a : Morce's Gap, 5000 ft., Underwood 530, 621, 632 (Y, NY); base of John Crow Peak, 5000-6000 ft., Underwood 2361 (Y, NY); John Crow Peak, 5500-5800 ft., Underwood 657, 659, 823, 2360 (Y, NY); Portland Gap, 1650 m., Maxon and Killip 1195 (H, Y, NY); New Haven Gap, Johnson 19 (Y); Cinchona, Miss Cummings 11 (NY); Green Hill Wood, 4000 ft., Harris 12 (NY) — M a r t i n i q u e · Mt. Pelée, Duss 638, as *M. cunei-folium* (NY). — P u e r t o R i c o . El Yunque, Luquillo Mountains, Evans 57 (Y, NY), without locality, Schwanecke, the type (B, H), El Yunque, Pagán 486 (NY), without locality, Sintenis, cited by Stephani (1908, 436); Sierra de Naguabo, 465-720 m., J. A. Shafer 3758 (NY); Rio de Maricao, 500-600 m , E G Britton 2682 (NY) — C o s t a R i c a Without locality, Werckle (Y, NY), Zurquí, Standley 48091, reported as *B. phyllobola* by Herzog (W). — G u a t e m a l a : Alta Verapaz near Coban, 1350 m., Turck-heim 5425 as *M. phyllobolum* (NY). — B r a s i l . Rio de Janeiro, Glaziou (NY); Rio de Janeiro, Glaziou 4532, the type of *M. parvum* (H), Rio Negro and Uaupés, Spruce, Hep. Spruc as *B. bidens* (Y, NY), Manáos and San Carlos, Spruce, Hep. Spruc. as *B. bidens* var. (Y, NY) — B r i t i s h G u i a n a : Mt Roraima, McConnell and Quelch, 334/11 p p., cited by Stephani (1901-05, 98) — E c u a d o r · Mt Chimborazo, Spruce, Hep. Spruc., a por-tion of the type of *B. trichodes* Spruce (NY); with *B. leptostipa*, Spruce, Hep Spruc (NY)

REFERENCES: Stephani (1888a, 279; 1901-05, 98; 1908, 436; *Icones, Mastigobryum* nos. 30, 32, 446); Pagán (1939, 39).

SUBGENUS TRIDENTATAE

This subgenus is characterized by having the leaves three-toothed or -lobed at the truncated apices They are never or only occasionally two-toothed. Several species, namely, *B. Schwaneckiana, B. diversicuspis* and *B. canelensis,* have most of the leaves entire or nearly so, but in each instance the species in question is very closely related to the species within one of the Sections listed below.

The Sections *Parvistipula** and *Cordistipula*† of STEPHANI have been discarded because they were purely artificial groupings based on highly variable characteristics.

The Section *Connata* of STEPHANI's older classification (1886, 245) has been revived to include all species in which the underleaves are connate with one or both leaves. All of the American species of his Section *Serrulata* as well as one species from his Section *Grandistipula* belong here.

Key to the Sections

1 Leaves with a conspicuous vitta .   . . . . .   5 **Vittatae** (p. 155)
1. Leaves without a vitta.
   2 Underleaves connate with one or both leaves; leaf margins entire, inconspicuously serrulate to strongly dentate .   2 **Connatae** (p. 103)
   2 Underleaves free from the leaves; leaf margins not serrulate.
      3 Underleaves divided to the middle into long lobes or teeth (no representatives reported for the Americas) 3. **Fissistipulae** (p 124)
      3 Underleaves more or less entire, or less than one-third divided into lobes or teeth.
         4. Leaves with a conspicuous, usually appendiculate ventral auricle; underleaves large, cordate, attached in a recurved line, the line of attachment of the leaf curved in the upper part, the dorsal end bent downward forming a hook,
                              4 **Appendiculatae** (p. 125)
        4 Auricles of the leaves, if conspicuous, never appendiculate; underleaves always attached in a straight line, the line of leaf insertion curved to hook-formed,
                              1. **Grandistipulae** (p. 38)

---

*The American species which STEPHANI included in the Section *Parvistipula* are included in the *Grandistipulae* section of this paper Of the five species which he included in the *Parvistipula, M. deciduum, M. elegantulum* and *M. Krugianum* are small, depauperate, or juvenile forms of *B longistipula,* p 81, and *M. tenue* is a small plant of *B. longa,* p 90 Since the small size of the plant, and the small, distant underleaves are the only criteria of the Section, it is often impossible to determine whether a specimen is an example of a species which is normally of small size, or is a juvenile or poorly developed form of a species of normally larger size, unless additional specific characteristics are taken into consideration For this reason, *M tricuspidatum* has also been transferred, and is treated under the Section *Grandistipulae,* p. 38

†All of the American members of this Section have also been transferred to other Sections and are discussed elsewhere.

Section 1. Grandistipulae

Plants large or small, leaves without a vitta or conspicuous ventral auricles or appendages, the teeth with entire margins, the underleaves attached in a straight line, free from the leaves.

Key to the Species

1   Underleaves made up in part of hyaline cells which may form a conspicuous border
- 2. Leaf cells uniformly thin-walled, trigones absent or minute, cell lumina rounded; underleaves hyaline except for a small internal area at the base . . . . 2 **B. affinis** (p 39)
- 2. Leaf cells thin-walled, trigones conspicuous, with bulging sides, cell lumina angular-rounded
  - 3   Underleaves longer than broad, one-third to three-fourths hyaline, lateral margins scarcely bulging, never hyaline to the base, leaves elongate-ovate, the teeth large . 9. **B. pallide-virens** (p 42)
  - 3. Underleaves subquadrate-rounded, the hyaline border continuous to the base.
    - 4   Hyaline cells thin-walled, chlorophyllose cells of the interior with conspicuous trigones . . . 10 B **stolonifera** (p. 44)
    - 4. Cell walls and trigones of the hyaline and chlorophyllose areas similar
      - 5   Hyaline border always narrow, of one to four rows of cells . . . . 11 **B. chilensis** (p. 51)
      - 5   Hyaline border variable, absent, broad, or including most of the underleaf   12 **B. taleana** (p. 54)
1. Underleaves chlorophyllose throughout.
- 2   Underleaves variously toothed or *deeply* lobed or divided in the apical portion and on the lateral margins.
  - 3. Underleaves abundantly spinose-dentate and ciliate, 13. **B. denticulata** (p 56)
  - 3. Underleaves coarsely toothed or lobed but never ciliate.
    - 4. Underleaves deeply four-lobed in the apical portion, 14. **B. quadricrenata** (p. 60)
    - 4   Underleaves variously toothed and lobed on the margins.
      - 5   Teeth of the leaves long, narrow, the margins crenulate . . . . 15. **B. aurescens** (p 63)
      - 5. Teeth of the leaves shorter, broad, the margins entire . . . . 16 **B. Glaziovii** (p 65)
- 2   Underleaves with entire margins, or only the apical margin retuse or with three or four undulations.
  - 3. Underleaves subquadrate.
    - 4. Plants large, green, underleaves often cordate.
      - 5. Lateral margins plane, entire, convex, the apex two or four-lobed or undulate . . 17 B **Breuteliana** (p. 68)
      - 5. Lateral margins recurved, convex, the apex retuse, 18. **B. acuminata** (p 75)
    - 4. Plants large, yellow-brown, underleaves cordate, attached in a recurved line (see Section *Appendiculatae, B Hookeri* and *B. robusta*).
    - 4. Plants smaller, not as above.
      - 5   Teeth of the leaves very small or obscure, 19. **B. diversicuspis** (p. 77)

    5. Teeth of the leaves well developed.
        6. Underleaves small, round, very distant on the stem; leaf apices broad, transversely truncate, trigones conspicuous* . . .   . 20 B. tricuspidata (p 79)
        6. Underleaves small to medium size, approximate to imbricated, broader than the stem.
           7 Leaves ascending, obliquely truncated, trigones conspicuous . . . 21 B. longistipula (p. 81)
           7 Leaves spreading or falcate, teeth very coarse, cells and trigones very large, plants red-brown . . . . .   23 B. longa (p. 90)
           7 Leaves spreading, cell walls thin, trigones inconspicuous, underleaves often in part hyaline,   12 B. taleana (p. 54)
 3 Underleaves longer than broad, rectangular in outline, the bases not cordate.
    4. Leaves ascendent, unequally three-toothed, cell walls thin, trigones conspicuous, plants green to yellow-brown,
                  21. B. longistipula (p 81)
    4 Leaves spreading to strongly falcate.
        5 Leaves spreading, long, teeth medium size; underleaves elongate, with parallel lateral margins, plants mostly golden yellow-brown . . . 22 B. latidens (p 88)
        5 Leaves falcate, sometimes spreading, unequally three-toothed, teeth large, coarse, cells and trigones very large; plants robust, yellow-brown to deep red-brown,   23 B. longa (p 90)
 3 Underleaves reniform, cordate at the bases.
    4 Underleaves inflated, appressed to the stem along the deeply pigmented margin, cells quadrate 24. B. jamaicensis (p 96)
    4. Underleaves plane, the margins not deeply pigmented, cells of the upper part elongate, with intermediate thickenings along the walls .   .   . 25. B. Wrightii (p 100)
 3 Underleaves ovate
    4. Apical margin entire.
        5 Underleaves inflated, appressed to the stem along the deeply pigmented margin, cells quadrate,
                  24. B. jamaicensis (p 96)
        5 Underleaves plane, the margins not pigmented, cells of the upper part elongate, with intermediate thickenings along the walls . . . 25 B. Wrightii (p. 100)
    4 Apical margin retuse, lateral margins recurved,
                  18 B. acuminata (p 75)

8. Bazzania affinis (Lindenb. & Gottsche) Trevis. Mem. Ist. Lomb. 13: 415. 1877.

Mastigobryum affine Lindenberg & Gottsche, in G. L & N., Syn. Hep. 720 1847. Not M affine Mitten, in Hooker, Bot. Ant. Voy. 2': Fl N. Zel. 147. pl C. fig. 4. 1854.
Mastigobryum inciso-bilobatum Stephani, in Herzog, Biblioth. Bot. 87: 224. fig. 165, a-b. 1916.

Plants scattered or growing in depressed mats, pale yellow-green to olive-green: stems slender, to 5 cm. or more in length, with leaves 2 mm. to 3 mm. broad, prostrate; in longitudinal section the cells elongate, the medullary cells averaging 0.18 mm. long,

---

*Depauperate forms of other species might be confused with **B. tricuspidata** unless a careful examination of the plants is made.

the cortical shorter, both averaging 0.18μ in diameter, the vertical walls uniformly thickened and containing frequent pits, the end walls thin; lateral branches 0.5 cm. to 1.5 cm. apart, diverging at a wide angle; flagelliform branches frequent, long; rhizoids scarce, arising on the underleaves at the base: leaf insertion little curved in the upper part; leaves spreading, approximate to densely imbricated, ascendent, becoming slightly falcate in robust plants, sometimes becoming deflexed when dry, unsymmetrically ovate, 1.0 mm. - 1.6 mm or more in length, mostly 0 56 mm. - 0 8 mm. broad at the base, narrowed a little to the transversely truncate, tridentate apex; the dorsal margin convex from a curved base which covers one-third to one-half the stem, the ventral margin convex, the base often more or less dilated; the apex broad, more or less equally tridentate; the teeth acute, deltoid, four to six cells long and broad, the sinuses lunulate to acute, the margins straight to undulate; the leaf cells quadrate to rectangular in outline, with equally thickened walls, the cell lumina rounded, the trigones very small or absent; cells of the dorsal base and apical portion quadrate, averaging 18μ × 18μ, those of the interior longer, averaging 36μ - 45μ × 18μ, not forming a vitta; the cuticle verruculose: underleaves distant to imbricated, in part hyaline, attached in a straight line, quadrate to oblong, mostly 0 48 mm. - 0.56 mm. long and wide, the apex straight to rounded, entire or with two to four short, broad teeth or lobes, the lateral margins nearly straight or bulging, entire or sometimes undulate, a little rounded at the bases; the cells with uniformly thickened walls and infrequent trigones, the hyaline cells occupying most of the leaf, the chlorophyllose cells making up a small, internal basal area: leaves of the flagelliform branches small, ovate, the apex mostly rounded· sexual branches not seen.

HABITAT· On decaying wood or on stones in woods

The distinguishing characteristics of the species are its dull, pale green prostrate stems, the tridentate leaves with quadrate cells and no or minute trigones; and the entire or slightly two- to four-lobed underleaves composed of hyaline cells throughout except for a small area of chlorophyllose cells in the basal region. (FIG. 10, nos. 1-12).

The portion of the type of *M. inciso-bilobatum* from the Rijksherbarium of Leiden was made up of plants identical with those of the type of *M. affine* from Mexico. Unfortunately, the illustrations which STEPHANI published with the original description of *M. inciso-bilobatum* and in the *Icones, Mastigobryum* no. 165 do

---

FIG. 10 — *Bazzania affinis* (Lindenb & Gottsche) Trevis. — 1. Portion of a plant, dorsal view, × 30. 2. Portion of a plant, ventral view, × 30. 3 Leaf, × 30 4 Apices of leaves, × 30 5 A cell from the apical region of a leaf, × 350. 6 Cells from an apical tooth of a leaf, × 260 7 Cells from the dorsal margin near the base, × 260 8 Cells from the ventral margin including some from the basal portion, × 260 9 Underleaves, × 30. 10 Portion of the base of an underleaf, including the margin, × 260 11. Portion of the apical region of an underleaf, × 260. 12. Portion of a cross-section of a stem, × 260 Nos. 1-11 drawn from a portion of the type material; no. 12 from material collected by A. C. SMITH in Fiji.

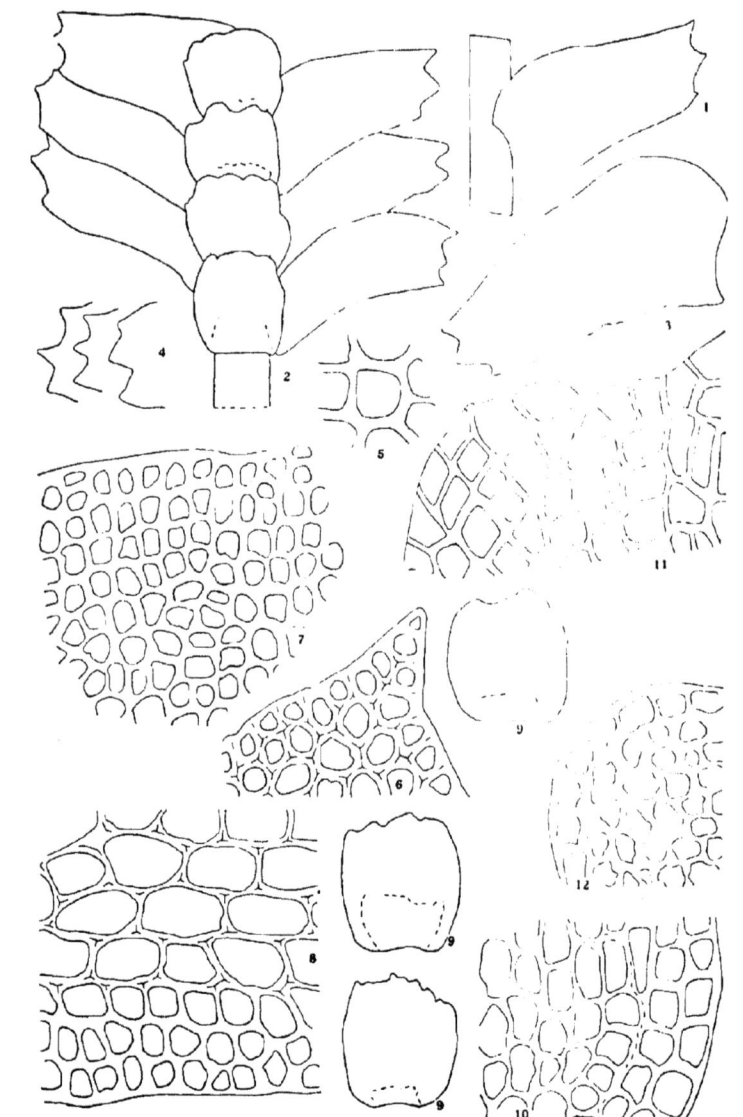

not agree with these plants. His illustrations indicate that the underleaves are cordate at the base and bilobed at the rounded apex. The underleaves of the material from Leiden are quadrate, not cordate at the base, and have truncate, entire or undulate apical margins.

DISTRIBUTION: M e x i c o : without locality or collector's name (NY). — C o l o m b i a · Bogotá, Andes, Weir (NY). — B o l i v i a : Rio Tocorani, no 4073, Herzog, the type of *M. inciso-bilobatum* (L). — P e r u . San Gavan, Lechler (NY). — F i j i I s l a n d s : Koro; Vanua Levu Thakaundrove, Smith (NY)

REFERENCES· Lindenberg & Gottsche (1856, 93); Gottsche (1863, 164); Stephani (1886, 242; 1908, 407; 1924, 468; *Icones, Mastigobryum* nos 151, 165).

9. Bazzania pallide-virens (Steph.) comb. nov.

Mastigobryum pallide-virens Stephani, Spec Hep 3· 473. 1908.

Plants medium size, olive-green to dark green, becoming slightly pigmented with brown in the older portions: stems slender, to 4 cm. or more long, with leaves to 3.5 mm. broad; flagelliform branches numerous; rhizoids colorless, occasional on the bases of leaves of the flagelliform branches: the line of leaf insertion curved in its upper part; leaves imbricated, mostly plane, unsymmetrical, ovate to elongate-oblong, straight to falcate, 1.8 mm. - 2.3 mm. long, 5 mm. - 6 mm. broad at the base, narrowed a little to the transversely truncate, tridentate apex; the dorsal margin convex from a curved base, covering one-half the stem, the ventral margins concave, the base little dilated, the apex sharply three-toothed, the teeth variable, three to eight cells long, three to six cells broad at the base, the sinuses deep, acute to lunulate, the margin entire; leaf cells thin-walled, the cell lumina angular-rounded, the trigones conspicuous, rarely becoming coalesced, the cuticle verruculose; cells of the apical region 20μ - $32\mu \times 22\mu$, those of the median portion larger, those of the base 48μ - $60\mu \times 24\mu$, a vitta not differentiated: underleaves distant to subimbricated, oblong, attached in a straight line, in part hyaline, the lateral margins nearly straight, entire, the apex truncate, entire, undulate or variously lobed, the hyaline border varying from several rows to the entire upper half of the leaf in width, the cells rectangular in outline, 24μ - $36\mu \times 20\mu$, those of the chlorophyllose area similar: the leaves of the flagelliform branches scale-like, ovate: male branches catkin-like, solitary, one to several on a stem, the bracts and bracteoles similar, concave, broadly ovate, shortly bifid, antheridia occurring singly: female branches and perianths not seen.

HABITAT: Not given.

The distinguishing characteristics of the species are its green color; the mostly elongate, tridentate leaves with thin-walled cells and distinct trigones; and the oblong underleaves, one-third to three-fourths convex, hyaline, with scarcely convex, entire, lateral margins and entire to variously lobed apices. (FIG. 11, nos. 1-6).

The species differs from *B. affinis* in that its leaves are longer, the leaf cells have conspicuous trigones with bulging sides, and the basal portions of the underleaves are not bordered by hyaline cells.

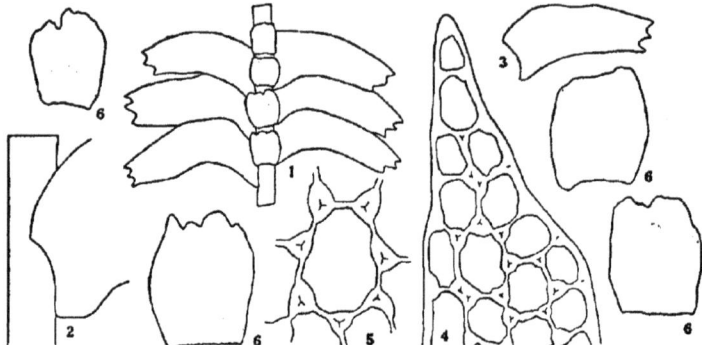

FIG 11. — *Bazzania pallide-virens* (Steph.) Fulford. — 1 Portion of a plant, ventral view, × 15. 2. Portion of a leaf and stem, dorsal view, × 30 3 A leaf, × 15 4. A tooth of a leaf, × 310. 5. A cell from the apical portion of a leaf, × 400. 6. Underleaves, × 30 Nos. 1-6 drawn from a portion of the type material

DISTRIBUTION B r a z i l : without locality, Glaziou, 14418, the type (H).
REFERENCES Stephani (*Icones, Mastigobryum* no. 172)

10. **Bazzania stolonifera** (Swartz) Trevis. Mem. Ist. Lomb. 13: 415. 1877.

Jungermannia stolonifera Swartz, Prodr Fl Ind. occ. 144 1788
Pleuroschisma stoloniferum Dumortier, Receuil d'obs Jungerm 20 1835
Herpetium stoloniferum Montagne in D'Orbigny, Voy. l'Amer Merid. 7'· 74. 1839
Mastigobryum stoloniferum Lindenberg in G. L & N, Syn Hep. 227. 1845
Jungermannia vincentiana Lehm & Lindenb. in Lehman, Pug. Pl 4. 59. 1832.
Herpetium vincentianum Mont. loc. cit
Mastigobryum vincentinum Lehm. & Lindenb in G L & N, op cit p 226
Bazzania vincentina Trevis. op. cit p. 414.
Mastigobryum Turkheimii Bvrd. in Stephani, Spec. Hep 6. 481 1924
Mastigobryum sylvaticum Stephani ms, non Gottsche, loc cit as synonym
Bazzania leptostipa Spruce, Trans & Proc Bot Soc. [Edinburgh] 15: 374. 1885.
Mastigobryum leptostipum Stephani, Spec Hep 3· 524. 1909.
Mastigobryum Lindigii Stephani, Hedwigia 25. 203 pl 3 fig 44-45. 1886.
Bazzania Lindigii Spruce, Mem Torrey Bot Club 1. 129. 1890.
Mastigobryum Quelchii Stephani, Spec. Hep 3. 471. 1908.

Plants large, dull olive-green to brownish green, light yellow-green at the growing tip: stems stout, to 10 cm. or more long, with leaves to 5 mm. wide, in deep tufts or depressed mats; stem cells in longitudinal section averaging 0.16 mm. long, the marginal cells shorter, both containing pits, the end walls thin, lateral branches numerous, 1 cm. or more apart, diverging at a wide angle; flagelliform branches numerous, long, often branched; rhizoids colorless, present only on the leaves of the flagelliform branches; the line of leaf insertion curved in the upper part, leaves widely spreading, imbricated, nearly plane, becoming convex on drying, sometimes strongly deflexed, unsymmetrically ovate, to 3 cm long on robust plants, to 1.5 mm. wide at the base, narrowing to the truncate, tridentate apex, the dorsal margin strongly convex from a rounded base which covers two-thirds the stem, the ventral margin somewhat concave, sometimes dilated at the base, the apex transversely truncate, strongly to faintly tridentate, the teeth spreading, deltoid, acute to subobtuse, mostly unequal, large, three to seven cells long, three to seven cells broad at the base, the sinuses broad, lunulate, to acute, the margins straight to undulate; the cell cavities angular-rounded to stellate, the cell walls thin, the trigones small to large, with convex sides, often becoming confluent, the cuticle verruculose; cells of the apical portion and dorsal base averaging 25μ long $\times$ 21μ wide, those of the median portion longer, those of the base mostly 45μ $\times$ 21μ, a vitta not differentiated: underleaves subimbricated to imbricated, attached in a straight

FIG. 12. — *Bazzania stolonifera* (Swartz) Trevis. — 1. Portion of stem, dorsal view, $\times$ 12. 2. Portion of stem, ventral view, $\times$ 12 3 Leaf, $\times$ 12 4. Apices of leaves, $\times$ 30 5. A cell from the apical portion of a leaf, $\times$ 350. 6. Apical tooth, $\times$ 260 7. Cells from the dorsal margin of a leaf, $\times$ 260. 8. Cells from the ventral margin of a leaf, $\times$ 260. 9. Cells from the basal portion of a leaf, $\times$ 260 10 Underleaf, $\times$ 30. 11. Cells from the lateral margin of an underleaf, $\times$ 260. 12. Cells from the apical portion of an underleaf, $\times$ 260. Nos. 1-12 drawn from the type, *J. stolonifera*, from Jamaica.

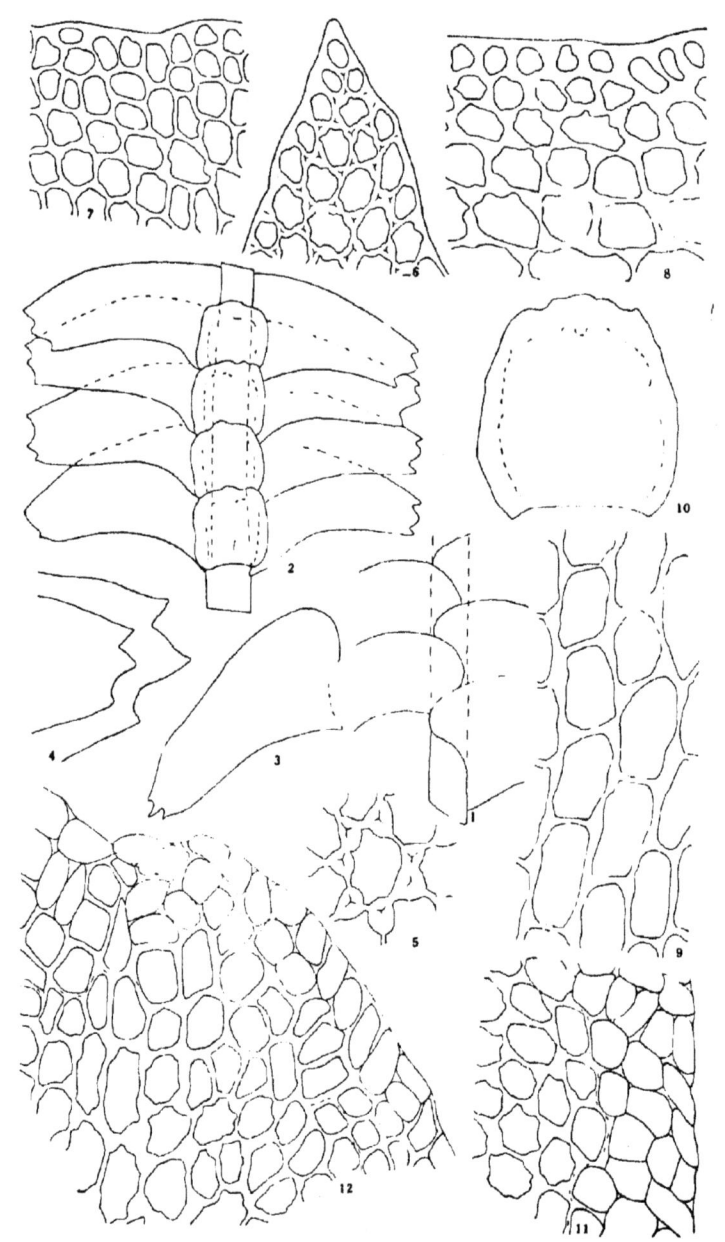

line, broadly round-quadrate, mostly 0.7 mm. - 0.8 mm. long, 0.8 mm. - 1 mm. wide, broader than the stem, with a hyaline border, the apex truncated, broadly undulate, slightly three- or four-lobed, the lateral margins convex, the bases rounded to semicordate; the hyaline border continuous, four to eight or more cells wide, the cells more or less rectangular, thin-walled, 18μ - 30μ long $\times$ 15μ - 18μ wide, trigones rare; cells of the chlorophyllose internal portion averaging 25μ in diameter, longer near the line of attachment, the trigones with bulging sides as in the leaf, the cell lumina angular-rounded: leaves of the flagelliform branches ovate, 0 22 mm. - 0.37 mm. long, squarrose-spreading, concave, the margins crenulate, the apex rounded to acute · male branches few to many on a stem, to 1 mm. long, ovoid, the bracteoles small, subquadrate, mostly 0.25 mm. long $\times$ 0 57 mm. wide, concave, mostly bilobed, the bracts larger, broadly ovate, mostly 0.6 mm. long $\times$ 0.5 mm. - 0.6 mm wide, strongly concave, the apex bi- or tridentate with short, broad teeth, the lateral margins crenulate; the antheridia borne singly or in pairs: female branches several on a stem; the bracts and bracteoles similar, oblanceolate, the outer series averaging 0.67 mm. long $\times$ 0.45 mm. wide, the apex shortly bi- or tridentate, the innermost series larger, 1.5 mm. - 1.8 mm. long $\times$ 0 85 mm. - 0 95 mm. wide at the base, the apex one-third to one-fourth divided into two to four long, narrow, crenulate teeth, the lateral margins crenulate, often crenulate, the cells all of one kind, rectangular in outline, mostly $78\mu \times 20\mu$, cell walls, for the most part uniform, but with occasional protuberances on the inner walls of some of the cells: perianth to 6 mm. long, ovoid-cylindrical, three-keeled in the median portion, contracted at the short-ciliate to dentate mouth: capsule 1.5 mm. long, ovoid-cylindrical, of four or five layers of cells, the thickenings similar to those of *B. trilobata;* elaters to 390μ long, 18μ wide, bispiral, the ends rounded; spores 15μ - 18μ, minutely punctate.

HABITAT: In deep tufts or mats or mixed with other bryophytes, on soil, trees and logs in woods.

The distinguishing characteristics of the species are its large size, the olive-green to brown-green color, the large, tridentate leaves with angular-rounded to stellate cell cavities and conspicuous

---

FIG. 13 — *Bazzania stolonifera* (Swartz) Trevis. — 1. Portion of a stem, ventral view, $\times$ 10 2 Stem and leaf, dorsal view, $\times$ 20 3 Cells from the apical portion of a leaf, $\times$ 200 4 A cell from the apical portion of a leaf, $\times$ 350. 5. Cells from the dorsal margin of a leaf, near the base, $\times$ 200. 6. Cells from the ventral margin of a leaf near the base, including those from the middle of the leaf, $\times$ 200. 7. Cells from the lateral margin of an underleaf, $\times$ 200. 8. Portion of a transverse section of a stem, $\times$ 230. 9 Apices of leaves, $\times$ 30 10. Cells from the apical portion of a leaf, $\times$ 350 11 Underleaf, $\times$ 30 12 Portion of a plant, ventral view, $\times$ 15. 13. A cell from the apical portion of a leaf, $\times$ 400 14. A leaf, $\times$ 15. 15. Cells from the apical portion of a leaf, $\times$ 400 16. Underleaves, $\times$ 15 17 A cell from the apical portion of a leaf, $\times$ 400 18. Underleaf, $\times$ 15. 19 A cell from the apical portion of a leaf, $\times$ 400 20 Underleaf, $\times$ 15. 21. A cell from the apical portion of a leaf, $\times$ 400. 22. Underleaf, $\times$ 15. Nos. 1-8 drawn from plants collected by EVANS, no. 110, in Puerto Rico; 9-11 from the type of *J. vincentiana,* from St. Vincent; 12-13 from the type of *M. Lindigii,* from Colombia; 14-16 from the type of *B leptostipa,* from Ecuador; 17-18 from the type of *M. Turkheimii,* from Guatemala; 19-20 from the type of *M. sylvaticum* Steph., from Guatemala; 21-22 from the type of *M. Quelchii,* from Guiana.

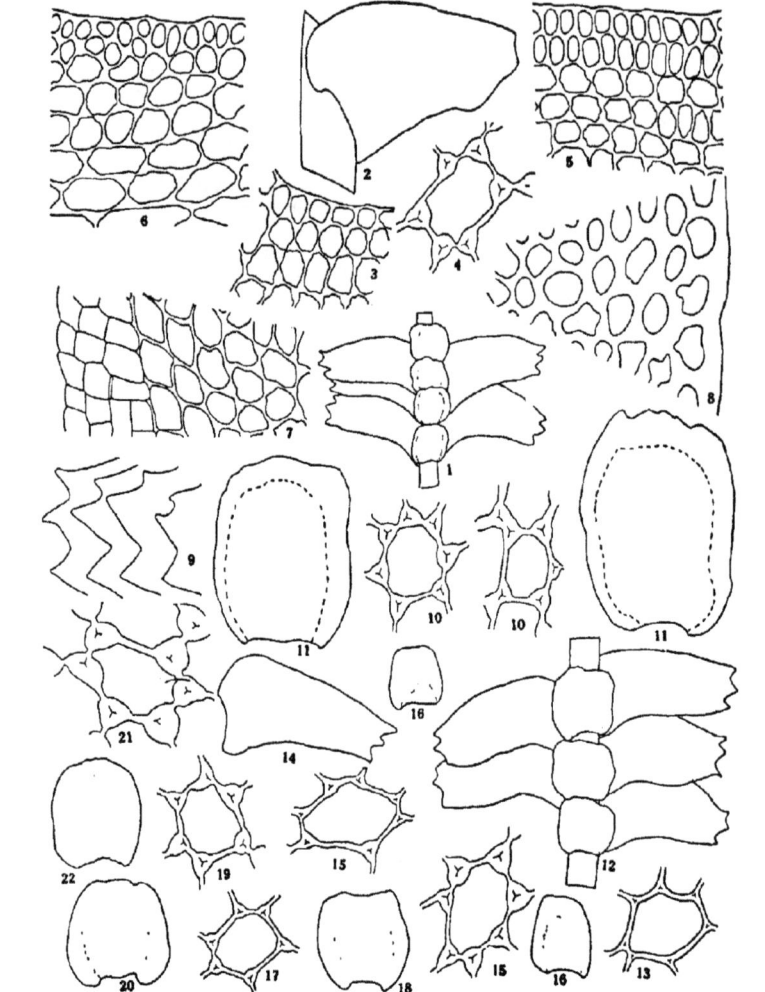

trigones; and the large, round-quadrate underleaves with continuous hyaline borders of thin-walled cells surrounding the chlorophyllose cells, the latter with conspicuous trigones. FIGS. 12, nos. 1-12; 13, nos. 1-22; 14, nos. 1-10).

The species is widespread throughout the West Indies and tropical South America, and because of its size and abundance is perhaps more frequently collected than most of the other species of this genus. As is the case of most of the other species, *B. stolonifera* also exhibits a wide variety of habitat modifications, particularly in the size of the trigones of the cells of the leaves, and in the width of the hyaline borders of the underleaves.

The type specimens of *J. stolonifera* from Jamaica (see FIG. 12, nos. 1-12) are large, dark green plants deeply pigmented with brown, with large, round-quadrate underleaves, semicordate at the bases, and having a border of hyaline cells. The trigones of the leaf cells are very strongly developed, with bulging sides, and often become coalesced. The cell cavities are more or less stellate.

In contrast to these are the plants of the type of *J. vincentiana* which agree in size, form, position of the leaves and underleaves, hyaline borders, etc., as is shown in FIG. 13, nos. 9-11, but differ in that they are less deeply pigmented and have a somewhat different cell pattern. The cell walls are thin, and the trigones are small with bulging sides, and do not often become confluent, so that the cell cavity is angular-rounded rather than stellate. Because the walls of the outer rows of cells are somewhat thicker than those of the internal cells, these cells appear to form a border around the leaf. While the marginal rows of cells of *J. stolonifera* also have thickened walls, the border is not conspicuous because of the large trigones and thick walls (coalesced trigones) throughout the leaf. This modification is not uncommon, and is illustrated further, FIG. 13, nos. 1-8, by plants from Puerto Rico.

Plants of *B. leptostipa* collected by SPRUCE in Ecuador (FIG. 13, nos. 14-16), are somewhat smaller and more lax in habit and more delicate than the plants of *J. stolonifera*. The brown pigmentation is pronounced. On one stem the trigones of the cells of a leaf near the growing tip were conspicuous while those of the cells of leaves 3 cm. farther down the stem were very much smaller. The underleaves are distant to subimbricated. Many of them, especially those associated with leaves in which the trigones were minute, were mostly hyaline, with the chlorophyllose cells restricted to a small area near the base, but those on the upper part of the stem — where the trigones of the leaves were larger — had a much larger area of chlorophyllose cells, and were typical for the species. SPRUCE says of the leaves that they are deciduous. While several plants of the material examined were without leaves over a part of the stem, most of the plants still retained them, so that there may be a question as to whether these leaves were truly caducous or had become detached through some accidental means. All of the plants are very brittle when dry. This modification of the species at first

FIG 14 — *Bazzania stolonifera* (Swartz) Trevis. — 1 Male bracteole,
× 40 2 Male bracts, × 40 3 Male bract with two antheridia, × 50 4. Tip
of male bract, × 100 5 Female bract of outermost series, × 40 6 Female
bracts of an intermediate series, × 40 7 Tip of female bract of intermediate series, × 200 8-9 Female bracts of the innermost series, × 40
10 Tip of female bract of innermost series, × 200. Nos. 1-4 drawn from
plants collected by UNDERWOOD, no. 825, on John Crow Peak, Jamaica, 5-10
drawn from plants collected by EVANS, no 110, at El Yunque, Puerto Rico

glance suggests *B. affinis* but a close examination will show that it does not belong to the latter, because of the trigone pattern of the cells of the leaves and the chlorophyllose cells of the underleaves of the more vigorous plants. The leaves of *B. affinis* have uniformly thickened walls without trigones, or with very inconspicuous ones, and the underleaves are made up mostly of hyaline cells with the trigones not conspicuous in the green cells.

A further degree of modification in this same direction is exhibited by plants of the type of *M. Türkheimii* and the ms. species *M. sylvaticum* of STEPHANI (FIG. 13, nos. 17-20), collected in Guatemala. These plants are light green in color, very large, the underleaves have very broad, hyaline borders, and the leaf cells are thin-walled, with very small trigones which have bulging sides. The walls of the marginal rows of cells are unthickened. Here again, the differences are a matter of slight degrees of modification and are probably due to a combination of habitat factors.

M. Lindigii collected in Colombia is also a representative of the extremely mesophytic modification of the species. The plants are light green with some degree of brown pigmentation. The cells of the leaves have thin walls and very small trigones (FIG. 13, no. 13). The underleaves are large and the hyaline borders well developed (FIG. 13, no. 12).

The plants of *M. Quelchii* collected in British Guiana are robust and golden brown in color. The cells of the leaves have thin walls but the trigones are large and are very often confluent, and the underleaves are distinctive, with the usual typical hyaline borders as is shown in FIG. 13, nos. 21 and 22.

The range of variation in trigone size seems to be due to a combination of the age of the plants and the habitat conditions, as has been shown by BUCH to be the condition in the genus *Scapania*. The degree of pigmentation also varies according to the habitat and age of the plant, as is the condition in other species of the genus.

Male and female branches are frequently present. The female bracts and bracteoles and the perianth mouth are distinctive and will furnish further diagnostic characteristics (see FIG. 14, nos. 1-10).

DISTRIBUTION. C u b a . without locality or collector's name, cited by Stephani (1909, 527); Santiago de Cuba, Funck & Schlim, 2097 (H). — D o m i n i c a : Morne Micotrin, 97, 99, Morne Couronne, 218, Elliott, cited by Spruce (1895, 356) — G u a d e l o u p e · without locality, Madianna (NY), without locality, l'Herminier 55, 119 (NY), without locality, Husnot, Pl Antilles, 212 (NY); Mornes des Deus Marnelles, Duss 282 p p. (NY); nos. 117, 282 p.p. from Morne Hirondelle are *B. Breuteliana*, without locality, l'Herminier, Gottsche & Rabenhorst, Hepat. eur. 561 (Y, NY); without locality, Grateloup, Hb. Montagne, cited by Bescherelle (1893, 186); St. Rose, l'Herminier (H); Soufrière, Duss 66, 205, 320 as *M. portoricense* (NY) — J a m a i c a . without locality, Swartz, the type (B, NY, H), without locality, Menzies 101 (NY); without locality, Wilson (NY), without locality, Hart, cited by Boswell (1887, 50); John Crow Peak, near Cinchona, E G Britton 213 (NY); base of John Crow Peak, 5000-5500 ft., Underwood 2327, 2328, 2370, 2421, 2426 (Y, NY), John Crow Peak, 5500-5800 ft , Underwood 684, 825, 832, 834, 2427, 2428 (Y, NY), Morce's Gap, 1500 m., Maxon & Killip

647 (Y, NY); Blue Mountain, Bennet (NY), Britton 1103, 1190, 1227 (Y, NY), Greenwich Woodlands, 4500 ft., Harris 11,170 (NY), New Haven Gap, Evans 537 (Y); near Hardware Gap, 4000 ft, Underwood 2240 (Y, NY); Doll Woods, Evans 495 (Y), road from Cinchona to Morce's Gap, 5000 ft, Underwood 273 (NY); without locality, Wilson 768 (NY); Morce's Gap, New Haven Gap, Patterson (F) — M a r t i n i q u e : without locality, Husnot, Pl. Antilles, 212 (NY); Calebasse, Mt Pelée, Duss 13, cited by Stephani (1903, 22), 117 (NY). — P u e r t o R i c o · El Yunque, Evans 110 (NY); Sierra Luquillo, Br Hioram 403 p.p. (NY), without locality, Sintenis, 16, cited by Stephani (1888a, 279); without locality, Sintenis 92, as *B. Wrightii* (NY), without locality, Schwanecke, cited by Hampe & Gottsche (1852, 350); Mt Britton, Jones 10978 (H). — S t K i t t s . without locality, Breutel (NY); Mt. Misery, Breutel (NY); Britton & Cowell 508 (NY); without locality or collector, cited by Stephani (1909, 527). — S t . V i n c e n t · without locality, Hb Hooker 170 (NY), St Andrews, Guilding, Hb Hooker, the type of *J. vincentiana* (NY); without locality, Menzies (NY); without locality, Hart, cited by Boswell (1887, 50); St. Andrews, Elliott 63, cited by Spruce (1895, 356), without locality, G. W. Smith (H). — M e x i c o . β *intermedia*, Vera Cruz, Liebmann 52, cited by Gottsche (1863, 231). — B r i t i s h H o n d u r a s · Camayaguam, 1800 m, Yuncker, Dawson & Youse, 6617, 6618 (F) — C o s t a R i c a : Cartago, Maxon 502 (NY); Yerba Buena, Standley 49949, 49882, 49842; forma *defolians* 49869; forma *minor*, *ramulosa* 49891; Laguna de la Chonta, Standley 42240, Alto de la Estrella, Standley 39101; Cerro de las Lajas, Standley 51612 f *rufescens* (W). — G u a t e m a l a : Cobán, Turkheim 5816, the type of *M. Turkheimii* (G), no 5582 as *M viridissimum*, no. 5418 as *M Quelchii* (H). — N i c a r a g u a · Segovia (Ocotal), Oersted, cited by Hampe (1851, 302) — B o l i v i a . without locality, D'Orbigny, cited by Montagne (1839, 74); also *H vincentianum* from the same reference; Corana, Herzog 3390a, cited by Stephani (1916, 225) as *M Lindigii*. — B r a z i l : Rio de Janeiro, Glaziou 4572 (NY), the same, cited by Nees von Esenbeck in Martius (1833, 1 337), Espirito, Santo, Ynes Mexia 4076 (H, NY). — C o l o m b i a Merida, Moritz, cited by Hampe (1847, 328), without locality, Lindig, the type of *M. Lindigii* (H); without locality, Wallace (NY), var. *granatensis* cited by Gottsche (1864, 140) — E c u a d o r · Mt. Tunguragua, Spruce (1885, 377); Mt. Chimboraza, Spruce, Hepat. Spruc., the type of *B leptostipa* (Y). — G u i a n a . var *irregulare* Nees et Mont. ms, Leprieur 292, cited by Montagne (1840, 333). — B r i t i s h G u i a n a : Mt Roraima, McConnell & Quelch, cited by Stephani (1901-05, 98); Mt Roraima, Quelch, the type of *M Quelchii* (H) — Listed also from the Island of Bourbon, Bory; Australia and Sandwich Islands.

REFERENCES· Swartz (1806, 3 · 1862); Weber & Mohr (1807, 409); Lunan (1814, 518); Schwaegrichen (1814, 19); Weber (1815, 43); Sprengel (1827, 4: 222); Nees von Esenbeck (1830, 61, 1833b, 376); Wallroth (1831, 75); Montagne (1840, 333; 1844-46, 242; 1855, 315); G. L. & N. (1844-47, 720); Hampe (1847, 328; 1851, 302; 1873, 227); Lindenberg & Gottsche (1851, 71, 78); Hampe & Gottsche (1852, 350); Gottsche (1863, 231, 1864, 140); Husnot (1875, 3); Spruce (1885, 377; 1895, 356); Boswell (1887, 50); Stephani (1888a, 279; 1901-05, 98, 1903, 22; 1908, 471; 1909, 526; 1924, 481; *Icones, Mastigobryum* nos. 168, 174, 176, 178, 391, 406); Bescherelle (1893, 186); Herzog (1938, 19); Pagán (1939, 39).

11. Bazzania chilensis (Steph.) comb. nov.

Mastigobryum chilense Stephani, Hedwigia 24 · 247. pl. 2. fig. 1. 1885.

Plants medium size, dark green, pigmented with brown: stems to 3 cm. (?) long, with leaves to 3 mm. broad; lateral branches frequent, diverging at a wide angle; flagelliform branches frequent; rhizoids colorless, present on the leaves of the flagelliform branches:

the line of leaf insertion curved in its upper part; leaves imbricated, plane, becoming a little deflexed when dry, unsymmetrically ovate, straight or nearly so, 1.4 mm. - 1.8 mm. long, 0.5 mm. broad at the base, narrowed to the transversely truncate, tridentate apex; the dorsal margin strongly arched from a rounded base, covering two-thirds of the stem, the ventral margin straight, the base scarcely dilated, the apex three-toothed, the teeth large, eight to twelve cells long, five to ten cells broad at the base, the sinuses deep, acute to lunulate, the margins entire; the leaf cells thin-walled, the trigones conspicuous, often confluent, the cell lumina angular-rounded, the cuticle strongly verruculose; cells of the apical portion mostly $20\mu \times 20\mu$, of the median portion larger, and of the base $40\mu \times 22\mu$, a vitta not differentiated: underleaves distant to imbricated, attached in a straight line, broader than the stem, round-quadrate in outline, mostly 0.43 mm long and 0 5 mm. broad, with a hyaline border, the lateral margins convex from a rounded base, the apex truncate, mostly straight, crenulate, the hyaline border of one or two rows of cells on the lateral margins, of two to four rows at the apex, the cells averaging 16μ in diameter, the walls thin, the trigones small but distinct, those of the chlorophyllose area similar. sexual branches not seen.

HABITAT: Not given.

The distinguishing characteristics of the species are its medium size, the dark green color; the strongly tridentate leaves with small, thin-walled cells with conspicuous trigones; and the round-quadrate underleaves with a border of one to three rows of hyaline cells not distinct from the chlorophyllose cells in size, wall thickness, or trigone structure. (FIG. 15, nos. 1-6).

The plants remind one of small forms of *B. stolonifera* but they differ from that species in several characteristics. The cells of the leaf are smaller, mostly $20\mu \times 20\mu$, while in *B. stolonifera* they are mostly 24μ - $30\mu \times 24\mu$. The cuticle is more strongly verruculose. The greatest difference between the two species is to be found in the underleaves In *B. chilensis* the underleaves are smaller and the hyaline margin is not nearly so distinct. This hyaline margin varies from one to four cells in width in the apical portion, and is only one or two cells wide along the lateral margins as is seen in FIG. 15, nos. 1, 5 and 6. Only rarely is it entirely absent from the basal portion of the margin. These hyaline cells do not differ from those of the chlorophyllose interior except in the absence of chlorophyll (FIG. 15, no. 16). The cell walls and trigones are similar in the two areas. This characteristic alone is sufficiently striking to immediately separate *B. chilensis* from *B. stolonifera*, for in the latter the cells of the hyaline part are very different from those of the chlorophyllose area.

STEPHANI listed several specimens, "Peru, Callao (NOLLNER), Tatanara (LECHLER), Chile (LECHLER), Nova Granada (SCHLIM 861)" in his original description of the species, and did not designate any one of them as the type. The plants collected by SCHLIM no. 861 in Colombia were the only ones available for study (see FIG. 15, nos. 1-6). They do not agree with the original description

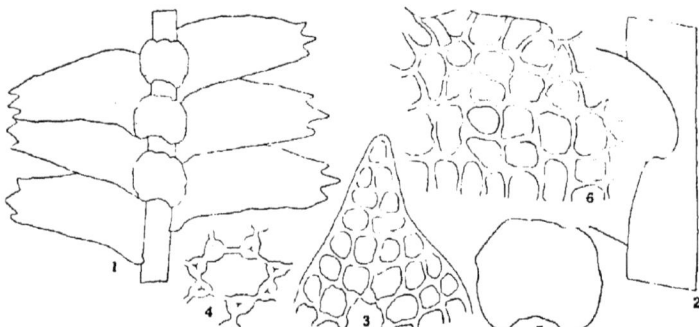

Fig 15 — *Bazzania chilensis* (Steph) Fulford — 1 Portion of a plant,
ventral view, × 15   2. Portion of a leaf and stem, dorsal view, × 30
3. Apical tooth of a leaf, × 310   4 A cell from the apical portion of a leaf,
× 400   5 Underleaf, × 30   6 Cells from the apical portion of an underleaf showing the hyaline margin, × 310. Nos. 1-6 drawn from a portion
of the type (?) material, collected by Schlim in Colombia

and figures in *Hedwigia* or with the figures in the unpublished
Icones, Mastigobryum no. 381, which were made from plants collected by Lechler in Chile. It may be that a study of the other
collections cited will bring to light plants of the sort illustrated by
Stephani. If that is the case, the plants described above represent
an up to now undescribed species. Stephani's illustrations
suggest robust plants of *B. Breuteliana.*

DISTRIBUTION. B o l i v i a : Yungas, Rusby, cited by Spruce (1890, 129).
— C h i l e · without locality, Lechler, cited by Stephani (1885, 247) —
C o l o m b i a · without locality, Schlim 861 (H). — P e r u · Callao,
Nollner, cited by Stephani (1885, 247), Tatanara, Lechler, cited by Stephani
(1885, 247).

REFERENCES· Stephani (1909, 522, *Icones, Mastigobryum* no 381).

12. Bazzania taleana (Gottsche) comb. nov.

Mastigobryum taleanum Gottsche, Mex. Leberm 131 1863
Mastigobryum longiscuspe Stephani, Spec. Hep 3: 472 1908.
Mastigobryum variedentatum Stephani, in Herzog, Biblioth. Bot. 87· 225
     Fig 166 1916

Plants delicate, medium size, olive-green, becoming pigmented
with brown in the older portions· stems to 3 cm. or more in length,
with leaves to 2.5 mm. broad· lateral branches frequent, mostly 5
cm apart, diverging at a wide angle· flagelliform branches frequent; rhizoids not seen the line of leaf insertion curved in its
upper part; leaves imbricated, plane to deflexed, unsymmetrically
ovate, ascendent, 1 mm. - 1.5 mm. long, 0 5 mm. broad at the base,
narrowed a little to the transversely truncate, tridentate apex; the
dorsal margin convex from a curved base, covering one-half the
stem, the ventral margin straight, the base scarcely dilated, the
apex more or less equally three-toothed, the teeth narrow, sharp,
five to eight cells long, four to six cells broad at the base, usually
ending in a row of two cells, the sinuses broad, lunulate, the
margins mostly entire; the leaf cells quadrate in outline, the walls
thin, the trigones minute, the cell lumina rounded, the cuticle faintly
verruculose; the cells of the apical region mostly 16μ - 20μ × 18μ,
of the median portion larger, and of the base to 40μ × 24μ, a vitta
not differentiated· the underleaves distant to imbricated, round-quadrate, attached in a straight line, broader than the stem, .55
mm. - .65 mm long × 55 mm. - 6 mm. broad, the lateral margins
entire, convex from a rounded base, the apex mostly entire, repand
to undulate, the cells as in the apical portion of the leaf, sometimes hyaline in part: leaves of the flagelliform branches scale-like, ovate, acute to bifid· sexual branches not seen.

HABITAT· Not given.
The distinguishing characteristics of the species are its medium
size and green color; the slightly ascendent leaves, transversely
truncate, and set with three, nearly equal, short teeth often ending
in two-celled points; the quadrate leaf cells with thin walls,
minute trigones and rounded cell lumina; and the round-quadrate,
repand underleaves with entire margins. The underleaves may be
in part or entirely devoid of chlorophyll. (FIG. 16, nos. 1-10).

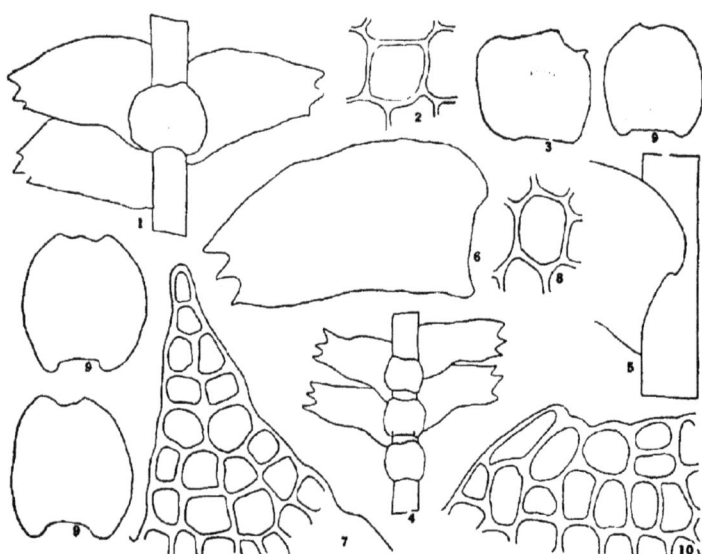

FIG. 16 — *Bazzania taleana* (Gottsche) Fulford — 1 Portion of a plant, ventral view, × 30   2 A cell from the apical portion of a leaf, × 400. 3 Underleaf, × 30.   4. Portion of a plant, ventral view, × 15.   5 Portion of a leaf and stem, dorsal view, × 30   6 A leaf, × 30.   7. A tooth of a leaf, × 310.   8. A cell from the apical portion of a leaf, × 400.   9. Underleaves, × 30.   10. A portion of the apical margin of an underleaf, × 310.   Nos 1-3 drawn from a portion of the type of *M. taleanum* (H), 4-10 from a portion of the type of *M. longicuspe* (H).

The plants of *M. longicuspe* from Brazil seem to be better developed than those of *M. taleanum* from Mexico, although all of the material is fragmentary (see FIG. 16, nos. 1 and 4). The two-celled points of the teeth of the leaves (FIG. 16, no. 7), seem to be a constant characteristic on the more robust plants.

The underleaves are round-quadrate, with the apex more or less retuse, and the margins entire, as is shown in FIG. 16, nos. 1, 3, 4, and 9. It is not unusual to find an underleaf one-half to two-thirds hyaline adjacent to an underleaf which is chlorophyllose throughout its entire area. Since not all of the underleaves on a stem are completely or in part hyaline, it would seem that for this species the hyaline characteristic may be due to external conditions. There is no differentiation in structure between the hyaline and chlorophyllose cells. The margins of the underleaves of poorly developed plants are in part crenulate or even occasionally dentate.

The plants of *M. variedentatum* collected by HERZOG in Bolivia are like those mentioned above except that none of the underleaves are hyaline. However, since this is a variable characteristic in both *M. taleanum* and *M. longicuspe*, there seems to be no justification for considering *M. variedentatum* a distinct species. B. *taleana* is readily distinguished from the other members of the *Grandistipulae* which have the underleaves in part hyaline, since the underleaves are retuse with entire margins, the hyaline areas of the underleaves of a stem vary in size and position, and the hyaline cells are not structurally distinct.

DISTRIBUTION Mexico· Oaxaca, Mt Talea, Liebmann, the type (H). The portion of the type from the Herb Boissier was a poorly preserved plant of some other species — Brazil. Apiahy, Puiggari, the type of *M longicuspe* (H). — Bolivia: Comarapa, Herzog, the type of *M. variedentatum* (L).

REFERENCES Stephani (1909, 519. 1924, 468, *Icones, Mastigobryum* nos 169, 180, 401).

13 Bazzania denticulata (Lindenb & Gottsche) Trevis. Mem. Ist. Lomb. 13: 414. 1877.

Mastigobryum denticulatum Lindenberg & Gottsche, in G L & N. Syn Hep 718 1847
Mastigobryum planiusculum Lindenberg & Gottsche, loc cit
Bazzania planiuscula Trevis loc cit
Bazzania Rusbyi Spruce, Mem Torrey Bot. Club 1: 129. 1890

Plants medium size, light green becoming slightly pigmented with brown in the older portions: stems stout, to 5 cm. or more in

FIG. 17. — *Bazzania denticulata* (Lindenb. & Gottsche) Trevis. — 1 Portion of a plant, ventral view, × 10. 2. Portion of a leaf and stem, dorsal view, × 25 3. Leaf, × 25 4. Cells from the dorsal base, × 300 5. A cell from the apical portion of a leaf, × 400. 6 Underleaves, × 25. 7. Portion of the apical area of an underleaf, × 300. 8. Female bracts of an outer series, × 40. 9 Female bract of an intermediate series, × 40 10 Portion of a lacinia of this bract, × 100 11. Female bract of the innermost series, × 40. 12. Portion of a lacinia of this bract, × 400 13 Portion of a transverse section of a stem, × 400. Drawn from plants collected by MAXON and KILLIP in Jamaica.

length, with leaves to 3.5 mm. broad, prostrate; stem cells in longitudinal section averaging 0.17 mm long, the cortical shorter, both averaging 20μ in diameter, the vertical walls uniformly thickened, containing frequent pits, the end walls thin; lateral branches frequent, 5 mm. or more apart, diverging at a wide angle; flagelliform branches numerous, short; rhizoids present on the leaves of flagelliform branches: the line of leaf insertion curved in its upper part, the leaves imbricated, plane, becoming a little convex on drying, unsymmetrically ovate, straight, 1.5 mm. - 2 mm. long, to 1 mm. broad at the base, narrowing to the more or less obliquely truncate, strongly tridentate apex, the dorsal margin strongly convex from a rounded base, covering one-half or more of the stem, the ventral margin concave, the base sometimes dilated, the apex equally three-toothed, the teeth spreading, large, six to eight cells long, five to seven cells broad at the base, the margins entire, the sinuses acute to rounded, deep; leaf cells uniformly thin-walled, trigones scarcely evident, the cell lumina rounded, the cuticle faintly verruculose; cells of the apical region averaging 20μ, of the median portion larger, and of the base 30μ - 40μ × 24μ, a vitta not differentiated. underleaves approximate to imbricated, squarrose, subquadrate, broader than the stem, attached in a straight line, not connate with the leaves, 0.5 mm. - 0.7 mm. long × 0.6 mm - 0.9 mm. broad, the apex and lateral margins variously toothed with numerous long, narrow, often ciliate teeth or spines, becoming crenulate near the curved bases, the cells as in the leaves · leaves of the flagelliform branches scale-like, narrowly ovate, to 0.3 mm. long, the apex bi-tridentate: female branches occasional, solitary, one to several on a stem, the bracts and bracteoles similar, the outermost series ovate-lanceolate, 0 65 mm. long × 0.45 mm. broad, the margins crenulate, occasionally toothed, the apex with two to four sharp teeth; the intermediate series larger, to 2 mm. or more long, ovate-lanceolate, the margins ciliate to dentate, the apex divided into two to four sharp teeth or dentate laciniae; the innermost series similar, larger, more deeply divided into usually four dentate-ciliate laciniae, the lateral margins dentate to short ciliate, the cells rectangular in outline, 52μ - 90μ × 26μ, thin-walled male branches and perianths not seen.

HABITAT: Over mosses, tree bases and logs in wooded areas.

The distinguishing characteristics of the species are its pale green color, the prostrate habit, the spreading, strongly dentate leaves with uniformly thin-walled cells and minute trigones; and the subquadrate underleaves with irregularly and variously spinose to ciliate, toothed margins. The underleaves are *not* connate with the leaves. (FIGS. 17, nos. 1-13; 18, nos. 1-6).

The plants of the type material of *M. planiusculum* are not quite so large and do not have so many ciliate teeth on the margins of the underleaves as are to be found in *M. denticulatum*, but these differences are not constant. The plants of *B. Rusbyi* are lighter green, larger, and often have more teeth on the underleaves than do those mentioned above. STEPHANI considered both *M. planiusculum* and *B. Rusbyi* identical with *M. denticulatum* and reduced them to synonymy. SPRUCE considered *B. Rusbyi* very close to the

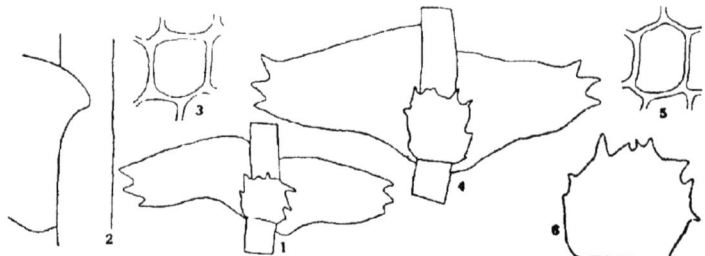

FIG 18 — *Bazzania denticulata* (Lindenb & Gottsche) Trevis. — 1 Portion of a plant, ventral view, × 15. 2. Portion of a leaf and stem, dorsal view, × 30 3 A cell from the apical portion of a leaf, × 400 4 Portion of a plant, ventral view, × 15 5 A cell from the apical portion of a leaf, × 400 6. Underleaf, × 30. Nos 1-3 drawn from a portion of the type of *M planiusculum* from Mexico, 4-6 from the type of *B. Rusbyi* from Bolivia.

Mexican *M. denticulatum*, and states (1890, 116), that the latter "is possibly its nearest congener, but is smaller, more opaque, and the underleaves are much less toothed, especially at the sides." There seems to be no adequate reason for keeping them distinct.

The species is easily distinguished from the other members of the *Tridentatae* because of its strongly three-toothed leaves, the uniform cell walls with inconspicuous trigones, and the ciliate, dentate underleaves. In appearance it resembles certain members of the West Indian *Connatae* Section, but the attachment of the underleaf, free from the leaves will at once distinguish it.

DISTRIBUTION: J a m a i c a John Crow Peak, Maxon & Killip 989 (NY); Morce's Gap, Evans 29 (Y), Cinchona, Earle (Y). — M e x i c o Oaxaca, Liebmann 298, the type (H), Oaxaca, Liebmann 295b, the type of *M. planusculum* (G). — B o l i v i a · Yungas, Rusby 3029, the type of *B. Rusbyi* (NY); also no 5029 from the same locality

REFERENCES. Lindenberg & Gottsche (1851, 62, 63); Gottsche (1863, 136, 137), Stephani (1886, 243, 1908, 506, *Icones, Mastigobryum* 345 a, b)

14. Bazzania quadricrenata (Gottsche) Pagán. Bryologist 42: 39. 1939.

Mastigobryum quadricrenatum Gottsche in Stephani, Hedwigia 25. 206 pl. 1, fig 1-4. 1886
Mastigobryum quadricrenatum forma *paupercula* G. A Lindberg, Hedwigia 25· 206. 1886 (nomen nudum)
Mastigobryum Martianum Gottsche in Stephani, Hedwigia 25 205. pl 1, fig 9-12. 1886

Plants medium size to large, olive-green to brownish green, becoming deeply pigmented with brown in the older portions· stems to 5 cm. or more long, with leaves to 3 5 mm. broad, prostrate to suberect stem cells in longitudinal section 0.17 mm. long, the cortical shorter, averaging 20μ in diameter, the vertical walls uniformly thickened and containing frequent pits, the end walls thin· lateral branches frequent, mostly 5 mm. apart, diverging at a wide angle; flagelliform branches frequent; rhizoids colorless, on the bases of leaves of the flagelliform branches· leaf insertion curved in its upper part; the leaves imbricated, plane to deflexed, unsymmetrically ovate to oblong-ovate, nearly straight, 1.5 mm. - 2 mm.

FIG 19 — *Bazzania quadricrenata* (Gottsche) Pagán — 1. Portion of a stem, ventral view, × 12. 2. Portion of a stem with leaf, dorsal view, × 30. 3 A cell from the apical portion of a leaf, × 400. 4. An apical tooth of a leaf, × 310. 5. Cells from the dorsal base of a leaf, × 310. 6. Cells from the ventral base of a leaf, × 310. 7 Cells from the basal portion of a leaf, × 310. 8. Underleaf, × 30 9. Cells from a lobe of an underleaf, × 310. 10. Female bracts of an outer series, × 30 11. Female bracts of the intermediate series, × 30 12 Female bract of the innermost series, × 30 13 One of the laciniae of a bract of this series, × 90 14 Portion of the mouth of the perianth (immature), × 90. 15 Portion of a plant, ventral view, × 15. 16 A cell from the apical portion of a leaf, × 400 17 Underleaf, × 30. 18 Portion of a plant, ventral view, × 15 19 A cell from the apical portion of a leaf, × 400 20 Underleaf, × 30. Nos 1-14 drawn from a portion of the type, from Guadeloupe; 15-17 from plants of forma *paupercula*, from Brazil, 18-20 from a portion of the type of *M. Martianum*, from Brazil.

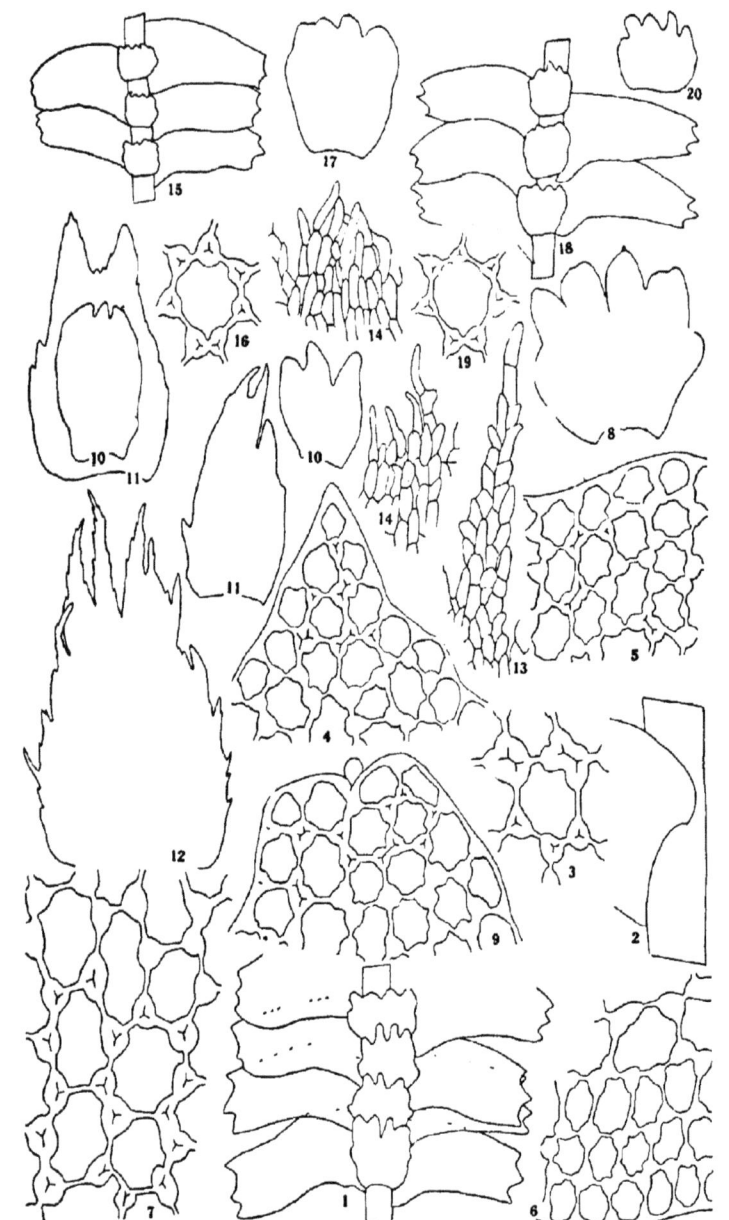

long, 0 8 mm. - 1 mm. broad at the base, narrowed a little to the transversely truncate, tridentate apex: the dorsal margin arched from a rounded base, covering one-half the stem, the ventral margin a little concave, the base rarely dilated, the apex irregularly three-toothed, the teeth mostly large, acute, four to six cells long and broad, the sinuses deep, acute to lunulate, the margins entire; leaf cells thin-walled, the trigones large, with bulging sides, often coalesced, the cell lumina angular-rounded to stellate, the cuticle slightly verruculose; cells of the apical region $22\mu \times 22\mu$, of the interior larger, and of the base 40μ - $48\mu \times 22\mu$, a vitta not differentiated underleaves approximate to imbricated, attached in a straight line, subquadrate, broader than the stem, mostly 0.56 mm long $\times$ 0.7 mm broad, the lateral margins deeply lobed, the apex distinctly four-lobed, the lobes broad, rounded, mostly 3 to 8 cells long, 6 to 8 cells broad, a slime papilla usually present at the apex of each lobe, the cells as in the leaf leaves of the flagelliform branches ovate, scale-like· male branches several on a stem, the bracts and bracteoles round-quadrate, bi-trifid, antheridia occurring singly· female branches occasional, solitary, one to several on a stem, the bracts and bracteoles similar, the outer series ovate, the apex shortly bi-trifid; the intermediate series ovate, longer, to one-fourth divided into two or three long, often serrulate teeth, the lateral margins serrulate to dentate, the innermost series long ovate, the apex divided into usually three, long, serrulate laciniae; the perianths mostly 5 mm. long, the mouth ciliate to laciniate.

HABITAT. In mats on logs and tree bases.

The distinguishing characteristics of the species are its large size, the olive-green to brown color, the tridentate leaves with conspicuous trigones and angular-rounded to stellate cell lumina, and the deeply four-lobed, subquadrate underleaves. (FIG. 19, nos. 1-20).

The forma *paupercula* collected by G. A. LINDBERG at Caldas, Brazil is much smaller, and shows evidence of having grown under unfavorable habitat conditions. The trigones are not so large but are, nevertheless, of the same form. The underleaves are smaller and while some of them are nearly entire with only a suggestion of lobing at the apex, others on the same plant are deeply four-lobed and identical with the underleaves on the large plants (see FIG. 19, nos. 15-17).

Mastigobryum Martianum Gottsche, also collected by G. A. LINDBERG at Caldas, Brazil is identical with the form *paupercula* mentioned above (compare FIG. 19, nos. 15-17 with nos. 18-20), and is therefore also to be considered a depauperate form of *B. quadricrenata*.

DISTRIBUTION Guadeloupe without locality, l'Herminier, the type (G). — Jamaica. John Crow Peak, Maxon 1240 (Y); Morce's Gap, Evans 465 (Y). — Brazil· Caldas, (forma *paupercula*), G. A. Lindberg (G); also type of *M. Martianum* (NY). — Venezuela. without locality, Korthals (G).

REFERENCES. Stephani (1908, 508, 1909, 525, *Icones, Mastigobryum* nos 348, 393), Bescherelle (1893, 186).

15. **Bazzania aurescens** Spruce, Trans. & Proc. Bot. Soc. [Edinburgh] 15: 374. 1885

Mastigobryum aurescens Stephani, Spec. Hep 3. 507 1908
Bazzania Hookeri var Spruce ms, Hepat. Spruc.

Plants medium to large, greenish brown, becoming dark yellow-brown in the older portions: stems slender, 6 cm or more in length, with leaves to 3 5 mm. broad, prostrate to ascending; lateral branches infrequent, diverging at a wide angle; flagelliform branches frequent, long; rhizoids colorless, present on some leaves of the flagelliform branches: the line of leaf insertion curved in its upper part, leaves approximate to subimbricated, plane, becoming deflexed when dry, unsymmetrically narrow-ovate to oblong, spreading, 1.5 mm. - 2 mm long, 0 7 mm. - 0 8 mm. broad at the base, narrowed a little to the transversely truncate, tridentate apex; the dorsal margin arched from a curved base, covering one-half the stem, the ventral margin straight to a little concave, the base scarcely dilated, the apex three-toothed, the teeth irregular, three to six cells long and broad, acute to acuminate, the sinuses lunulate, the margins usually crenulate; leaf cells thin-walled, the cell lumina angular-rounded to stellate, the trigones large, with convex sides, often becoming coalesced, the cuticle faintly verruculose; cells of the apical region 20μ - 24μ in diameter, and of the median portion larger, and of the basal portion to $40\mu \times 20\mu$, a vitta not differentiated: underleaves imbricated, subquadrate in outline, broader than the stem, the line of attachment straight, 0.6 mm. - 0 7 mm. long and broad, the lateral margins a little convex from a straight base, repand, the apex irregularly incised with unequal teeth and lobes, the cell pattern as in the leaf: leaves of the flagelliform branches, scale-like, ovate, the apex acute to shortly bifid· female branches occasional, solitary, one to several on a stem, the bracts and bracteoles similar, ovate; the outermost series short, the apex bifid, the intermediate series larger, divided to one-fourth into three long narrow laciniae, the innermost series long, one-sixth to one-fourth divided into three ciliate laciniae, the lateral margins dentate to short ciliate· perianth (immature) mouth fringed with long cilia: male branches not seen.

HABITAT. On shaded rocky slopes on Mount Guayrapurina, also on logs at higher altitudes in Jamaica.

The distinguishing characteristics of the species are its greenish brown color; the oblong to ovate leaves with transversely truncate, equally tridentate apices which have irregular, mostly crenate margins, and cells with thin walls and very large trigones; and the subquadrate underleaves, repand on the lateral margins and incised to form irregular teeth or lobes at the apex. (FIG. 20, nos. 1-11).

The plants of the type material are quite large and the yellow-brown pigmentation is strongly developed. The teeth of the leaves are long, usually acuminate, and the margins are conspicuously crenulate as is seen in FIG. 20, nos. 1, 3 and 7. This form of margin is present to some degree in all leaves but in the less well developed forms it is less obvious. The large cells with their very large,

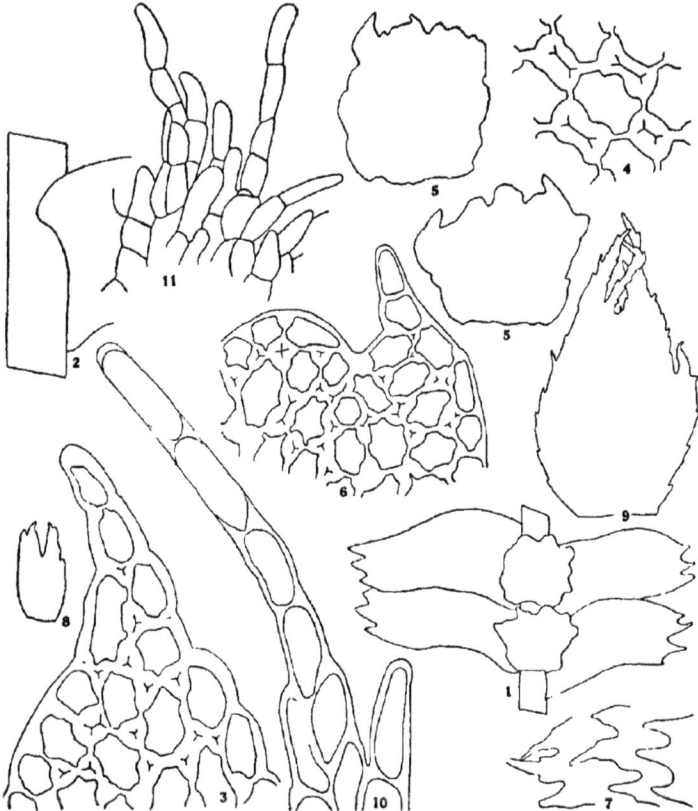

FIG 20 — *Bazzania aurescens* Spruce — 1 Portion of a plant, ventral
view, × 15   2 Portion of a leaf and stem, dorsal view, × 30   3 A tooth
of a leaf, × 310 4. A cell from the apical portion of a leaf, × 400. 5 Underleaves, × 30. 6 A portion of the apical margin of an underleaf, × 310
7. Apices of leaves, × 30   8 Female bract of the outermost series, × 30.
9 Female bract of the innermost series, × 30   10. One of the laciniae of a
bract of this series, × 310   11 Portion of the mouth of a perianth, × 100
Nos 1-6 drawn from a portion of the type material, from Peru, 7-11 from
plants of the type of *B. Hookeri* var Spruce, also from Peru

rounded trigones, are another conspicuous feature of the leaves. The cell walls are thin but usually this is not obvious because of the deposition of abundant secondary thickenings, so that only small, thin-walled pits remain (FIG. 20, nos. 3 and 4). The cell lumina are stellate.

The underleaves, FIG. 20, nos. 1, 5 and 6, are large. They are subquadrate in outline and are variously lobed and often irregularly toothed, with broad, blunt teeth along the margins. The cells are similar to those of the leaf.

Plants similar to those described above were distributed in the *Hepaticae Spruceana* as *B. Hookeri* var. Some of these plants have female branches in various stages of development. The laciniae of the intermediate and innermost series of bracts are long, and are short ciliate along the margins (see FIG. 20, nos. 8-10). The perianth mouth is fringed with numerous long cilia as is shown in FIG. 20, no. 11.

Plants from Jamaica are much smaller than those from South America. The stems with leaves average only 2.5 mm. - 3 mm. broad and are deeply pigmented with brown The teeth of the leaves are not nearly so long, but they are sharp, and many of them have more or less crenulate margins. The female bracts and the perianth mouths are like those of the plants from Peru. Many of the underleaves were not nearly so lobed and dentate as those shown in FIG. 20, nos. 1 and 5, but most of them showed some indication of lobing along the apical margins with two or more teeth at the apex. In this condition they are very similar to the underleaves of *B. Glaziovii* from Brazil. However, this latter species usually is more robust than even the plants from Peru and the teeth of the leaves are rather short and broad, with the margins not crenulate. Female branches and perianths have not been found in *B. Glaziovii* so that no comparisons of these characters can be made at this time.

Poorly developed plants may be confused with depauperate forms of *B. quadricrenata*. However, the larger cells and very large trigones of the leaves of *B. aurescens* should aid in the separation of the two species. If female branches are present the mouth of the perianth will furnish additional characteristics.

DISTRIBUTION J a m a i c a Morce's Gap, Underwood 622 (NY), John Crow Peak, Underwood 678, 2364 (NY). — P e r u · Mt. Guayrapurina, Spruce, Hepat Spruc, the type (H), the same, as *B Hookeri* var. (NY) — V e n e z u e l a . without locality, Fendler (as *M. scutigerum*), poor (H).

REFERENCES. Stephani (*Icones, Mastigobryum* no. 343).

16. Bazzania Glaziovii (Gottsche) comb. nov.

Mastigobryum Glaziovii Gottsche in Stephani, Hedwigia 25: 8 pl. 4. fig. 1-2 1886.

Plants medium to large, dark green, becoming pigmented with brown in the older portions: stems stout, to 5 cm. or more in

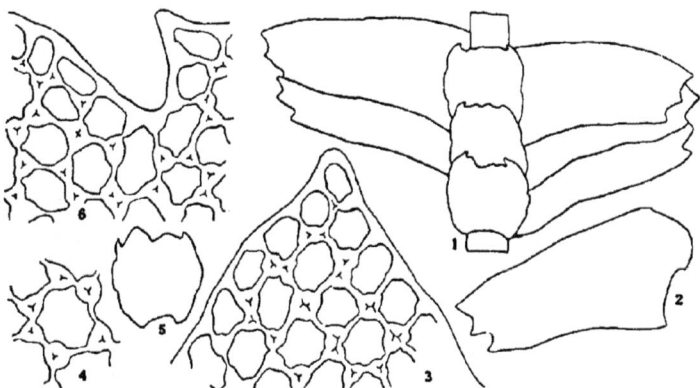

FIG 21 — *Bazzania Glaziovii* (Gottsche) Fulford — 1 Portion of a plant, ventral view, × 15 2. A leaf, × 15   3. A tooth of a leaf, × 310. 4. A cell from the apical portion of a leaf, × 400   5. Underleaf, × 15. 6. A portion of the apical margin of an underleaf, × 310. Drawn from the type material.

length, with leaves to 4 cm. broad, prostrate to suberect; lateral branches frequent, 1 cm. or more apart, diverging at a wide angle; flagelliform branches frequent; rhizoids colorless, present on the bases of the leaves of the flagelliform branches; the line of leaf insertion curved in the upper part; leaves imbricated, plane to deflexed, unsymmetrically ovate, spreading, 1.8 mm. - 2.3 mm. long, 1 mm. broad at the base, narrowed to the more or less obliquely truncate, tridentate apex; the dorsal margin strongly arched from a cordate base, extending across the stem and some-times beyond, the ventral margin straight to concave, the base scarcely dilated, the apex irregularly three-toothed, the teeth broad, three to five cells high, four to seven cells broad at the base, the sinuses lunulate, the margins entire; leaf cells thin-walled, the cell lumina angular-rounded, the trigones large, distinct, often becom-ing coalesced, the cuticle smooth to faintly verruculose; cells of the apical portion and dorsal base mostly 20μ - 24μ in diameter, those of the median portion larger, those of the base 40μ - 48μ $\times$ 24μ, a vitta not differentiated: underleaves imbricated, sub-quadrate in outline, attached in a straight line, broader than the stem, 0.7 mm. - 0.85 mm. long, 0.6 mm - 0.7 mm. wide, the lateral margins somewhat convex from a curved base, often lobed, the apex usually with a short, incurved tooth at either end, undulate to lobed between, the cells as in the apex of the leaf: leaves of the flagelliform branches scale-like, ovate: sexual branches not seen.

HABITAT: Not given.

The distinguishing characteristics of the species are its dark green color and large size; the large, obliquely truncate leaves with large, thin-walled cells and conspicuous trigones; and the large, subquadrate underleaves with entire or lobed lateral margins and truncate, several lobed apices which have an incurved tooth at either end. (FIG. 21, nos. 1-6).

The species is distinguished from well developed forms of *B. quadricrenata* because of the deeply four-lobed apices of the under-leaves of the latter. Poorly developed plants of the two species are very similar. The leaves, with their shorter, broader teeth with smaller cells and smaller trigones will separate it from *B. aurescens*.

The underleaves offer the most accurate guide in the recogni-tion of the species. They are large, broader than the stem and usually imbricated. The lateral margins are undulate to irregu-larly lobed. The apex is truncate and usually has a short, incurved tooth on each end, with several lobes between as is seen in FIG. 21, nos. 1, 5 and 6. The teeth of the leaves are always short and broad and separated by shallow sinuses (see FIG. 21, nos. 1, 2 and 3).

DISTRIBUTION: B r a z i l : Rio de Janeiro, Glaziou, the type (H). — B r i t i s h G u i a n a : Turkeit, Lutz (NY).

REFERENCES· Stephani (1909, 528, *Icones, Mastigobryum* no. 386).

17. **Bazzania Breuteliana** (Lindenb. & Gottsche) Trevis. Mem. Ist. Lomb. 13: 414. 1877.

Mastigobryum Breutelianum Lindenberg & Gottsche, in G L. & N , Syn. Hep. 226 1845.
Bazzania vincentina var *subrectifolia* Spruce ms p p
Mastigobryum portoricense Hampe & Gottsche, Linnaea 25 348 1852.
Mastigobryum Cuervi Gottsche, Ann. Sci Nat. Bot Ser V. 1: 141. 1864
Mastigobryum sylvaticum Gottsche, Husnot, Hep. Exsicc. (nomen nudum).
    Not *M. sylvaticum* Stephani.
Bazzania chimborazensis Spruce, Trans. & Proc. Bot Soc [Edinburgh] 15: 376. 1885.
Mastigobryum chimborazense Stephani, Spec Hep. 3. 527. 1909.
Bazzania viridissima Spruce, op. cit. p. 375.
Mastigobryum viridissimum Stephani, op. cit p 522.
Mastigobryum Uleanum Stephani, op. cit. p. 529
Bazzania portoricensis var. *pycnodictyon* Herzog, Rev. Bryol. et Lichén. 11: 19 1938.
Mastigobryum Harioti Stephani, in Herzog, Biblioth Bot 87: 224 Fig. 164, d-e. 1916.

Plants large, in deep tufts or mats, olive-green to brownish green, pigmented with brown: stems to 10 cm. or more in length, with leaves to 4.5 mm. broad, prostrate to suberect; stem cells in longitudinal section to 0.18 mm. long, the cortical shorter, both averaging 20μ in diameter, the vertical walls uniformly thickened and containing frequent pits, the end walls thin: lateral branches frequent, mostly more than 5 mm. apart, diverging at a wide angle; flagelliform branches frequent: rhizoids colorless, rare, on the bases of the leaves of the flagelliform branches: the line of leaf insertion curved in its upper part, the dorsal margin recurved forming a short hook; leaves distant to imbricated, plane to deflexed, unsymmetrically ovate, oblong on robust plants, spreading, often becoming a little falcate, 1 5 mm. to 2 6 mm. long, 0.8 mm. - 1 mm. broad at the base, narrowed a little to the transversely truncate, unequally tridentate apex; the dorsal margin arched from a strongly rounded base, extending the width of the stem and often beyond, the ventral margin straight to a little concave, the base scarcely dilated, the apex irregularly three-toothed, the teeth large, acute, two to eight cells long and broad, occasionally obscure, the sinuses deep, acute to lunulate, the margins entire; leaf cells thin-walled, the cell lumina angular-rounded, the trigones small, conspicuous, the cuticle verruculose; the cells tending to be in rows, those of the apical region and dorsal base $20\mu \times 20\mu$, of the interior larger, and of the base 36μ - $54\mu \times 18\mu$, a vitta not differentiated· underleaves distant to imbricated, subquadrate to elongate in outline, attached in a straight line, much broader than the stem, 0.8 mm. - 1 mm. long, 0.65 mm. - 1 mm. wide, the lateral margins convex, entire, repand, the base cordate, the apex usually two- to four-lobed, the lobes broad, rounded, the cells as in the leaf: leaves of the flagelliform branches spreading, small, ovate, the apex acute to shortly bifid: female branches occasional, solitary, one to several on a stem, the bracts and bracteoles similar, the outermost series oblong, bifid, the intermediate series ovate, the apex divided into three or four short, serrulate laciniae, the lateral margins serrulate to dentate; the innermost series ovate, one-third

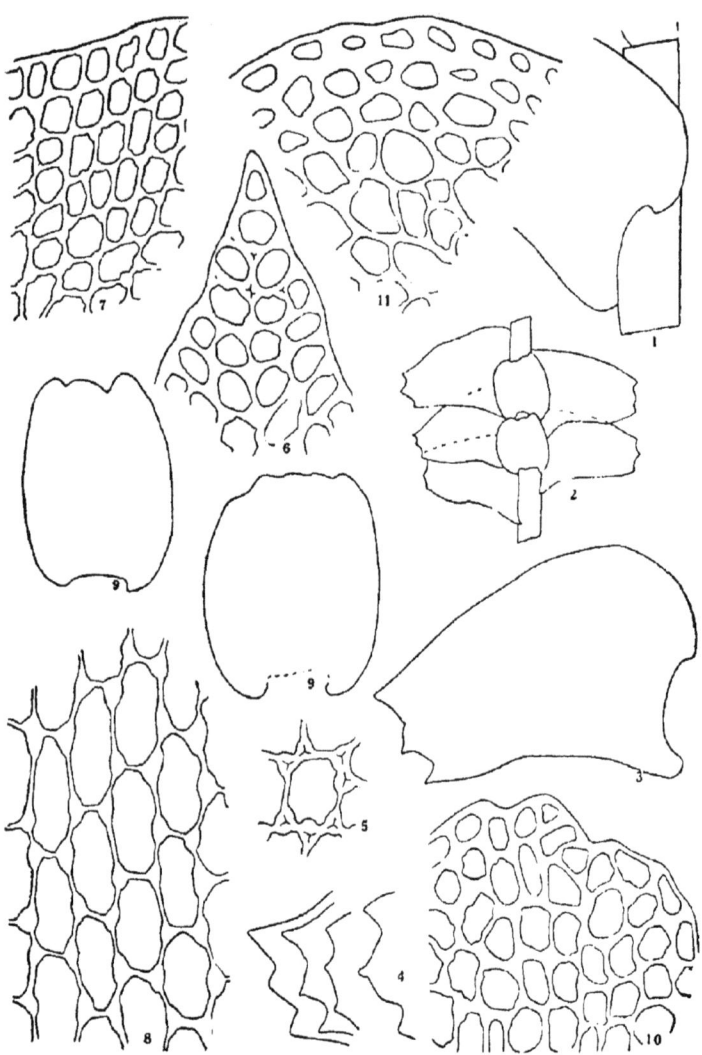

FIG. 22. — *Bazzania Breuteliana* (Lindenb. & Gottsche) Trevis. — 1. Portion of a leaf and stem, dorsal view, × 30 2 Portion of a plant, ventral view, × 12. 3. A leaf, × 30. 4. Apices of leaves, × 30. 5 A cell from the apical portion of a leaf, × 350. 6. Cells of an apical tooth, × 260. 7. Cells from the dorsal base, × 260. 8. Cells from the basal portion, × 260. 9. Underleaves, × 30 10 Cells from the apical portion of an underleaf, × 260. 11. Portion of a cross-section of a stem, × 260. Nos. 1-11 drawn from the type material.

to one-fourth divided into three or four long, serrulate laciniae, the margins serrulate to short ciliate or laciniate perianth mouth short laciniate: male branches not seen.

HABITAT· On logs, tree bases and branches in woods.

The distinguishing characteristics of the species are its large size, and olive-green color faintly tinged with brown; the large, spreading to slightly falcate leaves with irregularly tridentate apices, angular-rounded cell lumina, thin cell walls, and small, distinct trigones; and the quadrate to elongate, faintly two- to four-lobed underleaves, cordate at the base, with mostly repand lateral margins which are straight or a little convex. (FIGS. 22, nos. 1-11, 23, nos. 1-14; 24, nos. 1-11).

The plants exhibit the usual variations associated with differences in habitat. The stems are usually long, branched or unbranched, with the branches mostly from 0.5 mm. to 1.5 mm. apart. They are olive-green with a brown pigmentation which becomes more conspicuous with age. The leaves are distant to imbricated, unsymmetrically ovate (on the type material, FIG. 22, no. 3), to elongate on the robust plants (FIGS. 23, nos. 1, 7 and 9; 24, 3) and are usually spreading, even when dry The teeth vary in size and shape even on a single stem. The cells always have thin walls and small, distinct trigones In plants of exposed situations secondary thickenings are laid down to the extent that some of the trigones become coalesced.

The underleaves show a wide degree of variation. They may be distant on the unbranched elongate stems, but are usually imbricated. The bases are rounded from a straight line of attachment. On well developed plants definite auricles are formed but usually the bases are only rounded, and in a few instances are nearly straight. However, at least a few underleaves of a plant will show the well-rounded condition. The lateral margins are mostly a little convex, entire to undulate. On robust plants they are plane or only a little repand, but on the smaller, little branched plants they become strongly repand. The apex is characteristically broad and three- or four-lobed. These lobes are short and broad and the sinuses are lunulate. Some underleaves on a plant always show

---

FIG. 23 — *Bazzania Breuteliana* (Lindenb & Gottsche) Trevis — 1. Portion of a plant, ventral view, × 15. 2 Portion of a leaf and stem, dorsal view, × 30. 3 A cell from the apical portion of a leaf, × 400. 4 Portion of a plant, ventral view, × 10. 5. A cell from the apical portion of a leaf, × 400. 6 Underleaf, × 30 7. Portion of a plant, ventral view, × 15. 8. A cell from the apical portion of a leaf, × 400. 9. Portion of a plant, ventral view, × 15 10. A cell from the apical portion of a leaf, × 400. 11. Portion of a plant, ventral view, × 15. 12. Cells from the apical portion of a leaf, × 400. 13 Portion of a stem, ventral view, × 15. 14. A cell from the apical portion of a leaf, × 400. Nos. 1-3 drawn from a portion of the type of *M. portoricense*, from Puerto Rico; 4-6 from a portion of the type of *M. Cuervi*, from Colombia, 7-8 from a portion of the type of *B. chimborazensis*, from Ecuador, 9-10 from a portion of the type of *B. viridissima*, from Peru, 11-12 from a portion of the type of *M. Uleanum*, from Peru; 13-14 from a portion of the type of *B. portoricensis* var. *pycnodictyon*, from Costa Rica.

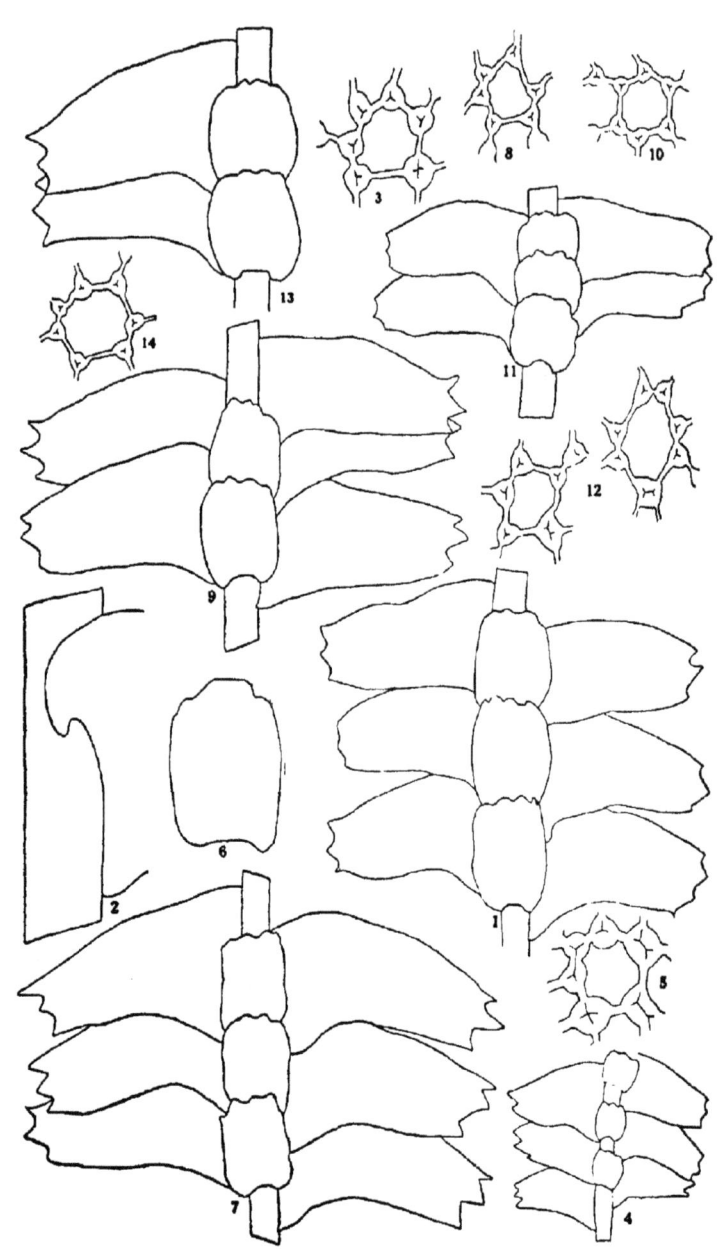

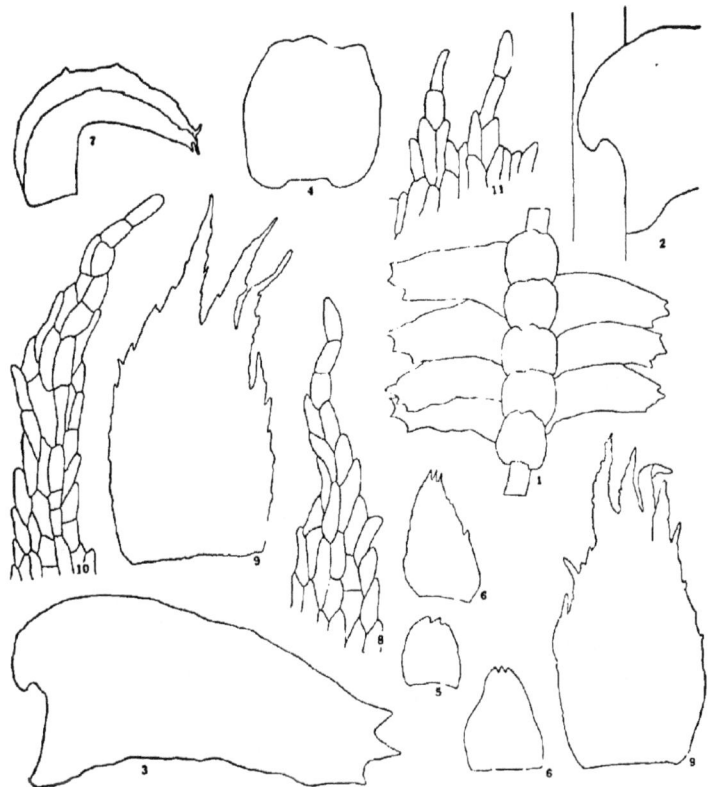

FIG 24 — *Bazzania Breuteliana* (Lindenb & Gottsche) Trevis — 1 Portion of stem, ventral view, × 12   2 Dorsal side of stem showing leaf attachment, × 30   3 Leaf, × 30   4 Underleaf, × 30   5 Female bract of outermost series, × 30   6-7 Female bracts of the intermediate series, × 30.   8. A tooth of a bract of an intermediate series, × 100   9. Female bracts of the innermost series, × 30   10 Portion of one of the laciniae of a bract of this series, × 100   11 Portion of the mouth of a perianth (immature), × 100   Nos 1-11 drawn from plants collected by WEBSTER in Jamaica

the characteristic lobed condition (FIG. 22, no. 9; FIG. 23, nos. 1, 4, 7, 9 and 11), of the apex. Female bracts and perianths were abundant on plants collected in Jamaica (see FIG. 24, nos. 5-11). When present, these will furnish additional diagnostic characters.

The plants of the type material (see FIG. 22, nos. 1-11), from St. Kitts are robust but the leaves are somewhat shorter than those of the other collections. They are very broad at the base, so that they are unsymmetrically ovate rather than elongate. Most of the teeth of the broad leaf apices are short and broad and separated by narrow sinuses. However, some of the leaves on a stem have much longer or larger teeth so that the short teeth cannot be used as a specific characteristic. The underleaves are large, rounded at the bases and uniformly truncate and three- or four-lobed or undulate at the apices.

The plants of the type collection of *M portoricense* (FIG. 23, nos. 1-3), from Puerto Rico, are a little larger and a little more deeply pigmented than those of *M. Breutelianum*. Most of the leaves are elongate. The underleaves are perhaps a little longer than those described above, but the apices are lobed in the characteristic manner.

M. Cuervi (FIG. 23, nos. 4-6), from Colombia, is a relatively small form with short, ovate leaves The teeth are irregularly developed, some very short and broad, others very long and acute. The underleaves are distant but have the same characteristic apices. The cell walls are somewhat thicker and the trigones a little larger than those of the leaves of *M. Breutelianum* or *M. portoricense* but the general cell pattern of the three is identical.

Plants of *B. chimborazensis* (FIG. 23, nos. 7-8), from Ecuador, are very large as is seen by a comparison of the habit sketches of FIGS. 22 and 23, no. 7. The leaves are elongate and very sharply toothed. The contrast between the size of these teeth and those of *M. Breutelianum* is so striking that at first glance one is apt to consider the two as distinct species. However, an examination of many plants from the West Indies and South America has revealed an overlapping series of gradations in the size of the teeth on individual plants, and *M. Breutelianum* with most of the teeth very short and broad is at one end of the series, while *B. chimborazensis* with most of the teeth large, is at the other. Some of the leaves of these plants have shorter teeth. The underleaves are very large, but typical for the species.

The plants of *M. Hariotii* from Bolivia also have sharply toothed leaves. The stems are not nearly so large as those of *B. chimborazensis* and the leaves are shorter and broader at the bases. The underleaves are distant.

B. viridissima (FIG. 23, nos. 9-10), from Peru, is another example of a very large form of the species. The teeth of the leaves are very large, often longer than those of *B. chimborazensis*. The underleaves are typical.

The plants of *M Uleanum* (FIG. 23, nos. 11-12), also from Peru, are more similar to *M. Breutelianum* than to the other South American plants described above. The leaves, while elongate, are for the most part tridentate with short, broad teeth. The under-leaves are mostly as broad as long, cordate at the base, undulate along the margins and three- or four-lobed at the apices. The presence of this form in Peru further substantiates the very close relationship of the various plants described above and besides, seems to indicate that the plants with very large teeth, *B. chimborazensis* and *B. viridissima* do not necessarily make up a geographic variety. Many of the representatives of the species of *Bazzania* which SPRUCE collected in the Amazon country of South America have the leaves more deeply toothed than plants of those same species collected elsewhere in tropical America.

The plants of *B. portoricensis* var *pycnodictyon* (FIG. 23, nos 13-14), from Costa Rica, differ only in that the cuticle is strongly verruculose. But since the cuticle of the plants of *M. Breutelianum* is slightly verruculose this characteristic seems not to be of sufficient importance to warrant a varietal name. The female bracts are identical with those of the species.

The species can readily be separated from the preceding species because of its large size, and large, subquadrate to elongate under-leaves with entire or faintly undulate lateral margins, rounded or cordate at the bases from a straight line of insertion, and the truncate, three- or four-lobed apices. Small forms might sometimes be confused with *B. acuminata*, a description of which follows.

DISTRIBUTION. C u b a   Oriente, Shafer 9116 (Y, NY). — D o m i n i c a · without locality, Eggers, cited by Stephani (1888b, 300); Morne Micotrin, Roseau Valley, Morne Diablotin, Elliott, cited by Spruce (1895, 356) — D o m i n i c a n R e p u b l i c   Pacificador, Abboy 2061a, 2063, 2126 (Y). — G u a d e l o u p e   Morne Hirondelle, Duss 282 (NY), without locality, Husnot, the type of *M. sylvaticum* Gottsche (H); without locality or collector's name (H); without locality, l'Herminier, Soufrière, Duss, cited by Stephani (1903, 22) — J a m a i c a · without locality, Webster (NY); Sir John's Peak, Harris 11, 135a (NY), Morce's Gap, Evans 41, 44, 390 (Y) — M a r t i n i q u e . Mt. Pelée, Duss 126, 127, 347 (NY), without locality, Hahn, cited by Bescherelle (1893, 186). — P u e r t o R i c o . without locality, Schwanecke, the type of *M. portoricense* (NY). El Yunque, Evans 11, 66, 132 (NY); Sierra Naguabo, Shafer, a, 3306, 3455, 3729 (NY); same locality, E G. Britton and Hess 2291 (NY), El Yunque, P. R College of Agri. 2792 (NY), Mt Britton, Jones 10976 (H), Alto de la Bandera, Britton and Marble 2175 (NY), Luquillo Mountains, E G. Britton 7753 (NY); Canóvanas, Pagán 291 (NY), Adjuntas, Sintenis 92, as *B. Wrightii* (NY); without locality, Sintenis 28, 87, cited by Stephani (1888a, 279) — S t K i t t s : Mt Misery, Britton & Cowell 783 (NY); Mt. Misery, Breutel, the type. — M e x i c o . Oaxaca, Liebmann 255 a & b, plants mixed with *M. taleanum* (G, H) — C o s t a R i c a   San Marcos de Data, Tonduz 11618 (NY); La Estrella 39106, 39117, 39403, El Muneco, Standley 51338, 50887, the type of *B. portoricensis* var. *pycnodictyon* (W). — B o l i v i a : Casapi, Mathews (H, NY); Comarapa, Herzog, the type of *M. Harriotii* (L) — B r a z i l · Manáos, Ule, the type of *M. Uleanum* (H); without locality, Sells as *M. Martianum* (H). — C o l o m b i a : Bogotá, Cuervo, the type of *M. Cuervi* (B); without locality, Wallace (NY). — B r i t i s h G u i a n a : Mt Roraima,

McConnell & Quelch 545, cited by Stephani (1901-05, 98) — E c u a d o r : Tunguragua, Spruce, Hepat. Spruc. as *B. vincentina* var. *subrectifolia* p p. (NY); Mt. Chimborazo, Spruce, the type of *B. chimborazensis* (NY). — P e r u . Campana, Spruce, the type of *B. viridissima* (H).

REFERENCES· Herzog (1938, 19); Lindenberg & Gottsche (1851, 75); Stephani (1888a, 279; 1888b, 300, 1901-05, 98; 1903, 22; 1908, 470; 1909, 519, 522, 526; *Icones Mastigobryum* nos 157, 164, 378, 382, 397*a, b,* 403, 407).

18. Bazzania acuminata (Lindenb. & Gottsche) Trevis. Mem. Ist. Lomb. 13: 414. 1877.

Mastigobryum acuminatum Lindenberg & Gottsche, in G L & N., Syn Hep. 719 1847.
Mastigobryum orizabense Gottsche, Mex Leberm. 130 1863
Mastigobryum Mullerianum Gottsche, op. cit. p. 129.

Plants medium size, olive-green, deeply pigmented with brown: stems to 5 cm. long, with leaves to 2.5 mm. or 3 mm broad; lateral branches frequent, diverging at an acute angle; flagelliform branches frequent, long: rhizoids colorless, abundant on the leaves of the flagelliform branches· the line of leaf insertion curved in its upper half, the dorsal extremity curved downward, forming a short hook; leaves distant to imbricated, strongly deflexed when dry, unsymmetrically and broadly ovate, ascendent, 1.5 mm - 2 mm long × 0.8 mm. - 1 mm. broad at the base, narrowed to the mostly obliquely truncate, unequally tridentate apex; the dorsal margin strongly arched from a cordate base, extending across the axis and somewhat beyond, the ventral margin nearly straight, the base scarcely dilated, the apex irregularly two- or three-toothed, the teeth acute, two to five cells long and broad, the sinuses mostly shallow, lunulate, the margins entire; leaf cells thin-walled, the trigones conspicuous, with bulging sides, sometimes coalesced, the cell lumina angular-rounded, the cuticle verruculose; cells of the apical region 18μ × 18μ, those of the interior larger, and those of the base 36μ - 46μ × 18μ, a vitta not differentiated: underleaves distant to approximate, orbicular, attached in a straight line, broader than the stem, 0 5 mm. - 0.56 mm. long × 0.45 mm. - 0.52 mm. broad, the lateral margins entire, strongly recurved, the apex entire, emarginate, sometimes with several undulations, the cells as in the leaf· leaves of the flagelliform branches ovate, scale-like, spreading: sexual branches not seen.

HABITAT: Not given.

The distinguishing characteristics of the species are its medium size, the brown pigmentation, the unsymmetrical, broadly ovate leaves with strongly cordate dorsal bases and hook-formed lines of attachment, and the orbicular, emarginate underleaves with strongly recurved lateral margins. (FIG. 25, nos. 1-11).

The type collection, from Mexico, in the Herb. Boissier contains two fragments of stems each less than 1 cm. in length. The characteristic hooked line of insertion of the leaves, the leaf shape, the trigones, and the orbicular, emarginate underleaves with re-curved lateral margins are distinctive (see FIG. 25, nos. 1-6).

FIG. 25 — *Bazzania acuminata* (Lindenb. & Gottsche) Trevis — 1 Portion of stem, ventral view, × 30. 2. Dorsal side of stem to show leaf attachment, × 30. 3. Leaf apices, × 30 4 A cell from the apical portion of a leaf, × 400 5. Underleaves, × 30 6 Cells from the apical portion of an underleaf, × 310 7 Portion of a plant, ventral view, × 15 8. A cell from the apical portion of a leaf, × 400. 9. Underleaf, × 30 10 Portion of a plant, ventral view, × 15. 11. A cell from the apical portion of a leaf, × 400. Nos. 1-6 drawn from a portion of the type, from Mexico, 7-9 from the type of *M. orizabense*, from Mexico, 10-11 from the type of *M. Mullerianum*, from Mexico.

The type collection of *M. orizabense* (FIG. 25, nos. 7-9), also from Mexico contains several stems, all with the same characteristics as are present in *M. acuminatum*. These stems are in a much better state of preservation.

M. Mullerianum (FIG. 25, nos. 10-11), from Mexico, is a little less pigmented with brown than *M. orizabense*, and some of the leaves have more conspicuous teeth, but the variation is so great, even on one stem that this characteristic is not of sufficient stability to separate *M. Mullerianum* as a distinct species.

The species is most similar to small plants of *B. Breuteliana*. However, the emarginate underleaves with strongly recurved lateral margins will usually serve to distinguish *B. acuminata* from all other species. In addition to this, the underleaves of *B. Breuteliana*, even though the lateral margins may be slightly recurved near the base, are always subquadrate to elongate in outline, rather than orbicular, and the truncate apices are three- or four-lobed rather than emarginate.

DISTRIBUTION· M e x i c o . Oaxaca, Liebmann 176b, the type (G), Vera Cruz, Orizaba, Muller 159, the type of *M. orizabense* (G), Orizaba, Muller 2361, the type of *M. Mullerianum* (NY) — V e n e z u e l a   Caracas, Burchel (NY).

REFERENCES· Lindenberg & Gottsche (1851, 69); Gottsche (1863, 131); Stephani (1909, 517, 518; *Icones, Mastigobryum* nos. 370, 394a, b, 395).

19. **Bazzania diversicuspis** Spruce, Trans. & Proc. Bot. Soc. [Edin-
burgh] 15: 373 1885.

Mastigobryum diversicuspe Stephani, Spec. Hep 3. 432. 1908.

Plants delicate, in depressed mats or scattered among other bryophytes, dull green to light brown: stems slender, to 4 cm. or 5 cm. long, with leaves to 3 mm. broad, prostrate; stem cells in longitudinal section elongate, to 0.17 mm. in length, the cortical shorter, both averaging 20μ in diameter, the vertical walls uniformly thickened and containing frequent pits, the end walls thin: lateral branches 1 cm. or more apart, diverging at a wide angle; flagelliform branches frequent, long: rhizoids colorless, present on the leaves of the flagelliform branches: the leaf insertion little curved in the upper part; leaves spreading, approximate to imbricated, straight to ascendant, unsymmetrically ovate, to 1 mm. long, 0.48 mm broad at the base, narrowed somewhat to the acute, rounded or transversely truncate apex, the dorsal margin convex from a slightly rounded base which covers one-half the stem, the ventral margin straight to slightly concave, the base scarcely dilated, the apex mostly broad, acute, rounded or obscurely bi- or tridentate; teeth when present, acute, three to eight cells broad at the base, two to four cells high, the sinuses lunulate, the margins entire; leaf cells more or less quadrate in outline, thin-walled, the trigones small, conspicuous, seldom becoming coalesced, the cuticle verruculose; cells of the apical region and dorsal base mostly $17\mu \times 17\mu$, those of the median portion a little larger, those of the base 27μ - $36\mu \times 18\mu$, not forming a vitta: underleaves distant to

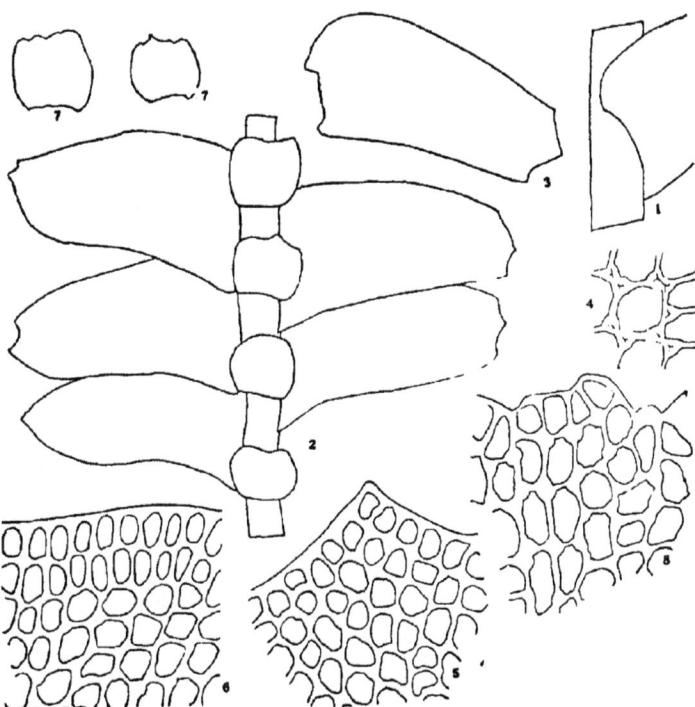

FIG. 26. — *Bazzania diversicuspis* Spruce. — 1. Portion of a stem and leaf, dorsal view, × 30. 2. Portion of a plant, ventral view, × 30. 3. A leaf, × 30 4. A cell from the apical portion of a leaf, × 350 5 Cells from an apical tooth of a leaf, × 260 6 Cells from the dorsal margin near the base, × 260 7. Underleaves, × 30. 8. Cells from the apical portion of an underleaf, × 260. Nos. 1-8 drawn from a portion of the type collection.

approximate, attached in a straight line, subquadrate in outline, a little broader than the stem, 0.28 mm. - 0.36 mm. long and broad, the lateral margins a little convex from a straight base, the apex straight, undulate, two- to four-lobed or occasionally with one or two short, sharp teeth, cells similar to those of the apical portion of the leaf: leaves of the flagelliform branches scale-like, acute, 0.9 mm. long: male and female branches not seen.

HABITAT: In depressed mats among ferns.

The distinguishing characteristics of the species are its dull green to brownish color, the small to medium size, the prostrate habit; the plane, mostly obscurely bi- or tridentate leaves with thin cell walls; and the small, quadrate, entire or faintly lobed underleaves. (FIG. 26, nos. 1-8).

The obscurely tridentate, acute or bidentate leaves and the small, distant to approximate underleaves will readily separate *B. diversicuspis* from all of the preceding species

DISTRIBUTION: T r i n i d a d : without locality or collector's name (NY). — B r a z i l : Tauáu near Pará, Spruce, *Hepat Spruc.*, the type (NY).

REFERENCES: Stephani (1886, 244; 1908, 432; *Icones, Mastigobryum* no. 8).

20. Bazzania tricuspidata (Steph.) comb. nov.

Mastigobryum tricuspidatum Stephani, Spec. Hep. 3: 448. 1908.

Plants small, golden brown, becoming darker in the older portions: stems slender, 3 cm. or more in length, with leaves to 2 mm. broad; lateral branches mostly more than 1 cm. apart, diverging at a wide angle; flagelliform branches occasional; rhizoids numerous from the bases of the leaves of flagelliform branches: the line of leaf insertion little curved in its upper part; leaves distant, strongly deflexed, unsymmetrically ovate, ascendent, mostly 1 mm. long, 0.5 mm broad at the base, narrowed a little to the broad, transversely truncate, tridentate apex; the dorsal margin arched from a straight base, covering one-half the stem, the ventral margin mostly straight, the base scarcely dilated, the apex more or less equally three-toothed, the teeth three to six cells long, three to five cells broad at the base, the sinuses acute to lunulate, the margins entire; leaf cells thin-walled, the cell lumina angular-rounded, the trigones conspicuous, sometimes becoming coalesced, the cuticle faintly verruculose; the cells of the apical region mostly $24\mu \times 24\mu$, of the interior larger, those of the base to $48\mu \times 24\mu$, a vitta not differentiated: underleaves distant, round-quadrate, entire, scarcely broader than the stem, attached in a straight line, 0.28 long and broad, the margins rounded, the cells 20μ - 24μ long $\times$ 16μ broad, the cell walls uniformly thickened, especially along the margin: leaves of the flagelliform branches scale-like, ovate: sexual branches not seen.

HABITAT: Not given.

The distinguishing characteristics of the species are its golden brown color, and the almost filiform habit of the stems; the ascendent, more or less equally three-toothed leaves with large,

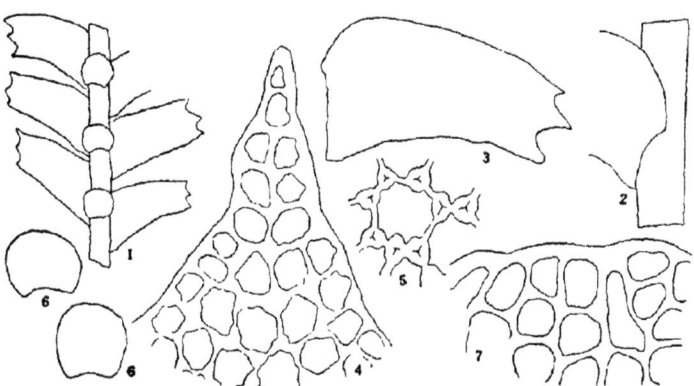

FIG. 27. — *Bazzania tricuspidata* (Steph) Fulford. — 1. Portion of a plant, ventral view, × 15   2 Portion of a leaf and stem, dorsal view, × 30. 3. A leaf, × 30. 4 A tooth of a leaf, × 310   5. A cell from the apical portion of a leaf, × 400. 6. Underleaves, × 30   7 Portion of the apical margin of an underleaf, × 310. Nos 1-7 drawn from a portion of the type material.

thin-walled cells and conspicuous trigones; and the small, round-quadrate underleaves with entire margins and uniformly thickened cell walls. (FIG. 27, nos. 1-7).

The plants are very small, and the leaves which are narrowed only a little from the base to the apex, are always ascendent and more or less equally three-toothed as seen in FIG. 27, nos. 1, 2 and 3. The teeth are sharply acute (FIG. 27, no. 4), and usually end in a two-celled point. The underleaves are always small, round-quadrate and entire. They are usually distant. The cells are mostly thick-walled, particularly along the margin (FIG. 27, no. 7).

The species can readily be separated from *B. diversicuspis*, the only other small species of this Section, because of its golden brown color, the smaller size, the very acute teeth of the leaves, and the rounded underleaves with thick-walled cells, particularly along the margin.

DISTRIBUTION. B r i t i s h   G u i a n a . without locality, Quelch, the type (H).

REFFRENCES. Stephani (*Icones, Mastigobryum* no 60).

21. **Bazzania longistipula** (Lindenb.) Trevis. Mem. Ist. Lomb. 13: 415. 1877.

Mastigobryum longistipulum Lindenberg, in G L & N., Syn. Hep. 228 1845.
Mastigobryum consanguineum Hampe & Lindenberg, in G. L. & N., op cit. p. 717 1847.
Bazzania consanguinea Trevis op cit p. 414.
Mastigobryum consanguineum var *brachyphyllum* Stephani, Hedwigia 24· 217 pl 2, fig. 2 1885
Mastigobryum brachyphyllum Gottsche in Stephani, loc. cit. (nomen nudum)
Bazzania teretiuscula Spruce, Trans & Proc. Bot. Soc [Edinburgh] 15. 375 1885 Not *M. teretiusculum* Lindenberg & Gottsche
Bazzania longistipula var Spruce ms., Hepat. Spruc.
Mastigobryum paludosum Gottsche in Stephani, Hedwigia 25. 243 1886 (nomen nudum)
Mastigobryum phyllobolum Gottsche in Stephani, loc cit. (nomen nudum) Not *Bazzania phyllobola* Spruce.
Mastigobryum saxatile Gottsche in Stephani, Spec Hep 3 470. 1908 (nomen nudum)
Mastigobryum elegantulum Gottsche, Ann Sci. Nat. Bot Ser V 1. 141 1864. (nomen nudum), in Stephani, Hedwigia 25. 5 pl 2 fig 1-3 1886 Not *M elegantulum* De Notaris, 1874
Bazzania Krugiana Stephani, Hedwigia 27 300. pl 13 fig. 40 1888
Mastigobryum Krugianum Stephani, Spec. Hep. 3. 447. 1908.
Mastigobryum Hansenii Stephani, op. cit. p 467
Bazzania longistipula var *polymastix* Spruce ms , Hepat. Spruc
Bazzania decidua Spruce, Trans & Proc Bot. Soc [Edinburgh] 15. 372 1885
Mastigobryum deciduum Stephani, op cit. p. 447.
Mastigobryum Puiggarii Stephani, op cit. p 472.

Plants in depressed mats or deep tufts, olive-green to golden brown or dark brown: stems slender to 6 cm or more long, with leaves 1.5 mm. to 3 mm. broad, prostrate to ascending or erect; in longitudinal section the cells elongate, the medullary averaging 0.16 mm. long, the cortical shorter, both averaging 18μ in diameter, the vertical walls uniformly thickened and containing frequent pits, the end walls thin: lateral branches 0.5 cm. to 1.5 cm. apart, diverging at a wide angle: flagelliform branches frequent, long: rhizoids colorless, present on some of the leaves of the flagelliform branches. leaf insertion curved in the upper part; the leaves approximate to densely imbricated, ascendent, often deflexed and becoming wrapped around the stem when dry, unsymmetrically ovate, 0.8 mm. - 2 mm. long, mostly 0.5 mm. - 1 mm broad at the base, narrowed to the obliquely truncate, tridentate apex; the dorsal margin strongly convex from a rounded base which covers one-half to the entire axis and sometimes extends beyond, the ventral margin straight or slightly concave, the base often more or less expanded; the apex broad to narrow, tridentate, in slender forms sometimes bidentate or acute; the teeth acute, two to six cells long and broad at the base, the acroscopic tooth the longest, the sinuses lunulate to deep and acute, the margins straight to undulate; leaf cells thin-walled, the cell lumina angular-rounded, the trigones conspicuous, with convex sides, often becoming coalesced; the cuticle faintly verruculose; cells of the apical portion averaging $24\mu \times 24\mu$, those of the median portion larger, those of the base 36μ - $40\mu \times 18\mu$, a vitta not differentiated: underleaves distant to imbricated, attached in a straight line, oblong-quadrate to quadrate, as broad or broader than the stem, 0.35 mm. - 1 mm. long $\times$ 0.35 mm. - 0.7 mm. wide, often squarrose, the apex straight to rounded-entire, or faintly two to four undulate or lobed, the lateral margins straight to slightly convex, rounded at the bases, the cells similar to those of the apical portion of the leaf: leaves of the flagelliform branches scale-like, ovate, to 0.3 mm. long, acute to bifid: female branches occasional, one to several on a stem, the bracts and bracteoles similar; the outermost series ovate, to 0.35 mm long, mostly bifid; the intermediate series larger, 0.8 mm. - 0 96 mm. long, 0.5 mm wide, the margins crenulate, dentate to ciliate, the apical portion divided into two to four laciniae, four to six cells long, the cells uniform throughout, averaging $54\mu \times 18\mu$; the innermost series larger, one-third to one-fourth divided into usually three, dentate to ciliate laciniae, the lateral margins dentate to ciliate, the cells uniform, 45μ - 72μ long $\times$ 18μ wide: perianth mouth laciniate, the laciniae crenulate, mostly three to five cells long: male branches and sporophyte not seen.

HABITAT: In tufts or depressed mats on logs and soil in woods.

The distinguishing characteristics of the species are its olive-green to yellow-brown color; the ascendent, obliquely truncated, tridentate leaves with thin cell walls, conspicuous trigones which

FIG. 28. — *Bazzania longistipula* (Lindenb.) Trevis. — 1 Dorsal side of stem showing leaf attachment, $\times$ 30   2 Portion of a stem, ventral view, $\times$ 12.   3. Leaves, $\times$ 30   4. Cells from an apical tooth, $\times$ 260.   4a. A cell from the apical part of a leaf, $\times$ 350.   5 Cells from the dorsal margin of a leaf near the base, $\times$ 260.   6. Cells from the basal portion of a leaf, $\times$ 260.   7. Underleaves, $\times$ 30   8. Cells from the apical portion of an underleaf, $\times$ 260.   9 Portion of a transverse section of a stem, $\times$ 260.   10 Portion of a stem, ventral view, $\times$ 12   11. Portion of a stem, ventral view, $\times$ 12.   12 Portion of a stem, ventral view, $\times$ 12.   13. Underleaf, $\times$ 30.   14. Portion of a stem, ventral view, $\times$ 12.   15. Underleaf, $\times$ 30.   Nos. 1-9 drawn from a portion of the type material, from St. Vincent, 10-11 from the type of *B. teretiuscula* Spruce, from Ecuador; 12-13 from the type of *M. paludosum*, from Guadeloupe, 14-15 from the type of *M. saxatile*, from Guadeloupe.

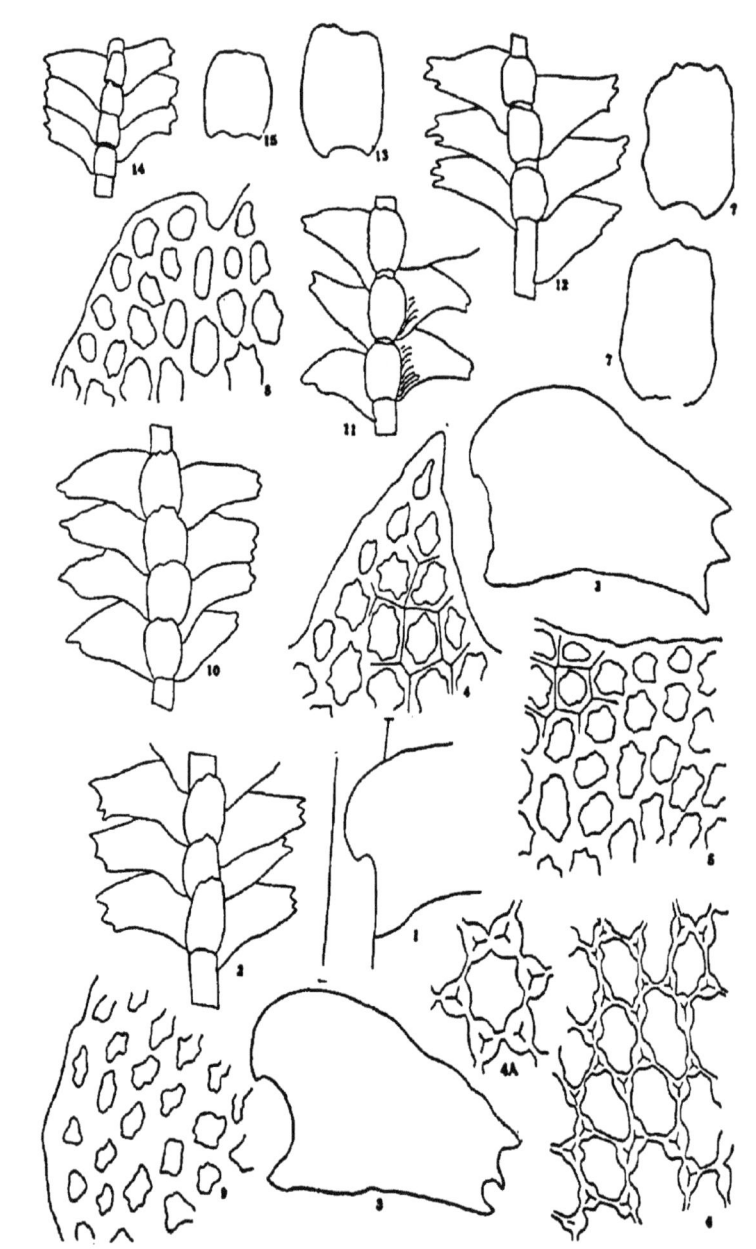

often become coalesced, and angular-rounded cell lumina; and the round-quadrate to elongate underleaves which may be distant to densely imbricated   (FIGS. 28, nos. 1-15; 29, nos. 1-16).

The plants show a high degree of variation in size and form of the leaves and underleaves. The variations in the underleaves are primarily in length and degree of convexity of the lateral margins, while those of the leaf are mostly in length, in the width of the apical portion, and in the size and shape of the teeth.

STEPHANI (1886, 243) called attention to this variation among the plants. He stated that after an examination of *Mastigobryum longistipulum* from the HOOKER Herbarium (the type material), he considered it to be the normal form and *M. consanguineum* as the more lax mountain form. He added further, that Dr. GOTTSCHE's Antilles species, *M paludosum* with somewhat tapering leaves, *M. brachyphyllum* with distant, shorter underleaves, and *M. phyllobolum* G., a distorted form with shorter leaves, were variations of this species   He said that all these plants show the same leaf outline, strongly developed teeth, the uppermost of which is by far the longest, elongate underleaves, and the same angular, strongly thickened leaf tissue. They all grew erect in densely compact, deep tufts of a reddish brown color. He stated further that he was convinced that here was a whole series of forms of a widespread species, such as had been observed in other liverworts and mosses. To the above forms he later (1908, 470) added *M. saxatile.*

An examination of the available material has led to the conclusion that *M. longistipulum, M. consanguineum, M. brachyphyllum, B. teretiuscula* Spruce, *M. paludosum, M. phyllobolum* G., *M. saxatile, M elegantulum, B. Krugiana, M. Hansenii, B decidua, B. longistipula* var. *polymastix* and *M. Puiggarii* are, in part, different expressions of the species under differing conditions of growth, a situation similar to that found in the more northern *B. tricrentata* (FULFORD, 1936).

The plants of the type collection of *M longistipulum*, from St. Vincent (see FIG. 28, nos. 1-9), are robust, but the stems are rarely over 6 cm long and 3 mm. broad, and are copiously branched, with the branches diverging at a wide angle. The leaves are ascendent, the underleaves densely imbricated, and elongate, with rounded to faintly two- to four-lobed apices, and nearly straight sides from slightly rounded bases.

Most of the plants of *B teretiuscula* Spruce, from Ecuador, are very similar (FIG. 28, nos. 10-11), except that they are less robust and the branches occur less frequently, although a few of the stems are as well developed as those of *M. longistipulum* (compare nos. 2 and 10). The underleaves are distant to imbricated, and while most of them are elongate with nearly straight sides, a few are shorter and have bulging sides. The apices often tend to be more deeply lobed. *M. paludosum* (FIG. 28, nos. 12-13), from the Antilles is very similar but not so large.

M. elegantulum (FIG. 29, nos. 6-12), collected in Jamaica approximates *B. teretiuscula* in appearance, although the stems are not so long. The leaves are short, ascending, and the underleaves are mostly approximate and quadrate, with straight to bulging sides. *M. saxatile* (FIG. 28, nos 14-15), from Guadeloupe, *M. Hansenii* (FIG. 29, nos. 3-5), from Jamaica, and *B. decidua* (FIG. 29, nos. 13-14), from Ecuador, are very similar. (*B. decidua* is lighter in color than most of the other plants, and the leaves and underleaves are well developed but distant. The stems are long and little branched.) *B. Krugiana* (FIG. 29, nos. 1-2), collected in Santo Domingo, differs only in that the underleaves are less well developed and are distant. A cross section of the stem shows that the walls of the stem cells are not so thick as in the other variations, but this too is a variable characteristic, dependent in part at least on the type of habitat in which the plant grows.

M. Puiggarii (FIG 29, nos. 15-16), from Brazil, is rather small and yellow-brown, with the underleaves mostly four-lobed at the apex.

STEPHANI's figures (1885, 217-218. pl. 2, fig. 2), of *M. consanguineum* var *brachyphyllum*, from Guadeloupe, suggests that this plant is a variation similar to that shown by *B. Krugiana*. His figures of *M. consanguineum* drawn from the type collected by MORITZ in Colombia show a plant with leaves little imbricated, and underleaves approximate, elongate, with nearly parallel margins, a plant with the characteristics of *M. longistipulum* but not so robust.

The stems may be very slender to medium size and are usually branched. The poorly developed plants and the growing tips of the more robust forms are olive-green but most plants soon become strongly pigmented with brown. Those from the higher altitudes often take on a golden brown color. Some tend to grow in deep patches while others are found in depressed mats or scattered among mosses.

The leaves may be distant to densely imbricated and are ascendent, with the lower margins nearly straight. They may be nearly plane or deflexed and sometimes are tightly wrapped around the stem when dry. They are unsymmetrically ovate with a mostly obliquely truncate, tridentate apex. The length varies from 0.8 mm. or less on poorly developed forms to as much as 1.5 mm. on robust stems. The teeth vary in shape and size but are usually strongly developed, with the acroscopic tooth the longest The leaf cells are thin-walled, with conspicuous trigones. The size of the trigones varies with the age of the plant and its conditions of growth. They have bulging sides and when large may become coalesced.

The underleaves also exhibit much variation. They may be distant to densely imbricated, and as wide or wider than the stem. The insertion forms a straight line. On many plants, most of them are rectangular in outline, with nearly straight lateral margins and an entire, faintly two- to four-lobed apex. On the same plant may also be found shorter underleaves, quadrate, with sometimes straight, but more often bulging sides. On some stems only this latter sort occur. Sometimes they are much reduced and very distant, and tend to be more deeply lobed or cut.

The female branches are not common. The bracts and bracteoles are of the usual sort, ovate to oblong-ovate, with crenulate to dentate margins, and divided at the apex into two to four laciniae. The perianths were not mature. The mouth is laciniate, with the laciniae three to five cells long (see Fig. 29, nos. 8-12).

The species is distinguished from B. Breuteliana and B acuminata because of its much smaller size, its brown color, the ascendent, obliquely truncate leaves which become conspicuously narrowed toward the apex, and its smaller underleaves. It differs from B. tricuspidata in its mostly larger size, the narrow, obliquely truncate leaf apices, and in the cells of the underleaf. Regardless of the shape of the underleaves of depauperate forms of B. longistipula the marginal rows of cells are never noticeably thick-walled, but instead are thin-walled with small but distinct trigones.

DISTRIBUTION Dominica· Morne Diablotin, Elliott 672, cited by Spruce (1895, 356). — Guadeloupe· without locality, Hb. Gottsche, the type of M paludosum (H), without locality, Hb Gottsche, the type of M. saxatile (H); without locality, Parker (NY); Soufrière, Duss 136 (NY), Matouba, Duss 211 (NY), without locality, l'Herminier, Germain, cited by Stephani (1908, 470), without locality, l'Herminier, the type of M consanguinium var. brachyphyllum, cited by Stephani (1885, 217) — Jamaica· without locality, Harris (NY), summit of Blue Mountain Peak, Maxon & Killip 1104 (Y, NY), Blue Mountain Peak, 6500-7325 ft, Underwood 1784 (NY); Sir John's Peak, E G. Britton 1197 (NY), without locality, Hansen, the type of M. Hansenii (H), without locality, Rheder, the type of M. elegantulum G. (H, B), New Haven Gap, Patterson (F) — Puerto Rico: Rio de Maricao, E G Britton 2682 (Y) — Santo Domingo (Dominican Republic) without locality, Eggers, the type of B. Krugiana (H, B) — St. Vincent without locality, Guilding (NY), without locality, Hooker Hb, the type of M. longistipulum (H, V) — Trinidad: without locality, Beyrick, cited by G L & N. (1845, 231). — Colombia "Sierra Nevada, Prov Merida", Moritz, the type of M consanguineum (H). — Ecuador: Mt Tunguaragua, Spruce, the type of B. teretiuscula Spruce, Hepat Spruc. (Y, NY); the same locality, Spruce, the type of B decidua, Hepat. Spruc. (NY) — Peru Mt Campana, Spruce, the type of B. longistipula var polymastix (NY) — Bolivia. Yungas, Jay (Y) — Brazil Serra

FIG 29 — *Bazzania longistipula* (Lindenb.) Trevis — 1. Portion of a stem, ventral view, × 30. 2. A cell from the apical portion of a leaf, × 400. 3. Portion of a stem, dorsal view, × 30 4. Portion of a plant, ventral view, × 30 5 A cell from the apical portion of a leaf, × 400 6. Portion of a plant, ventral view, × 30 7. A cell from the apical portion of a leaf, × 400 8. Female bract of an intermediate series (immature), × 30 9. A lacinia of a bract of this series, × 260. 10. Female bract of the innermost series (immature), × 30 11 Portion of a lacinia of a bract of this series, × 260. 12 Portion of the perianth mouth, × 260 13. Portion of a plant, ventral view, × 15. 14. A cell from the apical portion of a leaf, × 400. 15. Portion of a plant, ventral view, × 15. 16. A cell from the apical portion of a leaf, × 400. Nos. 1-2 drawn from a portion of the type of *B. Krugiana*; 3-5 from a portion of the type of *M. Hansenii*, 6-12 from a portion of the type of *M. elegantulum*; 13-14 from a portion of the type of *B. decidua*, 15-16 from a portion of the type of *M. Puiggarii*.

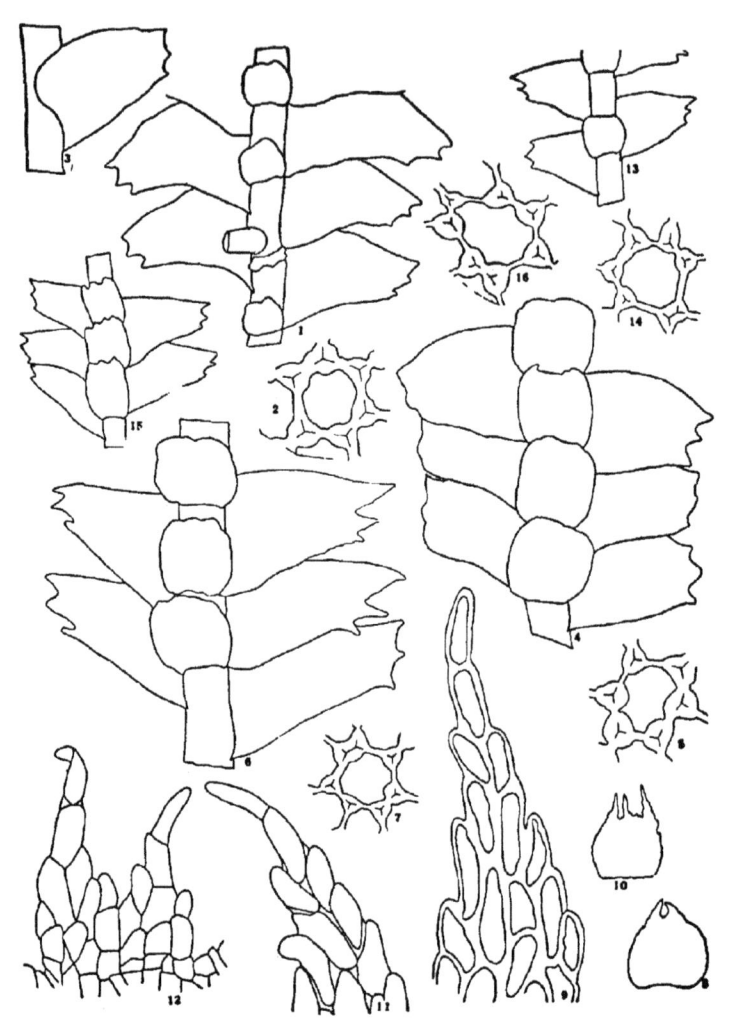

do Mar, Dusén, the type of *M. Puiggarii* (H); Apiahy, Puiggari, cited by Stephani (1908, 472).

REFERENCES: Bescherelle (1893, 187); Hampe (1847, 328), Lindenberg & Gottsche (1851, 60, 88); Spruce (1895, 356); Stephani (1886, 243, 1901-05, 98; 1903, 23; 1908, 447, 467, 470, 472; *Icones, Mastigobryum* nos 56, 57, 58, 163, 171 a, b, c, d, 173)

22. Bazzania latidens (Gottsche) comb. nov.

Mastigobryum latidens Gottsche in Stephani, Hedwigia 25 134 pl. 5 fig 7-9. 1886

Plants medium to large, golden yellow to yellow-brown, tinged with red in the older portions. stems to 5 cm. or more in length, with leaves to 4 mm. broad: lateral branches frequent, 1 cm. or more apart, diverging at a wide angle; flagelliform branches occasional; rhizoid not seen the line of leaf insertion curved in its upper part; the leaves subimbricated to imbricated, plane to deflexed, unsymmetrically ovate to elongate, straight to ascendent, becoming a little falcate, mostly 2 mm. long, 0 8 mm. broad at the base, narrowed a little to the obliquely truncate, tridentate apex; the dorsal margin strongly arched from a cordate base, extending across the stem, the ventral margin concave, the base little dilated, the apex three-toothed, the teeth variable, mostly large, six to eight cells long, five to eight cells broad at the base, the sinuses deep, acute to lunulate, the margins entire; the leaf cells thin-walled, the cell lumina angular-rounded, the trigones conspicuous, with convex sides, sometimes becoming coalesced, the cuticle verruculose; the cells of the apical region 20μ - 24μ in diameter, of the medium portion larger, and of the base 40μ - $48\mu \times 24\mu$, a vitta not differentiated: underleaves approximate to imbricated, rectangular in outline, attached in a straight line, broader than the stem, 0.6 mm. - 0.9 mm. long, 0.55 mm. broad, the lateral margins nearly straight, entire, the apex truncate, entire, undulate to slightly two- to four-lobed, the cells tending to be in rows, mostly 16μ - 24μ $\times 16\mu$, the trigones conspicuous: sexual branches not seen

HABITAT: Over rocks.

The distinguishing characteristics of the species are its medium to large size, the golden brown color, the plane to deflexed leaves which are elongate, spreading, and strongly three-toothed, with cells 20μ - 24μ in diameter, thin-walled and with conspicuous trigones; and the rectangular underleaves with nearly straight, entire lateral margins, and truncate, entire, undulate to faintly lobed apices. (FIG. 30, nos. 1-6).

The type in the STEPHANI Collection at Harvard consists of one robust stem about 4 cm. long. The outstanding characteristics of the plant are its elongate leaves, and rectangular underleaves which are only a little curved at the base, and are entire to faintly two- to four-lobed at the apices.

Plants with similar characteristics were collected by UNDERWOOD on Blue Mountain Peak in Jamaica. These plants grew in mats or tufts and are light green at the growing tips and golden

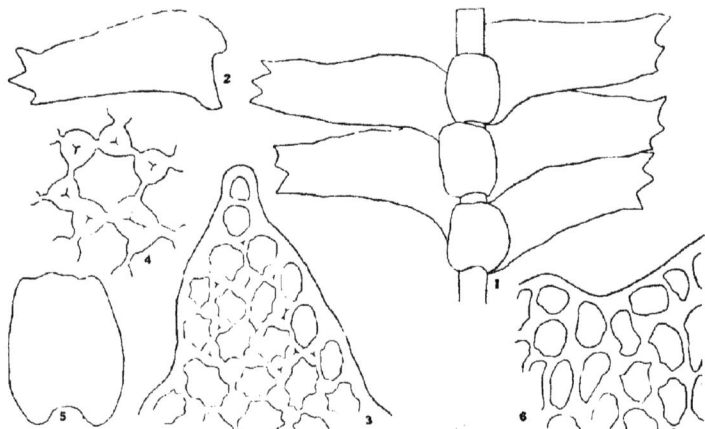

Fɪɢ 30. — *Bazzania latidens* (Gottsche) Fulford — 1. Portion of a
plant, ventral view, × 15. 2 A leaf, × 15. 3 A tooth of a leaf, × 310.
4 A cell from the apical portion of a leaf, × 400 5 An underleaf, × 30.
6. A portion of the apical margin of an underleaf, × 310. Nos 1-6 drawn
from a portion of the type material

brown tinged with red in the older portions. The leaves are not quite so long but are of the same shape, with similar teeth and cell configuration. The underleaves are long-rectangular, with the cells arranged more or less in rows as in the type. On some of the stunted plants in which the internodes are very short, the under-leaves tend to be a little shorter, but otherwise the characteristics are the same.

The species has spreading leaves and elongate underleaves with apices truncate and three- or four-lobed, similar to those of *B. Breuteliana.* However, the yellow-green to brown color, the well defined teeth of the leaves, and the larger trigones of the leaf-cells of *B. latidens* are usually sufficiently distinctive to easily separate the two.

The species is perhaps more closely related to *B. longistipula* and is intermediate between that species and *B longa B latidens* is always larger than *B. longistipula* and the leaves are usually elongate and spreading. The leaves of *B. longistipula* are always ascendent, and very obliquely truncate at the apices The under-leaves of *B. latidens* are always elongate, with the lateral margins more or less parallel. This characteristic is also present in the robust forms of *B. longistipula.*

DISTRIBUTION · J a m a i c a : Blue Mountain Peak, 6500-7325 ft , Underwood 1483, 1484, 1490, 1512 (NY), Cinchona, Harris 11, 135a (NY). — B r a z i l · without locality, Glaziou 1792, the type (H)

REFERENCES. Stephani (1909, 529; *Icones, Mastigobryum* no 390)

23. Bazzania longa (Nees) Trevis. Mem. Ist. Lomb. 13: 415. 1877.

Jungermannia longa Nees, Linnaea 6. 623. 1831.
Jungermannia stolonifera Sieb. Pl. crypt. exsicc. n 35. Linnaea, loc cit. Not J stolonifera Swartz.
Mastigobryum longum Nees, in G. L. & N., Syn. Hep. 231. 1845.
Mastigobryum Gottscheanum Lindenberg, op. cit p 224
Bazzania Gottscheana Trevisan, op cit. p 414.
Mastigobryum speciosum Gottsche, Husnot Pl Antilles no 213. 1868 Husnot, Rev. Bryol 2: 3. 1875. Gottsche in Stephani, Hedwigia 25: 233. pl 1. fig 1-3. 1886.
Mastigobryum subfalcatum Gottsche in Stephani, op. cit. p 234, pl. 1. fig. 4-6.
Bazzania subfalcata Spruce, Jour. Linnean Soc Bot. 30. 356. 1895
Mastigobryum tenue Stephani, Spec. Hep. 3. 448. 1908.
Mastigobryum trinitatis Stephani, Spec. Hep. 6. 483. 1924

Plants medium to robust, dark green becoming deep red-brown: stems stout, to 10 cm. long, with leaves to 5.5 mm. broad, ascending to erect; in longitudinal section the cells elongate, averaging 0.16 mm. long, the cortical shorter, both averaging 16μ in diameter, the vertical walls strongly thickened and containing frequent pits, the end walls thin, the cells of the outer layers strongly pigmented: lateral branches distant, diverging at a wide angle: flagelliform branches frequent, long: rhizoids numerous, present on the bases of the leaves of the flagelliform branches: the line of leaf insertion curved in its upper half; leaves imbricated, strongly falcate, de-

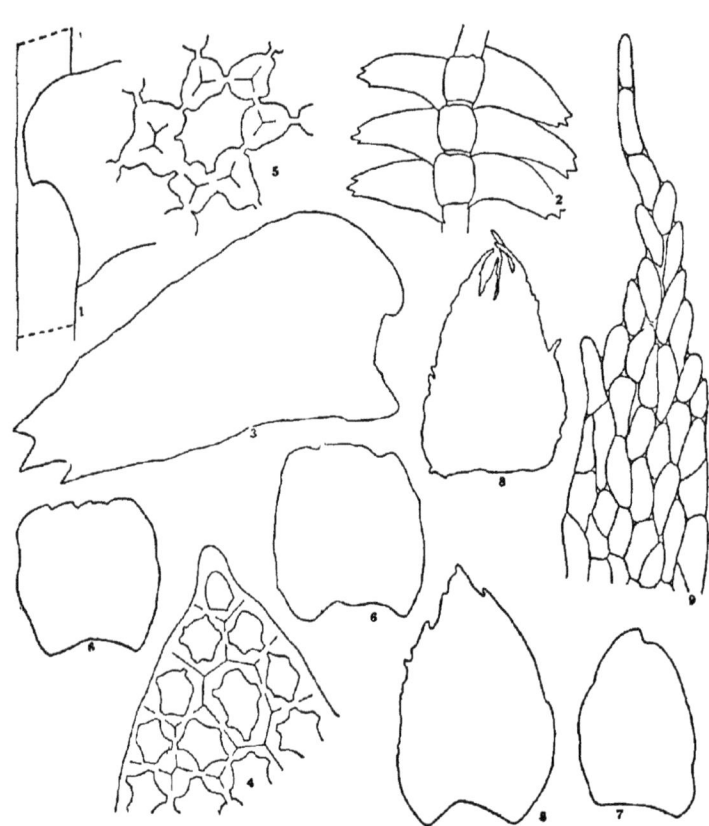

FIG. 31 — *Bazzania longa* (Nees) Trevis. — 1 Portion of leaf and stem, dorsal view, × 30. 2 Portion of plant, ventral view, × 12 3. Leaf, × 30 4. Cells from an apical tooth of a leaf, × 260 5 A cell from the apical portion of a leaf, × 350 6 Underleaves, × 30. 7 Female bract of the outermost series, × 30. 8. Female bracts of intermediate series, × 30 9. One of the laciniae of a female bract of the innermost series (immature), × 100. Nos 1-9 drawn from the type material

flexed, often becoming connivent when dry, unsymmetrically ovate, often elongate, 1.5 mm. - 2.5 mm. long, to 1.5 mm. broad at the base, narrowing to the obliquely truncate, tridentate apex; the dorsal margin strongly convex from a rounded base which extends across the stem, the ventral margin concave, the base a little dilated; the teeth large, unequal, the acroscopic tooth longer than the others, four to eight cells long, three to five cells broad at the base, the sinuses deep, acute to rounded, the margins straight to repand; leaf cells thin-walled, the cell cavities stellate, the trigones very large, with strongly convex sides, soon becoming coalesced by the deposition of secondary thickenings, the cuticle verruculose; cells of the apical portion and dorsal lobe 24μ - $34\mu \times 24\mu$, of the median portion larger, and of the base $54\mu \times 18\mu$, a vitta not differentiated: underleaves distant to imbricated, the line of attachment straight, round-quadrate to elongate, 0.45 mm. - 1.2 mm. long, 0.45 mm. - 0.8 mm. broad, the lateral margins entire, often convex from a rounded base, the apex rounded, entire, to faintly two- or four-lobed: leaves of the flagelliform branches small, ovate, to 0.28 mm. long, spreading, the apex acute to shortly bifid, the cells very large: female branches occasional, solitary, one to several on a stem, the bracts and bracteoles similar, ovate, the outermost series short, rounded to shortly bifid; the intermediate series longer, shortly trifid, the teeth and margins mostly entire; the innermost series to 1.25 mm. long, to one-seventh divided into three short, crenate laciniae, the cells to 48μ long, 18μ wide, thick-walled, the lateral margins crenate to short spinose. perianths to 6 mm. long, the mouth short-spinose, the cells thick-walled. male branches not seen.

HABITAT: On rocks, logs and over tree bases.

The distinguishing characteristics of the species are its large size and dark red-brown color; the large, mostly falcate, obliquely truncate, unequally tridentate leaves with large teeth, large cells, stellate cell-cavities, and very large trigones; and the subquadrate to elongate underleaves which have convex to straight lateral margins and rounded or faintly lobed apices. (FIGS. 31, nos. 1-9; 32, nos. 1-16; 33, nos. 1-12).

The plants of *J. longa* (FIG. 31, nos. 1-9), collected by SIEBER in Martinique, are robust, to 10 cm. or more in length, and 4 mm. or more broad, and are unbranched. They are light to dark green at the growing tips but are characteristically a deep red-brown in the older portions. The leaves are long, unsymmetrically ovate, slightly to strongly falcate, and narrowed to the tridentate apices. The teeth are mostly large, often spreading, with the acroscopic tooth often the longest. The cell walls are at first thin, but soon become thickened by the deposition of secondary thickenings, and the trigones are large and very often coalesced. The cell lumina are stellate as shown in FIG. 31, nos. 4 and 5. The underleaves are distant, quadrate to elongate, broader than the stem, with the lateral margins entire and more or less parallel from a curved base, and the apices entire or faintly two- to four-lobed.

The plants of the type collection of *M. Gottscheanum* (FIG 32, nos. 13-16) are slightly smaller, to 6 cm. long, dark red-brown,

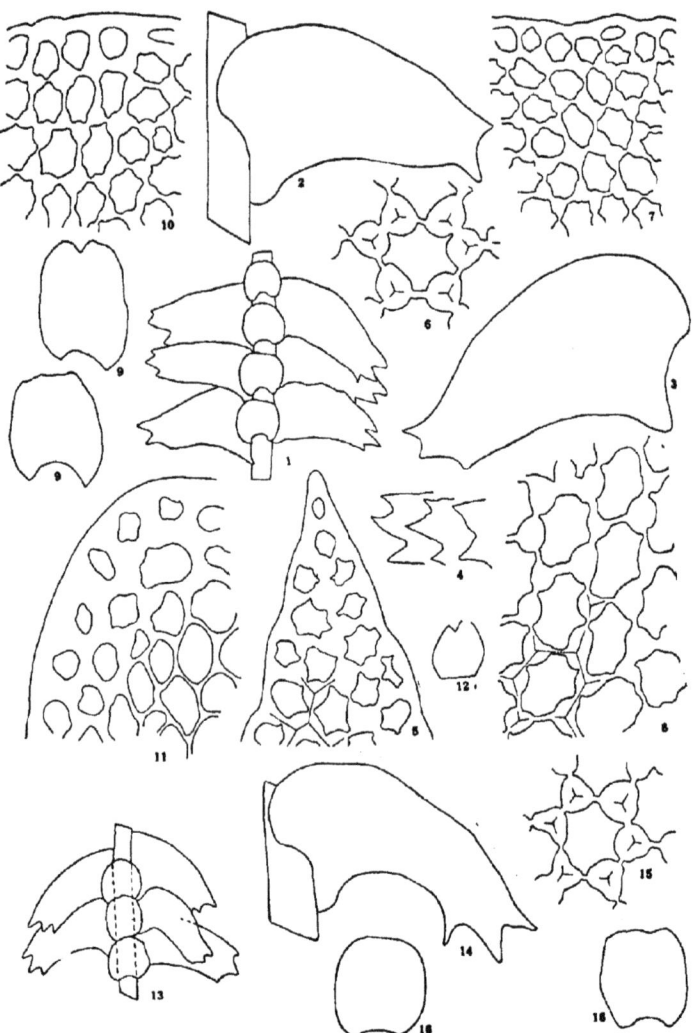

FIG. 32 — *Bazzania longa* (Nees) Trevis. — 1. Portion of a stem, ventral view, × 12 2. Portion of a stem, dorsal view, × 30 3 Leaf, × 30. 4 Leaf apices, × 30. 5 Apical tooth, × 260 6 A cell from the apical portion of a leaf, × 350 7 Cells from the dorsal margin of a leaf, × 260. 8. Cells from the basal portion of a leaf, × 260 9. Underleaves, × 30. 10 Cells from the upper margin of an underleaf, × 260. 11. Portion of a transverse section of a stem, × 260. 12. Male bract, × 30. 13. Portion of a stem, ventral view, × 12 14 Portion of a stem, dorsal view, × 30 15 A cell from the apical portion of a leaf, × 350. 16. Underleaves, × 30. Nos. 1-12 from a portion of the type of *M tenue*, 13-16 from a portion of the type of *M. Gottscheanum*.

and the leaves are deflexed and usually strongly falcate, although some leaves are only slightly so. The leaf cells are large, with very large, rounded trigones and stellate cell lumina. The underleaves are round-quadrate, with the lateral margins entire, and the apices rounded or faintly lobed. The plants of the type of *M. tenue* (FIG. 32, nos. 1-12) are also red-brown, approximately the same size, but most of the leaves are not quite so falcate, and many of the underleaves are longer. The plants of *M. subfalcatum* (FIG. 33, nos. 1-6) are also large and reddish brown, with deflexed, falcate leaves and mostly round-quadrate underleaves. They are identical with those of *J. longa.*

Most of the plants of the type collection of *M. speciosum* (FIG. 33, nos. 7-8) are very large, to 10 cm. long and 4 mm broad, a deep red-brown to black color, with the underleaves elongate rather than round-quadrate. In the other characteristics, leaf insertion, leaf shape, teeth, trigones, and the margins of the underleaves, the plants agree with those described above. Smaller plants in the same collection are intermediate or practically identical with *M. Gottscheanum,* while the larger ones are typical of large plants of *J longa.* The female bracts of plants collected by ELLIOTT in Dominica, no. 1080, are identical with those of the type of *M. subfalcatum.*

M. trinitatis (FIG. 33, nos. 9-10) collected by CRUGER in Trinidad must also be included here The plants are rather small, the pigmentation is not so strongly developed, and many of the leaves are not so falcate, but the coloration, type of leaf, and cell pattern are the same. It is obvious that the plants are poorly developed.

In some instances the above species have been identical, in others they have differed in size, leaf curvature, degree of pigmentation, length of underleaves, etc., with much variation in the individuals of one mat, so that no definite limits of variation can be assigned to any one of them They appear to represent mostly habitat variations of one unit, *J. longa.*

var. papillata (Steph.) comb. nov.

Mastigobryum papillatum Stephani, Spec. Hep. 3: 526. 1909

This variety, collected in Dominica (FIG. 33, nos. 11-12), differs from the species in that the cuticle of the leaves and underleaves is very conspicuously roughened by large, coarse, wart-like protuberances. The cuticle of *J. longa* and of the synonyms described above varies from faintly to strongly verruculose, but in no instance are the verruculae even half so large as those of the variety.

DISTRIBUTION. D o m i n i c a . without locality or collector's name (NY); Morne Diablotin, Elliott 678, cited by Spruce (1895, 356); without locality, Elliott 1080 (G); without locality, Elliott, the type of *M papillatum* (H); without locality, Elliott, as *M. arcuatum* (G). — C u b a : without locality, Wright, Hep. Cubensis Wrightianae, as *M. brasiliense* (H). — G u a d e l o u p e : without locality, l'Herminier (NY); without locality, l'Herminier, the type of *M. tenue* (H), without locality, Richard (NY); without locality,

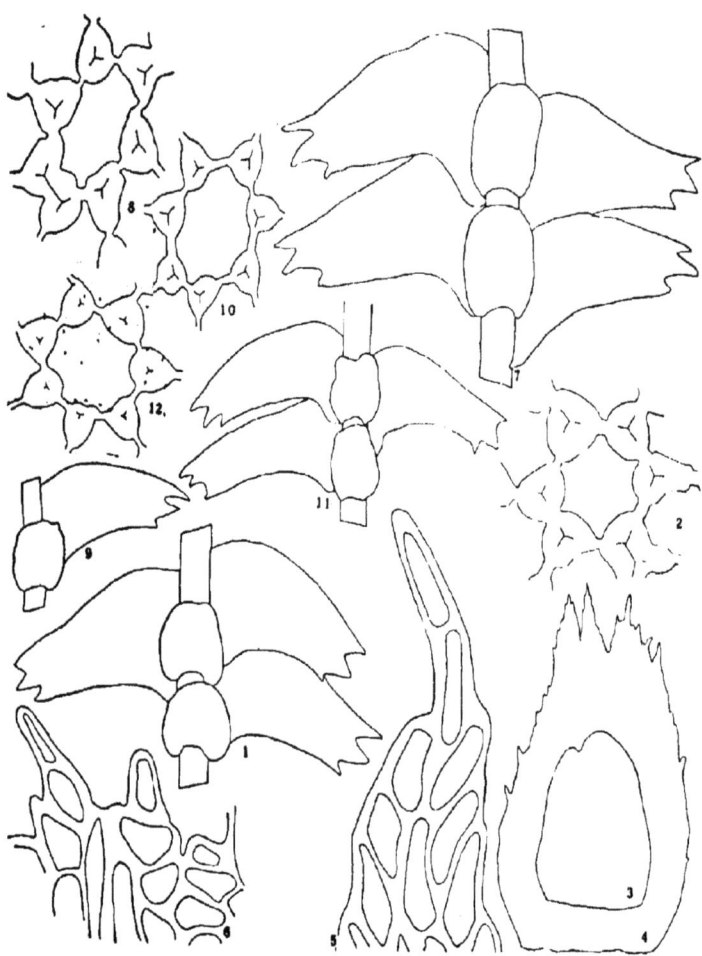

FIG. 33. — *Bazzania longa* (Nees) Trevis. — 1 Portion of a stem, ventral view, × 15. 2. A cell from the apical portion of a leaf, × 400. 3. A female bract, outermost series, × 30. 4. A female bract, innermost series, × 30. 5. A portion of an apical tooth of a bract of this series, × 300. 6. A portion of the perianth mouth, × 310. 7. Portion of a plant, ventral view, × 15. 8. A cell from the apical portion of a leaf, × 400 9. Portion of a plant, ventral view, × 15. 10. A cell from the apical portion of a leaf, × 400. — *B. longa* var. *papillata* (Steph.) *Fulford.* — 11. Portion of a plant, ventral view, × 15. 12. A cell from the apical portion of a leaf, × 400. Nos. 1-6 drawn from a portion of the type of *M. subfalcatum;* 7-8 from a portion of the type of *M. speciosum;* 9-10 from a portion of the type of *M. trinitatis,* 11-12 from a portion of the type of *M. papillatum.*

l'Hermmier, the type of *M. subfalcatum* (G, H); Morne-l'Echelle, Duss 394 (NY); Soufrière, Duss 83 (NY). — J a m a i c a : John Crow Peak, Underwood 680 (NY); Tweedside, Underwood 2042 (Y) — M a r t i n i q u e · without locality, Sieber 35, the type (H, NY), Mt Pelée, Husnot, Pl Antilles 213, the type of *M speciosum* (G); Mt. Pelée, Duss 394, 395, 584, 606 (NY); without locality, Bordaz, cited by Stephani (1908, 469), without locality or collector's name (H). — P u e r t o R i c o . Sierra de Naguabo, Shafer 3750 (NY); the same, Johnson 1620 (NY) — S t. K i t t s : without locality, Breutel, the type of *M. Gottscheanum* (B), without locality, Breutel (NY). — T r i n i d a d . without locality, Cruger, the type of *M trinitatis* (G), without locality, Cruger (NY), without locality or collector's name, Hb. Jack (G).

REFERENCES: Montagne (1843, 253); Lindenberg & Gottsche (1851, 66, 105), Stephani (1903, 22; 1908, 468, 472, 1909, 519, 520; *Icones, Mastigobryum* nos 59, 162, 170, 179, 396, 399, 400), Spruce (1895, 356)

24. **Bazzania jamaicensis** (Lehm. & Lindenb.) Trevis. Mem. Ist. Lomb. 13. 414. 1877.

Herpetium jamaicense Lehmann et Lindenberg, in Lehmann, Pug Pl. 7. 7. 1838
Mastigobryum jamaicense Lehm et Lindenb., in G. L. & N , Syn. Hep. 223. 1845
Mastigobryum chamaecardion Herzog ms (nomen nudum)
Bazzania jamaicensis var *chamaecardia* Herzog, Rev Bryol. et Lichén 11 19 1938.
Mastigobryum caracanum Stephani, Spec Hep 3: 525. 1909.

Plants large, in deep tufts or mats, olive-green to brownish green, strongly pigmented with brown: stems stout, to 10 cm. or more long, with leaves 4 mm. broad, prostrate to suberect; stem cells in longitudinal section elongate, averaging 0.2 mm. long, the cortical shorter, both averaging 18μ in diameter, the vertical walls strongly thickened and containing frequent pits, the end walls thin; lateral branches frequent, mostly more than 5 mm. apart, diverging at a wide angle; flagelliform branches frequent, long, often branched; rhizoids colorless, present on the bases of some of the leaves of the flagelliform branches. the leaf insertion curved in its upper part; leaves imbricated, convex, strongly deflexed even when moist, unsymmetrically ovate, a little falcate, to 2 mm. long, 1 mm. - 1.5 mm broad at the base, narrowing to the rather broad, transversely truncate, tridentate, apex; the dorsal margin arched from a strongly rounded base, extending the width of the stem, the ventral margin concave, the base a little dilated, the apex irregularly three-toothed, the teeth acute, narrow to broad, two to six cells long, two to nine cells broad, some obscure, the sinuses narrow, acute to lunulate, the margins entire, straight to undulate; the leaf cells thin-walled, the cell lumina angular-rounded, the trigones

FIG 34. — *Bazzania jamaicensis* (Lehm. & Lindenb.) Trevis — 1. Portion of leaf and stem, dorsal view, $\times$ 30. 2. Portion of plant, ventral view, $\times$ 10. 3. Leaf, $\times$ 30 4. A cell from the apical portion of a leaf, $\times$ 350 5. Cells of an apical tooth, $\times$ 260 6 Cells from the dorsal base of a leaf, $\times$ 260 7. Underleaves, $\times$ 30 8 Cells from the apical portion of an underleaf, $\times$ 260 9 Portion of a cross-section of the stem, $\times$ 260 10 Male bracteoles, $\times$ 30. 11. Male bracts, $\times$ 30. 12. Cells from the apical portion of a male bract, $\times$ 260 Nos. 1-9 drawn from a portion of the type material, 10-12 drawn from plants collected in Peru by LECHLER.

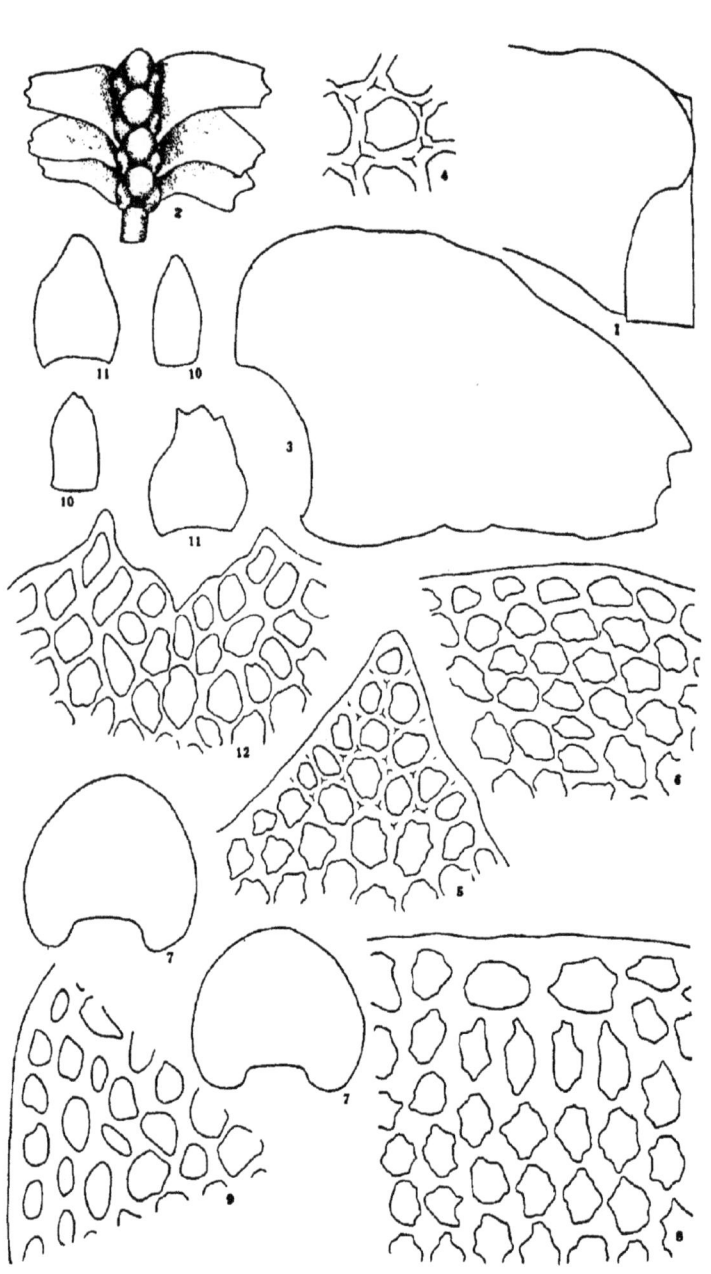

small, conspicuous, with convex sides, soon becoming coalesced in the marginal and apical regions, the cuticle smooth to faintly verruculose; cells of the apical region and dorsal base averaging $20\mu \times 20\mu$, those of the median portion a little larger, those of the base 45μ - $54\mu \times 27\mu$: underleaves approximate to imbricated, broader than the stem, attached in a straight line, appressed, broadly ovate from an auricled base, very concave when seen from above, 0.65 mm. long $\times$ 0.8 mm. - 1 mm. broad at the base, the margin entire; the cells of the interior 22μ - 32μ long and broad, the cell lumina angular-rounded, the trigones small, conspicuous, the walls thin, soon becoming thick by deposits of secondary thickenings and coalesced trigones, the marginal rows slightly larger, the walls more uniformly thickened, deeply pigmented with brown: leaves of the flagelliform branches ovate, to 0.32 mm. long, mostly entire: male branches one to several on a stem; the bracteoles small, oblong, averaging 0.56 mm. long $\times$ 0.28 mm. wide, somewhat concave from above, the apex rounded or with one or two obscure teeth; the bracts larger, ovate, to 0.56 mm. long - 0.64 mm. broad at the base, the apex entire, or with two or three short teeth; antheridia occurring singly: female branches and sporophytes not seen.

HABITAT: On tree trunks.

The species is distinguished by its large size, the olive-green color and brown pigmentation; the unsymmetrically ovate, transversely truncate, irregularly tridentate leaves; and the inflated, entire, ovate, auricled underleaves with dark borders which are appressed to the stem. (FIGS. 34, nos. 1-12; 35, nos. 1-4).

B. jamaicensis is one of the easiest of the American species to recognize. The plants are robust, dark green with some brown pigmentation, and usually grow in prostrate mats. The leaves are large, broadly ovate, and the teeth while conspicuous, are short and broad. The underleaves offer the best diagnostic characteristics. They are broadly ovate from a cordate base. They are strongly concave when seen from above, and the margin, which is entire, is tightly appressed to the stem, so that they appear to be inflated. The marginal cells are often a little larger than the others, and become pigmented with brown or red-brown, the degree of coloring apparently dependent on the habitat. The underleaves of robust plants always have the borders deeply pigmented.

M. caracanum, from Brazil, is not quite so robust as *H. jamaicense* from Jamaica, but in other respects is identical with it.

B. jamaicensis var. *chamaecardia*, from Costa Rica, is much less robust. The stems are long, and the leaves and underleaves are distant. The concavity of the underleaves is not nearly so conspicuous, nor is the pigmentation of the marginal rows of cells so well developed. Since however, many intermediate stages between this form and the more robust type occur, it would seem that the *variety* is probably the result of the special conditions under which it grew.

The underleaves will serve to distinguish the species from all of those already described. It might possibly be confused with *B. Wrightii*, a description of which follows.

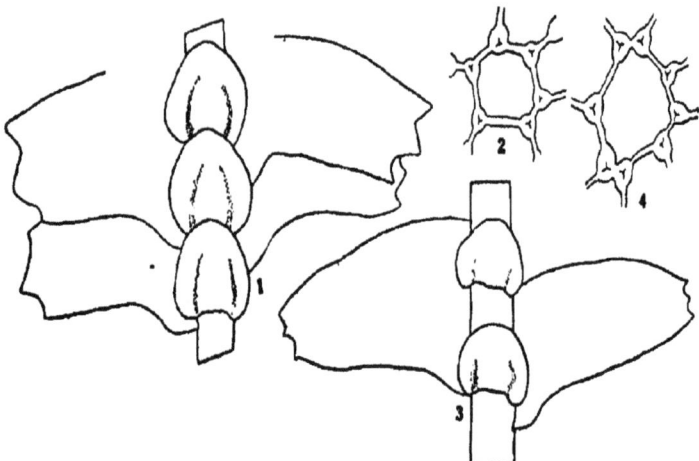

FIG. 35. — *Bazzania jamaicensis* (Lehm. & Lindenb.) Trevis. — 1. Portion of a plant, ventral view, × 15. 2. A cell from the apical portion of a leaf, × 400. 3. Portion of plant, ventral view, × 15. 4. A cell from the apical portion of a leaf, × 400. Nos. 1-2 drawn from a portion of the type of *M. caracanum* from Brazil; 3-4 from a portion of the type of *M. chamaecardion* from Costa Rica.

DISTRIBUTION. J a m a i c a : without locality, Swartz, cited by Stephani (1909, 525), without locality, Hart, cited by Boswell (1875, 50); without locality or collector's name, Hb Hooker, the type (NY); Blue Mountain Peak, 7300 ft, Harris 20, 11060 (Y, NY), summit of Blue Mountain Peak, Underwood 2505 (NY), slopes of Sir John, E G Britton 1209 (NY); Blue Mountain, Evans 239 (Y). — C o s t a R i c a . Cerro de las Lajas, Standley & Valerio 49949, 50713, 51446, 51643a, 51645, 52117, 52267, the type of var. *chamaecardia* (W); Segovia, Oersted, cited by Hampe (1851, 302). — B r a z i l . Rio de Janeiro, Guadichaud (NY), Caracas, Vainio, the type of *M. caracanum* (H). — E c u a d o r : Cayambe, Jameson (NY) — P e r u : Tatanara, Lechler 3112 (NY). — V e n e z u e l a without locality, Fendler, cited by Stephani (1909, 525); Caracas, Funck & Schlim (NY).

REFERENCES: Montagne (1844-46, 244); Hampe (1851, 302); Lindenberg & Gottsche (1851, 52); Boswell (1887, 50), Stephani (1909, 525, *Icones, Mastigobryum* nos. 380, 388).

25. Bazzania Wrightii (Gottsche) comb. nov.

Mastigobryum Wrightii Gottsche in Stephani, Hedwigia 25. 237. pl 2, fig 24-26. 1886.
Mastigobryum stoloniferum var. *cubense* Gottsche ms, Hep. Cub. Wrightianae.

Plants medium size to large, light yellow-green, becoming deeply pigmented with yellow-brown in the older portions: stems slender to robust, 5 cm. or more in length, with leaves to 4.5 mm. broad, prostrate to ascending. stem cells in longitudinal section elongate, to 0.17 mm. long, the cortical shorter, both averaging 18μ in diameter, the vertical walls uniformly thickened and containing frequent pits, the end walls thin, lateral branches frequent, diverging at a wide angle; flagelliform branches numerous, long: rhizoids colorless, from the basal cells of the leaves of the flagelliform branches: the line of leaf insertion curved in its upper part, leaves distant to imbricated, falcate, often becoming deflexed when dry, unsymmetrically ovate, 1.5 mm. - 3 mm. long, 1 mm. - 1.5 mm. broad at the base, narrowed a little to the more or less obliquely truncate, tridentate apex; the dorsal margin arched from a curved base, covering one-half or more of the stem, often extending beyond, the ventral margin concave, the base dilated, the apex irregularly three-toothed, the teeth mostly small, acute, to six cells long, three to five cells broad at the base, the sinuses shallow, lunulate, the margins entire; leaf cells thin-walled, the cell lumina angular-rounded, the trigones conspicuous, with convex sides, soon becoming coalesced through the deposition of secondary thickenings, the cuticle faintly verruculose; cells of the apical portion and dorsal base mostly 24μ × 24μ, those of the median portion larger, those of the basal area 32μ - 48μ × 24μ, a vitta not distinct: underleaves distant to imbricated, subquadrate to orbicular, broader than the stem, attached in a straight line, 0.5 mm. - 1.2 mm. long, 0.5 mm. - 0.95 mm. broad at the base, the lateral margins convex from a rounded to cordate base, entire, the apical portion rounded, entire, straight to four-lobed, a little squarrose, the cells 24μ - 32μ, thin-walled, the trigones large, often coalesced, intermediate thickenings developed in the elongate cells of the apical portion: leaves of the flagelliform branches scale-like, ovate, acute to shortly bifid, spreading, female branches occasional, solitary, one to several on a stem, the bracts and bracteoles similar, the outermost series small, bluntly

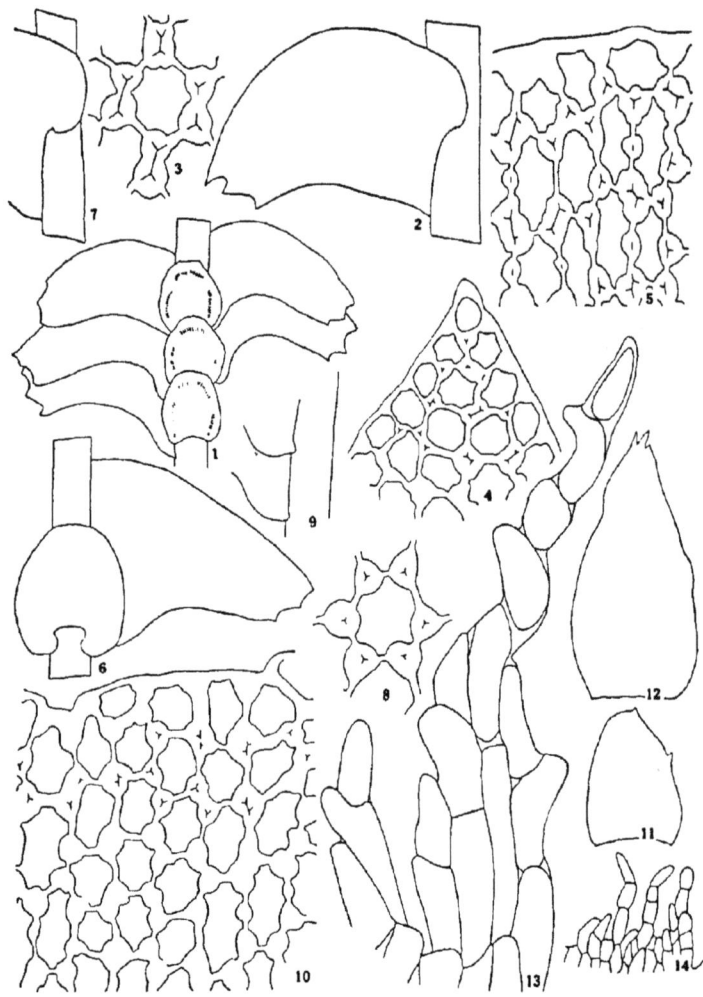

FIG. 36. — *Bazzania Wrightii* (Gottsche) Fulford. — 1 Portion of a
plant, ventral view, × 15   2 Portion of a stem and a leaf, dorsal view, × 30.
3 A cell from the apical portion of a leaf, × 400. 4. A tooth of a leaf, × 310
5. Cells from the apical margin of an underleaf, × 310. 6. Portion of a plant,
ventral view, × 15. 7. Portion of a leaf and stem, dorsal view, × 15. 8. A
cell from the apical portion of a leaf, × 400. 9. Ventral bases of leaves
attached to the stem, × 15. 10 Cells from the apical margin of an underleaf, × 310 11 Female bract of an outer series, × 30 12 Female bract of
an intermediate series, × 30   13. One of the laciniae of a bract of the innermost series, × 310   14 Portion of the mouth of the perianth, × 100. Nos.
1-5 drawn from a portion of the type material; 6-14 from a portion of the
type of *M. stoloniferum* var. *cubense* Gottsche, from Cuba.

ovate to shortly bifid; the intermediate series longer, shortly bi-
trifid, the lateral margins entire; the innermost series larger, to
one-sixth divided into two or three crenulate laciniae, the lateral
margins crenulate to short ciliate, the cells to 48μ long, 24μ wide,
with irregularly thickened walls: perianth (immature) mouth long
laciniate-ciliate: male branches not seen.

HABITAT: On logs and tree bases.

The distinguishing characteristics of the species are its size
and yellow- to brownish green color; the more or less falcate leaves
with short teeth and shallow sinuses; the thin-walled leaf cells,
with conspicuous trigones which soon become coalesced, and
angular-rounded cell lumina; and the subquadrate to orbicular
underleaves, attached in a straight line, with lateral margins convex from a rounded to cordate base, and apices rounded to undulate
or lobed and made up of rather large, elongate cells with thin walls,
large trigones, and intermediate thickenings. (FIG. 36, nos. 1-14).

The plants of the type collection (FIG. 36, nos. 1-5) are greenish
yellow-brown in color, the stems are large, and with leaves 3 mm.
or more broad, but they are for the most part, quite fragile and
break readily. The leaves are approximate to imbricated and the
underleaves are distant or approximate. The underleaves are
rounded at the bases, and the mostly rounded apical margins very
often show a deeper red-brown pigmentation than the interior
or base.

The only difference between these plants and those of *M.
stoloniferum* var *cubense* (FIG. 36, nos. 6-14), also collected in
Cuba by WRIGHT, is that the latter are more robust, mostly but not
always, light yellow-green in color, they are not brittle, and the
underleaves are larger and densely imbricated. The bases of the
underleaves are mostly strongly cordate instead of rounded as in
M. Wrightii, but I believe that this is a characteristic of the species
in its luxuriant form. The leaf shape, the teeth, cell size, walls
and trigones, as well as the cell configuration, including the presence of intermediate thickenings in the larger, elongate cells of the
underleaves are identical and the two should therefore, I believe,
be considered as different expressions, perhaps due to habitat
conditions, of one species.

The species is somewhat similar in several respects to *B.
jamaicensis*. The two species differ in that the leaves of *B. Wrightii*
are falcate, while the underleaves while often somewhat concave
when seen from above, never appear to be inflated, and the
margins are never closely appressed to the stem. The presence of
intermediate thickenings in the elongate cells of the apical portion
will also aid in separating the two.

DISTRIBUTION· C u b a : Mt. Verde, Wright, Hep Cub., the type (H, Y,
NY); without locality, Wright, Hep. Cub., as *M. stoloniferum* var *cubense*
(H, Y, NY); Loma del Gato, Fr. Clément 351 (NY).—J a m a i c a : Morse's
Gap, Evans 48 (Y); Tweedside, Underwood 2042 (NY). — P u e r t o R i c o :
without locality, Sintenis 3, 18, 33, 62, 84, 124, 130, cited by Stephani
(1888a, 279).

REFERENCES: Stephani (1888a, 279; 1909, 524; *Icones, Mastigobryum*
no. 408).

Section 2. Connatae

This Section includes plants with more or less three-toothed leaves which are entire to more or less serrulate or spinose along the margins in the apical part. The underleaves are entire to variously and irregularly incised, serrate and toothed along the margins, and may have a hyaline border of several rows of cells or may be chlorophyllose throughout. The underleaves are attached in a straight line and are *connate* with the *ventral base* of *one* or a *pair* of leaves. This attachment with the leaf is often not conspicuous except under high magnification.

The American species of this Section show three distinct tendencies of development within the group. One of these, exemplified by only one species, *B. Fendleri* from Brazil, Ecuador and Venezuela, has leaves only faintly three-lobed, with the margins entire, and the cells thick-walled and with large trigones; the underleaves are round-quadrate, faintly four-lobed, with entire margins, and *connate* with *one leaf*.

A second tendency is to be found in the species of the West Indies. The five species are very closely related and show a considerable degree of variation in their characters. The leaves vary from obscurely to strongly three-toothed; from entire to serrulate or spinose in the apical region; and the underleaves may be entire to sharply dentate or spinose, with a hyaline border, or chlorophyllose throughout. All are *connate* by a few cells with *one leaf*. The distribution of some of the species is limited to one or two of the islands.

The third tendency appears in the group of species which occurs south of the Equator from Peru to the Straits of Magellan with some of the species or their near relatives also in South Africa, Australia and New Zealand. This group is characterized by having the underleaves *connate* with a *pair of leaves*. The leaf apices may be obscurely to strongly three-toothed, entire to spinose, and the underleaves which are usually spinose-dentate have hyaline borders or are chlorophyllose throughout.

Key to the Species

1. Underleaves connate with a pair of leaves
    2. Hyaline cells of the underleaves forming a conspicuous, broad border, on at least some of the underleaves . . . 32 B. peruviana (p 119)
    2. Hyaline cells of the underleaves restricted to a marginal row, or scattered, or absent; the cuticle noticeably verruculose,
                                                        33. B. Skottsbergii (p. 122)
1. Underleaves inconspicuously connate by a few (often only one or two) cells with one leaf only.
    2 Underleaves chlorophyllose throughout.

FIG. 37. — *Bazzania Fendleri* (Steph) Fulford — 1. Portion of a plant, ventral view, × 15. 2. Portion of a leaf and stem, dorsal view, × 30   3 A leaf, × 15. 4. A cell from the apical portion of a leaf, × 400. 5 Cells from the basal portion of a leaf, × 310   6 Underleaf, × 15   Drawn from the type material.

26   Bazzania Fendleri (Steph.) comb. nov.

Mastigobryum Fendleri Stephani, Spec Hep. 3. 436, 468. 1908.

Plants medium to large, light greenish brown, more strongly pigmented in the older portions: stems to 5 cm. long, with leaves to 3.5 mm. broad, prostrate to ascending; lateral branches 5 mm. or more apart, diverging at a wide angle; flagelliform branches numerous, long; rhizoids on the bases of the leaves of flagelliform branches · the line of leaf insertion little curved in its upper part; the leaves imbricated, convex, ascendent, a little deflexed when dry, unsymmetrically ovate, to 1.5 mm. long, 0.7 mm. broad at the base, narrowed a little to the more or less transversely truncate, obscurely tridentate apex; the dorsal margin convex from a curved base, extending half way across the stem, the ventral margin nearly straight, the base scarcely dilated, the apex irregularly and obscurely one-, two-, or three-toothed, the teeth one to three cells high, two or three cells broad at the base, the sinuses lunulate, the margins entire; leaf cells thick-walled, the trigones large, with irregular, rounded sides, often becoming confluent, intermediate thickenings sometimes present, the cell lumina angular-rounded, the cuticle verruculose; cells of the apical portion averaging 16μ in diameter, those of the interior larger, those of the base 32μ $\times$ 16μ, a vitta not differentiated: underleaves large, imbricated, broader than the stem, round-quadrate, connate with one leaf, the line of attachment on the stem a straight line, 0.9 mm. broad and long, narrowed a little to the base, the margins recurved, the lateral margins convex, entire, the apical margin entire to faintly four-lobed, the cells as in the leaf: leaves of the flagelliform branches scale-like, to 0.2 mm. long, acute to shortly bifid: sexual branches not seen.

HABITAT: Not given.

The distinguishing characteristics of the species are its size, and light greenish brown color; the obscurely two- or three-toothed leaves with thick-walled cells with angular-rounded lumina, and large trigones with irregular, convex sides; and the large, round-quadrate underleaves, connate with one leaf, with entire lateral margins and faintly four-lobed apices. (FIG. 37, nos. 1-5).

DISTRIBUTION. B r a z i l : Rio de Janeiro, Gaudichaud (NY). — E c u a - d o r : Cayambe, Jameson (NY). — V e n e z u e l a : Valencia, Fendler, the type (H).

REFERENCES: Stephani (*Icones, Mastigobryum* no. 161).

27. Bazzania Schwaneckiana (Hampe & Gottsche) Trevis. Mem.
Ist. Lomb. 13: 414. 1877.

Mastigobryum Schwaneckianum Hampe & Gottsche, Linnaea 25: 345. 1852.

Plants scattered or growing in depressed mats, sometimes without leaves, mostly medium size, light green to olive-green, becoming brownish in the older portions: stems to 5 cm. long, with leaves mostly 1.5 mm. - 2.5 mm. wide, prostrate; in longitudinal section the cells elongate, the medullary cells averaging 0.17 mm. long, the cortical shorter, both averaging 16μ in diameter, the end walls thin, the vertical walls uniformly thickened and containing frequent pits: the lateral branches mostly 5 mm. or more apart, diverging at a wide angle: flagelliform branches frequent, long, occasionally branched: rhizoids colorless, sparingly produced on the leaves of the flagelliform branches: the leaf-insertion curved in its upper half; leaves approximate to imbricated, spreading, plane or nearly so, becoming deflexed on drying, unsymmetrically ovate, mostly 1.2 mm. long, 0.56 mm. wide at the base, narrowing somewhat to the transversely truncate apex; the dorsal margin convex from a slightly rounded base, extending over one-half the stem, the ventral margin straight to slightly concave from a scarcely dilated base, the apex broad, rounded, entire to undulate or truncate, sometimes tending to become faintly two- to three-toothed, the margins entire to crenulate; the leaf cells of the marginal one or two rows often forming a border, uniformly thick-walled, mostly 16μ × 10μ, the cells of the apical region 20μ - 24μ, thin-walled, the trigones very small, the median cells larger, those of the base to 50μ × 30μ, a vitta not differentiated, the cuticle verruculose: underleaves subimbricated, squarrose, attached in a straight line, connate by several cells with one leaf, quadrate to quadrate-orbicular, broader than the stem, mostly 0.34 mm. - 0.38 mm. long × 0.32 mm. - 0.38 mm. wide, the apex undulate to two- or four-toothed or -lobed, the sinuses acute, narrow, the lateral margins lobed, convex from a straight base, the hyaline border complete, two to four cells wide, broadest at the apex, the cells similar to those of the chlorophyllose area but with thinner walls: leaves of the flagelliform branches ovate, mostly 0.16 mm. long, convex, the apices acute to bifid: sexual branches not seen.

HABITAT: In depressed mats over logs and shaded banks.

The species is best characterized by its medium size, the light green color, the rounded-entire or nearly entire leaf apices with crenulate margins, and the subquadrate, usually lobed underleaves with hyaline borders several cells wide, which are connate by a few cells with one leaf. (FIG. 38, nos. 1-14).

The leaves while usually entire occasionally show a tendency to become three-toothed at the apex. These teeth are broad, obtuse, one or two cells high, with shallow, lunulate sinuses. The margins may be entire or more or less crenulate (FIG. 38, no. 6). The cells of the apical region are thin-walled, with small but distinct trigones, and the cell lumina are always rounded. The cells of the margin (one to several rows) are often longer and narrower, and have the walls

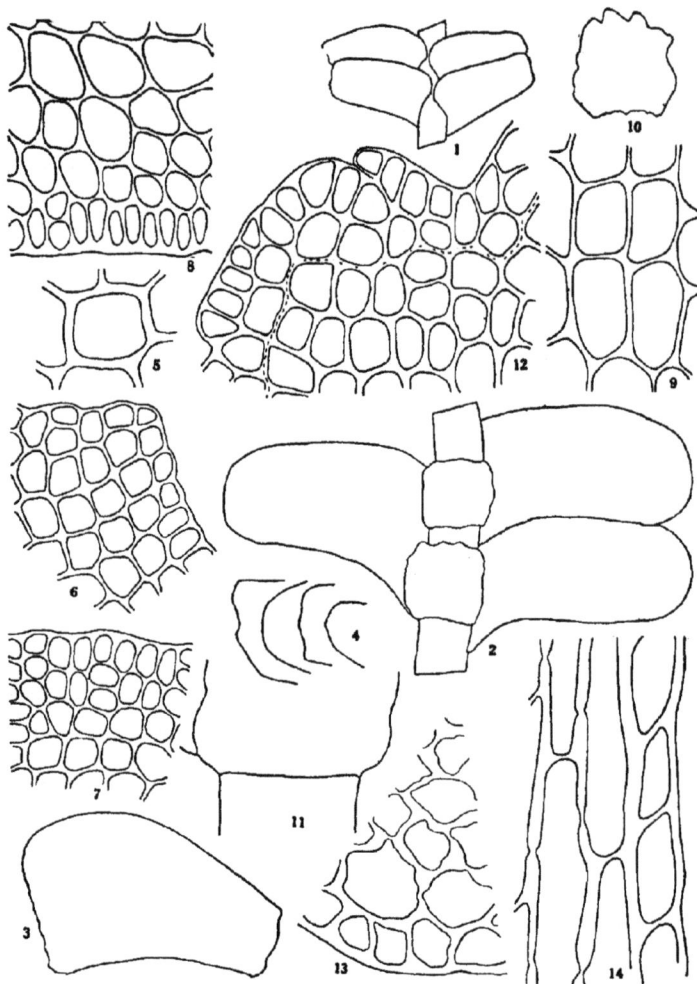

FIG. 38. — *Bazzania Schwaneckiana* (Hampe & Gottsche) Trevis —
1 Dorsal view of portion of a stem, × 12   2 Ventral view of portion of stem,
× 30. 3. A leaf, × 30. 4. Leaf apices, × 30. 5. A cell from the apical
portion of a leaf, × 400. 6. Cells from the apical portion of a leaf, × 260.
7 Cells from the dorsal margin of a leaf, × 260. 8. Cells from the ventral
margin of a leaf, × 260. 9. Cells from the basal portion of a leaf, × 260.
10 Underleaf, × 30. 11 Underleaf and portion of a stem and leaf to show
attachment, × 45. 12. Cells from the apical portion of an underleaf, the
outer part hyaline, × 260. 13. Portion of a cross-section of a stem, × 260.
14. Portion of a longitudinal section of a stem, × 260. Nos. 1, 3-14 drawn
from material collected by EVANS 166 in Puerto Rico; no. 2 from a portion
of the type material.

uniformly thicker than those of the rest of the leaf, so that they form a border. This marginal border is best developed in plants growing in the more xerophytic situations. The cuticle is very rough. Large oil bodies were present in some of the plants collected by PAGÁN, no. 274, in Puerto Rico.

The vitta, which is characteristic of the leaves of many of the tropical species, is in *B. Schwaneckiana* not differentiated. While the basal portion of the leaf consists of a group of elongated cells arranged in rows, they are not sufficiently differentiated from the adjacent cells to form a distinctly differentiated area. The cell walls are thin and uniform (FIG. 38, nos. 5, 6, 7, 8 and 9) and the trigones are small but distinct.

The underleaves are especially distinctive. They are subquadrate in outline, broader than the stem, and are usually four-lobed at the apex (FIG. 38, nos. 2 and 10). The hyaline margin is two to four or five cells wide (FIG. 38, no. 12), continuous, and the cell pattern is the same as that of the chlorophyllose area. This hyaline border is often difficult to detect in the older underleaves where the chlorophyll content has disappeared or where the cell walls have become brown. It is always conspicuous in the younger leaves. The line of attachment on the stem is a straight line, in optical view the width of the stem, and in addition, a few cells of the ventral basal margin of one leaf. This latter character is not noticeable unless the plants are examined under high magnification (see FIG. 38, no. 11). It is always restricted to one side of the stem on a branch, and is especially conspicuous on that underleaf and leaf at the junction of the branch and stem.

Many of the plants collected by EVANS and later PAGÁN in Puerto Rico, and by DUSS in Guadeloupe exhibit a tendency to shed their leaves, and many of the stems are without leaves throughout much of their length. This caducous habit seems to be restricted to the leaves only, for in no case were the underleaves absent even on those stems almost completely devoid of leaves.

STEPHANI included this species under his subgenus *Integrifolia* because of the more or less entire character of its leaf apices. *B. Schwaneckiana* is without doubt very closely related to a small group of species restricted locally in the West Indies, namely *B. Eggersiana*, *B. pycnophylla*, *B. armatastipula* and *B. cubensis*. It shares with them size, habit of growth, color, texture, cell configuration and similarity of underleaves. All of them have the underleaf connate by a few cells with one leaf. In addition, all except *B. cubensis* have underleaves with conspicuous hyaline borders. Because of this close natural relationship of the species with members of the *Connatae* it seems logical to transfer it to this group even though the leaf outline is not strongly serrate or the three teeth well defined.

DISTRIBUTION: D o m i n i c a : Four Hand, Fishlock 12a (NY), without locality, Elliott, cited by Stephani (1908, 431). — G u a d e l o u p e : without locality, l'Herminier (H, Y, NY); Pointe Noire, Duss 43, 57 (NY). — M a r-t i n i q u e . Calebasse, Morne Paillasse; Duss 38, 369 (NY). Duss 662 from Deux-Choux (NY), is a species of *Frullania*. — P u e r t o R i c o . without locality, Schwanecke, the type, 608 of Gottsche & Rabenhorst, Hep. eur (Y, NY); near Adjuntas, E G Britton & Marble 2175 (NY); Luquillo Mountains, Heller 1158, 4653, 4654, 4717 (NY), El Yunque, Evans 166, 185 (Y, NY), Rio de Maricao, E G Britton 2503 (NY), without locality, Sintenis 12, cited by Stephani (1888a, 279); Orocovis, Pagán 22, 23 (C); Canóvanas, Pagán 274 (C)

REFERENCES. Bescherelle (1893, 186), Stephani (1888a, 279; 1903, 22, 1908, 431; *Icones, Mastigobryum* no. 22); Pagán (1939, 39)

28. **Bazzania pycnophylla** (Taylor) Trevis. Mem. Ist. Lomb. 13: 414. 1877.

Mastigobryum pycnophyllum Taylor, London Jour. Bot 5: 371 1846

Plants growing in depressed mats, light green to olive-green, becoming tinged with brown; stems slender, with leaves to 3 mm. broad, prostrate · the lateral branches 0 5 cm. or more apart, diverging at a wide angle; flagelliform branches frequent; rhizoids colorless, present on the bases of leaves of the flagelliform branches: the leaf insertion little curved in the upper part; leaves imbricated, spreading, becoming somewhat deflexed on drying, unsymmetrically ovate, to 1.4 mm. long, 0.55 mm. broad at the base, narrowing a little to the transversely truncate, serrulate to spinose, obscurely tridentate apex; the dorsal margin convex from a curved base which covers one-half the stem, the ventral margin straight to slightly concave, the base little dilated; the apex broad, mostly obscurely tridentate, the teeth very short, acute, broad, the sinuses lunulate, the margins serrulate to spinose; the leaf cells subquadrate to rectangular in outline, the cell lumina rounded, the cell walls of the apical portion and margins uniformly thickened, those of the interior thin with small but distinct trigones, cells of the apical portion 18μ × 18μ, of the dorsal lobe smaller, those of the base 36μ - 54μ × 27μ; a vitta not differentiated; the cuticle verruculose: underleaves imbricated, a little broader than the stem, attached in a straight line, connate by several cells with one leaf, partly hyaline, quadrate, mostly 0.48 mm × 0 48 mm , the lateral margins entire, serrate or dentate, the apex three- to six-toothed, the teeth two to five cells broad at the base, two to four cells high, the margins mostly serrate to dentate; the cells of two sorts, those of the marginal rows (mostly of the teeth) hyaline, the walls uniformly thin, verruculose, those of the interior chlorophyllose, the walls thicker, trigones small: leaves of the flagelliform branches scale-like, ovate: male and female branches and sporophyte not seen.

HABITAT: In depressed mats on logs and tree bases in woods.

The distinguishing characteristics of the species are its prostrate habit and olive-green color; the blunt, obscurely tridentate leaves which are serrulate to dentate in the apical portion; and the quadrate underleaves, connate by a few cells to one leaf, with hyaline margins which are incised to form three to six, serrate to dentate teeth. (FIG. 39, nos. 1-10).

The species is of the size and habit of the other tropical American *Connatae*. Its leaves are spreading and do not become deflexed on drying. The outstanding characteristic of the plant is its blunt, rarely obscurely tridentate leaves with conspicuously serrulate to spinose margins as shown in FIG. 39, nos. 2, 3, 4, 6.

STEPHANI included the species among the *Fissistipula* but for obvious reasons it does not belong in that Section.

B. pycnophylla is easily distinguished from *B. Schwaneckiana* because of its blunt, serrulate to spinose leaf apices.

DISTRIBUTION: J a m a i c a : without locality, Swartz, the type (H, NY). — P u e r t o R i c o : Maricao, Pagán no 247*; Mt. Torrecillas, Bro. Hioram, 12 (NY). — G u a d e l o u p e : without locality, l'Herminier (H).

REFERENCES: G. L. & N. (1847, 719); Lindenberg in Gottsche (1851, 73); Stephani (1908, 507, *Icones, Mastigobryum* no. 347).

*I determined this specimen as *B. Eggersiana* for Dr PAGÁN, Bryol 42· 39. 1939, but until more material is available for study, it seems advisable to transfer it to *B. pycnophylla* because of the very short teeth on the leaves and the strongly serrate leaf apices

29. **Bazzania Eggersiana** (Steph.) Pagán, Bryol. 42: 39. 1939.
Mastigobryum Eggersianum Stephani, Spec Hep 3· 468 1908.

Plants growing in depressed mats, medium size, light green to olive-green, a little pigmented with brown in the older portions: stems slender, to 5 cm. long, with leaves to 3 cm. broad, prostrate; in longitudinal section the medullary cells averaging 0.17 mm. in length, the cortical shorter, both averaging 20μ in diameter, the end walls thin, the vertical walls thickened and containing frequent pits· lateral branches mostly 5 mm. apart, diverging at a wide angle; flagelliform branches numerous, long: rhizoids not seen: the leaf-insertion curved in its upper half; the leaves imbricated, spreading, plane or nearly so, sometimes a little deflexed on drying, unsymmetrical, ovate, mostly 1.4 mm. long, 0.65 mm. wide at the base, narrowing somewhat to the transversely truncate, tridentate apex; the dorsal margin convex from a curved base, extending over nearly one-half the stem, the ventral margin straight to slightly concave from a more or less dilated base, the apex broad, three-toothed, occasionally nearly rounded, the teeth mostly one to three cells long and two to four cells broad, the sinuses lunulate, the margins entire to serrulate, the leaf cells quadrate to rectangular in outline, the cells of the apical region averaging $25\mu \times 25\mu$, those of the interior larger, those of the basal section $54\mu \times 30\mu$, not forming a vitta; cell walls thin, the trigones small but distinct, the cell lumina rounded, the cuticle verruculose: underleaves imbricated, a little squarrose in the upper part, attached in a straight line and connate by a few cells with one leaf, subquadrate, partly hyaline, as broad or broader than the stem, mostly 0.48 mm. - 0.56

FIG. 39. — *Bazzania pycnophylla* (Taylor) Trevis. — 1. Portion of a plant, dorsal view, $\times$ 30 2 Portion of a plant, ventral view, $\times$ 30 3 Leaf, $\times$ 30. 4 Apices of leaves, $\times$ 30. 5. A cell from the apical portion of a leaf, $\times$ 350. 6-6a Cells from the apical margin of a leaf, $\times$ 260. 7. Cells from the dorsal base of a leaf, $\times$ 260 8. Cells from the basal portion of a leaf, $\times$ 260 9. Underleaves, $\times$ 30 10 Cells from the apical portion of an underleaf showing the hyaline margin, $\times$ 260. Nos. 1-10 drawn from plants of the type material.

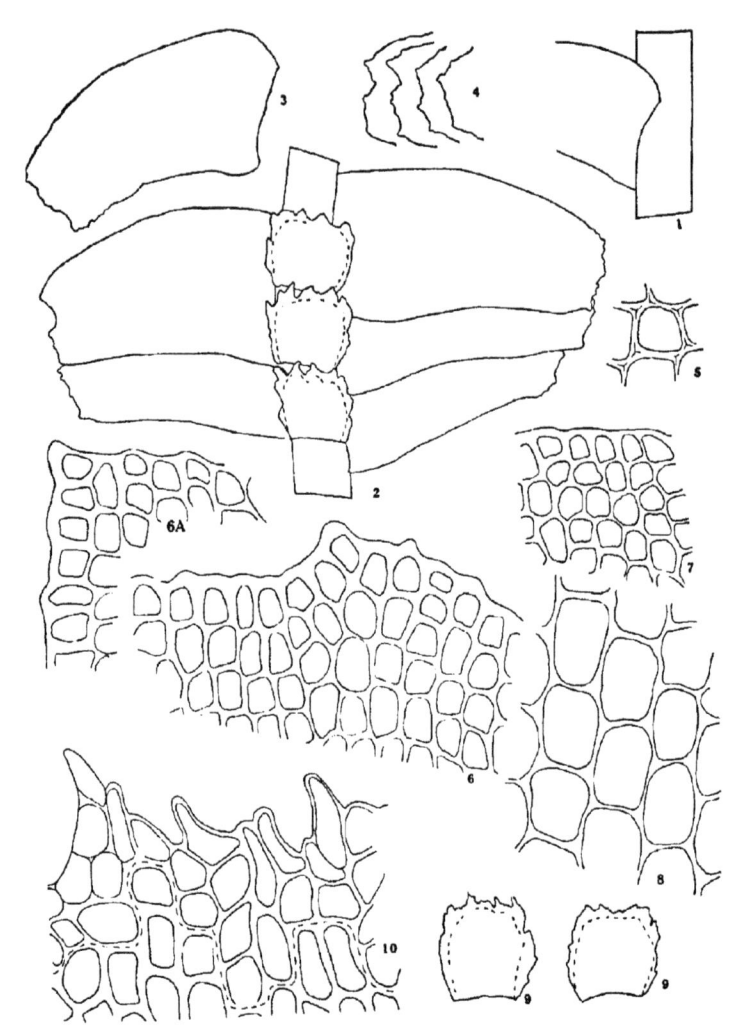

mm long × 0 56 mm. - 0.64 mm. broad, the apex with three to six, serrate to spinose-dentate teeth or lobes, the teeth to four cells broad, two to four cells high, the sinuses narrow, acute, the lateral margins serrate or with one to three teeth similar to those of the apex; the cells of two sorts, those of the marginal one to four rows (mostly of the teeth), hyaline, strongly verruculose, with uniformly thickened cell-walls and no trigones, those of the interior chlorophyllose, thin-walled, the trigones conspicuous, small· leaves of the flagelliform branches small, averaging 0.16 mm. long, the apex rounded, entire to crenulate: sexual branches not seen.

HABITAT: On logs and bases of trees, woods.

The species is best characterized by the dull green color; the transversely truncated leaf apices with mostly short, broad, entire to serrulate teeth; and the subquadrate underleaves with three to six, mostly hyaline, irregular, spinose-dentate teeth, three to six cells long, along the apical margins. (FIG. 40, nos. 1-10).

The leaves, while not caducous are often brittle when dry and are easily broken, so that stems without leaves are not uncommon. The teeth show a wide degree of variation. There are usually three distinct teeth two to four cells broad and two to four cells high, but broad undulations with one of the cells forming the apex are frequent. The sinuses are mostly shallow and rounded. The margins are entire to serrulate, straight or occasionally undulate.

The underleaves also, are variable. They are mostly subquadrate in outline and as broad or broader than the stem. They are attached in a straight line and are connate by several cells to one leaf. The hyaline border is conspicuous and varies from one to three cells along the upper lateral margins and three to five cells at the apex. The three to six irregular lobes or teeth are usually entirely hyaline (see FIG. 40, nos. 2, 8, 9). The border is more conspicuous in young underleaves, mostly because in the older plants the walls of the hyaline cells become somewhat pigmented, while the chlorophyll content of the green cells of the interior tends to disappear, so that the strong contrast is lost.

The color, size and habit of the plant, as well as its leaf apices and underleaves suggest a close relationship to B. Schwaneckiana. However, the teeth of the leaves are usually pronounced. The hyaline border of the underleaf of B Schwaneckiana is continuous, and the apical portion undulate or lobed, with the margin entire, while in B. Eggersiana the hyaline border is restricted to the apex, and is toothed, and has a spinose-dentate margin.

The species is distinguished from B. cubensis because of the hyaline margins of its underleaves, and from B. pycnophylla be-

FIG. 40 — Bazzania Eggersiana (Steph.) Pagán — 1. Portion of a plant, dorsal view, × 30. 2 Portion of a plant, ventral view, × 30 3. Leaf apices, × 30 4. Cells from an apical tooth of a leaf, × 260 5 A cell from the apical portion of a leaf, × 350. 6. Cells from the dorsal margin of a leaf, × 260. 7. Cells from the ventral margin, including some from the basal portion of a leaf, × 260 8. Underleaves, × 30. 9. Portion of the margin of an underleaf near the apex, × 260 10. Portion of a transverse section of a stem, × 260. Nos. 1-10 drawn from a part of the type material.

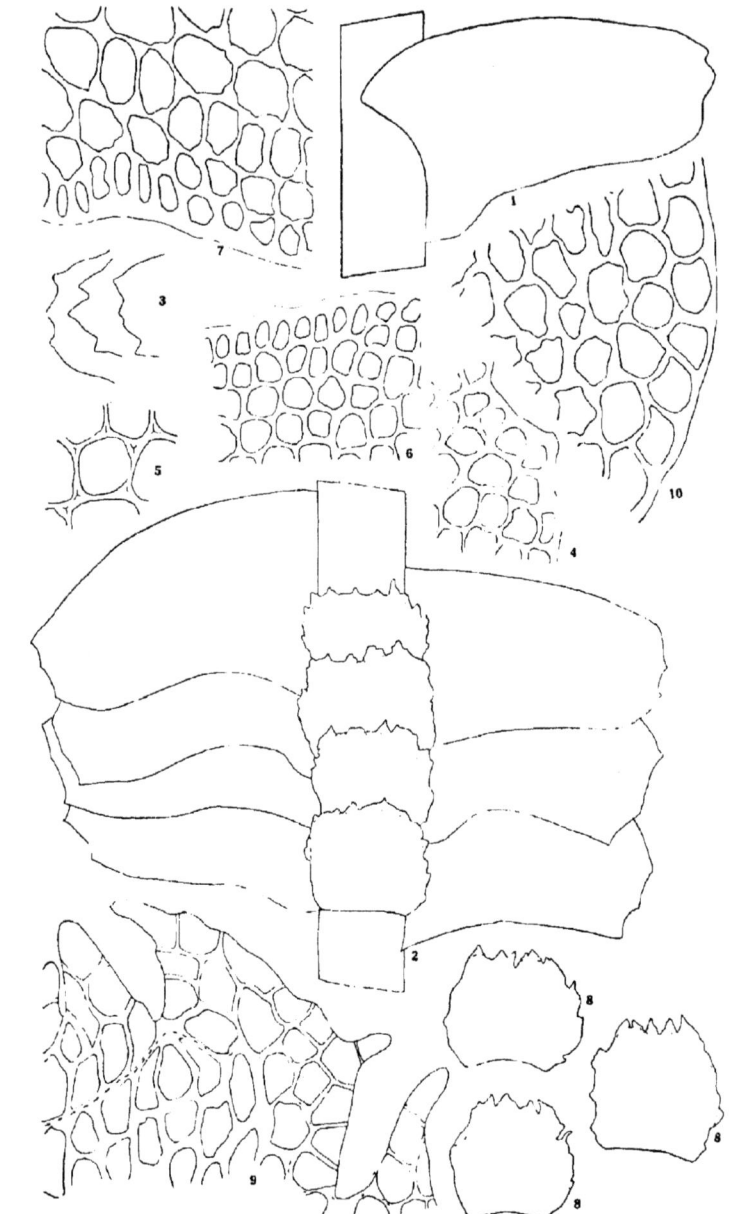

cause of the more pronounced teeth of its leaves, which have much less conspicuously serrulate or entire margins. STEPHANI included the species among the *Grandistipula*. This is the logical conclusion if one is not too careful in the examination of the margins of the leaf apices, for on some of the stems many of the leaves show so few serrations that these are apt to be overlooked. On careful examination the *connate* habit of the underleaves also becomes evident. This character, together with the cell pattern of the leaves, the general habit, and the leaf margins, especially those with many serrations, point to a closer relationship to *B. pycnophylla* and *B. armatastipula*, than to any member of the *Grandistipulae*.

DISTRIBUTION. C u b a : Pinal de Santa Anna, 2400', Eggers, the type (H); Monte de la Prenda, 2400', Eggers, 5191c (NY); Banao Mountain, Brother Léon & Per. Roca, 8340 (NY) The specimen collected by PAGÁN 247 at Maricao, Puerto Rico, should be referred to *B. pycnophylla*.

REFERENCES: Stephani (*Icones, Mastigobryum* no. 160).

30.   Bazzania armatistipula (Steph.) comb. nov.

Mastigobryum armatistipulum Stephani, Spec. Hep 3: 490. 1908

Plants growing in depressed mats, medium size, light green to olive-green, becoming pigmented with brown in the older portions: stems slender, to 5 cm. long, with leaves to 3 mm. broad, prostrate; in longitudinal section the cells elongate, the medullary cells averaging 0.17 mm. long, the cortical shorter, both averaging 20μ in diameter, the end walls thin, the vertical walls thickened and containing frequent pits; lateral branches 5 mm. or more apart, diverging at a wide angle; the flagelliform branches frequent, long; rhizoids not seen· the leaf insertion curved in its upper part; the leaves approximate to imbricated, spreading, plane or nearly so, unsymmetrical, ovate, mostly 1 4 mm. long, 0.65 mm. wide at the base, narrowing somewhat to the transversely truncate, tridentate apex; the dorsal margin convex from a curved base, extending over nearly one-half the stem, the ventral margin straight to slightly concave from a more or less dilated base; the apex broad, the teeth acute, one to five cells broad at the base, two to five cells long, the sinuses lunulate, the margins serrate; the leaf cells quadrate to rectangular in outline, the cells of the apical region averaging $25\mu \times 25\mu$, those of the interior larger, those of the basal portion $54\mu \times 36\mu$, not forming a vitta, the walls of the marginal rows more or less uniformly thickened, those of the interior cells thin with small but distinct trigones, the cell lumina rounded, the cuticle verruculose: underleaves approximate to imbricated, attached in a straight line, connate by a few cells with one leaf, subquadrate, mostly 0.56 mm. $\times$ 0.56 mm. - 0.64 mm. broad, with a hyaline border, the lateral margins bulging, dentate to serrate, the apex of three to six spinose-dentate teeth or lobes, the teeth to four cells broad, two to four cells high; the hyaline border one to five cells broad, the cells averaging $18\mu \times 12\mu$; the chlorophyllose cells averaging 20μ, the trigones conspicuous, the cuticle verruculose: leaves of the flagelliform branches scale-like, ovate, the apex mostly rounded: sexual branches not seen.

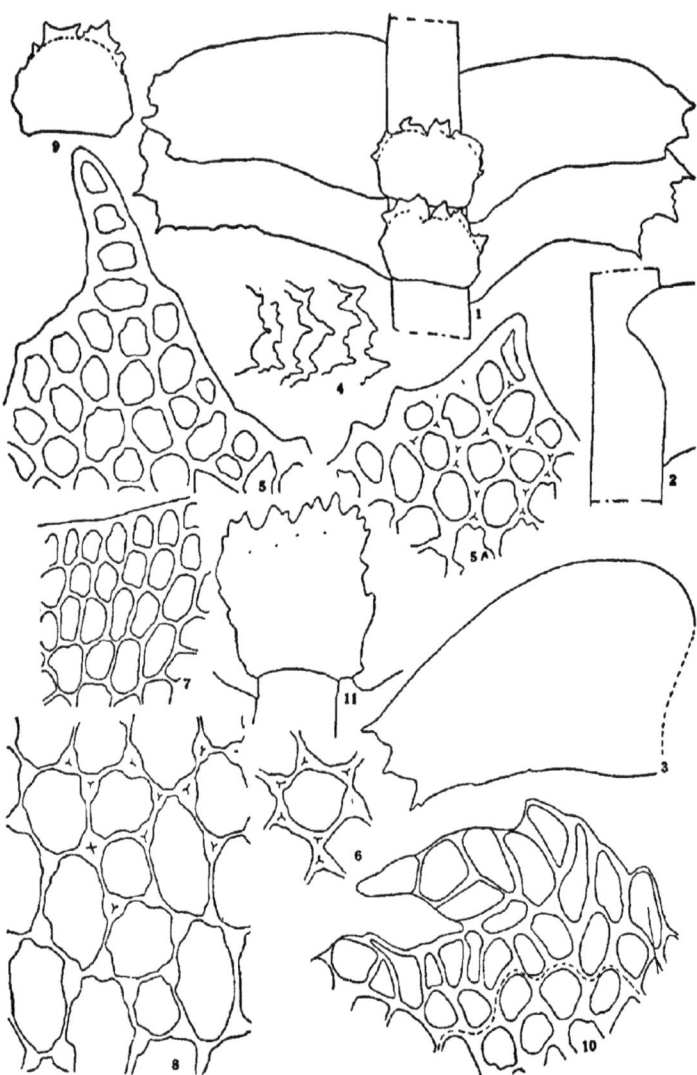

FIG. 41 — *Bazzania armatistipula* (Steph) Fulford. — 1. Portion of a stem, ventral view, × 30. 2. Portion of a stem, dorsal view, × 30. 3. Leaf, × 30. 4. Leaf apices, × 30. 5-5a. Apical teeth, × 260. 6. A cell from the apical portion of a leaf, × 350. 7. Cells from the dorsal margin of a leaf, × 260 8. Cells from the basal portion of a leaf, × 260. 9. Underleaf, × 30. 10. Portion of the apical region of an underleaf showing the hyaline border, × 260. 11. Underleaf and portion of stem and a leaf to show line of attachment, × 30. Nos. 1-11 drawn from a portion of the type material.

HABITAT: In depressed mats over logs and tree bases in woods. The distinguishing characteristics of the species are its light to olive-green color; the spreading, tridentate leaves with conspicuously serrulate to dentate apical margins; and the variously spinose-serrate, toothed underleaves which are bordered by several rows of hyaline cells in the apical regions. (FIG. 41, nos. 1-11).

The species has much the same habit as the other members of the *Connatae* just described. It can, nevertheless, readily be distinguished from them because of its strongly three-toothed leaf apices which have conspicuously serrulate to spinose margins as is shown in FIG. 41, nos. 1, 4, 5. The leaf apices of *B. cubensis* sometimes are very similar but the underleaves are always chlorophyllose throughout so that the two need never be confused.

The underleaves are similar to those of *B. pycnophylla* and *B Eggersiana*, and cannot be used as a diagnostic characteristic distinguishing these species from one another. They are always connate by a few cells with the ventral base of one leaf as is shown in FIG. 41, no. 11.

STEPHANI included *M. armatastipulum* as the only American species of the *Serrulata* but did not consider it among the connate group.

DISTRIBUTION C u b a Sierra Maestro, Bro León, Clément, and M Roca, 10471 (NY), Banao Mountains, Bro León and M Roca, 8075 (Y, NY). (?). — J a m a i c a · without locality, Burgensen, the type (H), near Hardware Gap, 4000 ft., Underwood 2242 (Y, NY), John Crow Peak, 5500-5800 ft, Underwood 855 (NY), Blue Mountains, Elizabeth Britton 1193 (NY); Chapelton to Bull Head, Underwood 3400 (NY); without locality, Wilson 186 (NY). — P u e r t o R i c o Monte Alegrillo, 500-900 m, Elizabeth Britton, 2650 (Y, NY); Maricao, Britton and Cowell 4251 (NY)

REFERENCES: Stephani (*Icones, Mastigobryum* no. 262).

31. Bazzania cubensis (Gottsche) Pagán, Bryologist 42: 38. 1939.

Mastigobryum cubense Gottsche, in Stephani, Hedwigia 24: 248 pl 3, fig. 1. 1885.

Plants in depressed mats, medium size, olive-green tinged with brown: stems slender, to 6 cm. long, with leaves to 3.5 mm. broad, prostrate; in longitudinal section the cells elongate, the medullary cells averaging 0.17 mm. long, the cortical cells shorter, both averaging 20μ in diameter, the vertical walls uniformly thickened and containing frequent pits, the end walls thin; lateral branches mostly 1 cm or more apart, diverging at a wide angle; flagelliform branches frequent, long; rhizoids colorless, present on the leaves

FIG. 42. — *Bazzania cubensis* (Gottsche) Pagán. — 1. Portion of a stem, dorsal view, × 30. 2 Portion of a stem, ventral view, × 30. 3. A leaf, × 30. 4. Leaf apices, × 30 5 A cell from the apical portion of a leaf, × 350. 6. Cells from an apical tooth of a leaf, × 260. 7. Cells from the dorsal margin of a leaf, × 260 8 Cells from the basal portion of a leaf, × 260. 9 Underleaves, × 30 10 Cells from the apical portions of two underleaves, × 260 11. Underleaf and portion of a stem and leaf to show attachment, × 30 Nos 1-11 drawn from a portion of the type material.

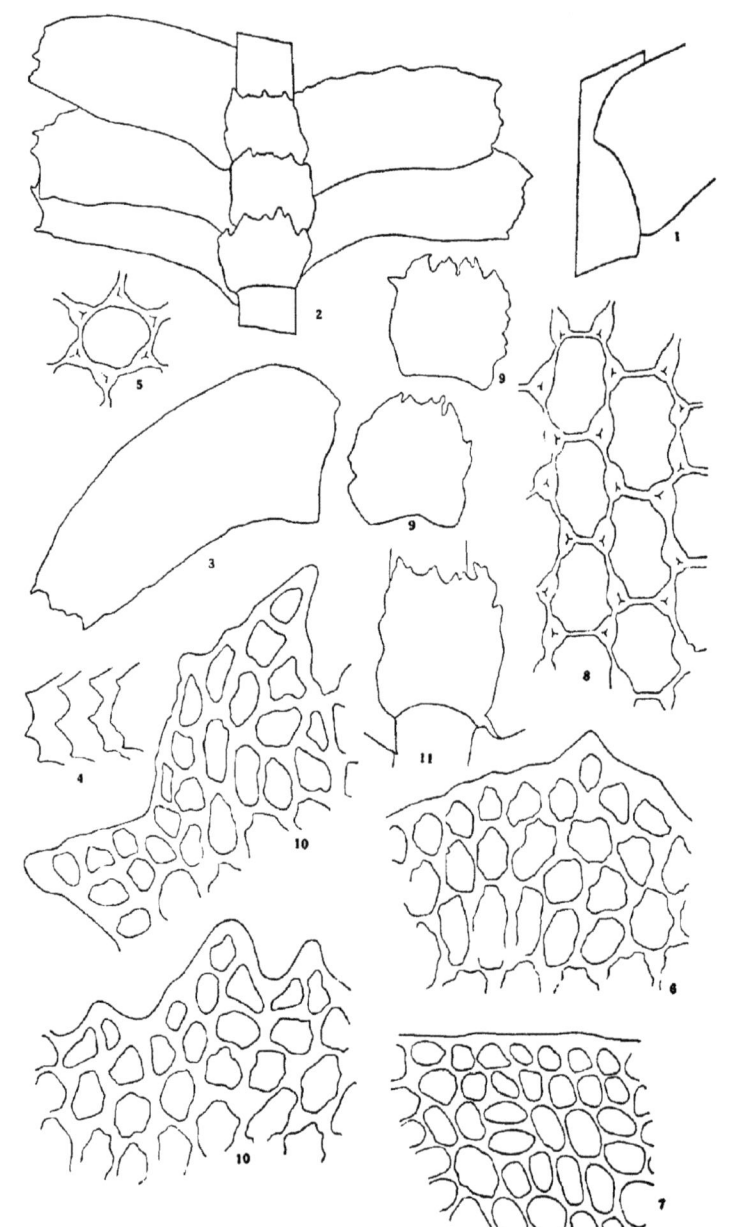

of flagelliform branches; leaf insertion little curved in the upper part; leaves imbricated, spreading, a little convex, deflexed when dry, unsymmetrically ovate, 0.9 mm. - 1.6 mm. long, 0.6 mm. - 0.7 mm. broad at the base, narrowed a little to the mostly transversely truncate, tridentate apex; the dorsal margin convex from a curved base which covers one-half the stem, the ventral margin straight or slightly concave, the base scarcely dilated; the apex broad, the teeth acute, large to obscure, two to eight cells long and three to six cells broad at the base, the sinuses lunulate, the margins mostly slightly serrulate; the leaf cells thin-walled, the cell lumina angular-rounded, the trigones conspicuous, small, rarely coalesced, the cells of the apical portion 22μ - 25μ $\times$ 25μ - 30μ, the marginal row smaller and with thicker walls, the cells of the median portion larger, those of the basal area 36μ - 54μ $\times$ 27μ; a vitta not differentiated; the cuticle very strongly verruculose; underleaves quadrate, little broader than the stem, imbricated, attached in a straight line, narrowly connate with one leaf, squarrose in the upper part, the lateral margins straight or slightly convex, serrate and lobed, the apex toothed, the teeth irregular, two to five cells broad at the base, two to four cells high, the margins entire to serrate; the cells 25μ $\times$ 25μ, becoming longer in the central portion, the cell walls thin, the trigones conspicuous, often becoming coalesced, the cell lumina angular-rounded, the cuticle strongly verruculose · male and female branches and sporophytes not seen.

HABITAT: On logs and bases of trees, woods.

The distinguishing characteristics of the species are its olive-green to brown color; the deflexed leaves, with irregularly tridentate, mostly serrate apices, and large thin-walled cells with conspicuous trigones; and the quadrate underleaves, connate by a few cells with one leaf, coarsely toothed and incised at the apex and often along the margins. There are no hyaline cells in the underleaf. (FIG. 42, nos. 1-11).

The plants are approximately the same size as the other tropical American members of this Section, but they differ in appearance, in that the leaves are always strongly deflexed when dry, and the green color is always tinged with brown, even at the growing tip, so that the plants are olive-green or darker brown.

The leaves are usually tridentate, with the teeth large, usually broadly triangular. However, on a single stem it is not unusual to find all sorts of variations in the size and shape of the teeth, from the large sort mentioned above, to small ones of one or two cells (see FIG. 42, nos. 2, 3, 4). The margins are serrate to a greater or lesser degree. The marginal cells have thick walls (see FIG. 42, no. 6), and the cuticle is conspicuously verruculose to rough papillose.

The underleaves are very similar to those of the other American species of the *Connatae* except that all of the cells are chlorophyllose. They are attached in a straight line to the stem and to several cells of the ventral base of one leaf (see FIG. 42, no. 11). As in the case of *B. Schwaneckiana* this attachment to the leaves is not noticeable except under high magnification.

STEPHANI considered *M. cubense* to be a member of the *Fissistipula* Section. The species certainly does not belong to that group since the underleaves are not deeply incised (see FIG. 42, no. 9). He likewise did not recognize the fact that the leaves are serrate, some of them strongly so, and that an underleaf is connate with one leaf for a short distance (see FIG. 42, nos. 2, 4, 11).

DISTRIBUTION C u b a · Mt Verde, Wright, Hep Cub Wrightianae, the type (Y, NY); Sierra Nipe, near Woodfred, Oriente, 450-550 m., Shafer 8344, 3434 (NY), Sierra Maestra, Bro Clément 343 (NY). — J a m a i c a summit Bull Head, Underwood 3390 (NY). — P u e r t o R i c o : Maricao, Pagán 216a, 237, 251 (F).

REFERENCES Stephani (1908, 507; *Icones, Mastigobryum* no 344).

32. **Bazzania peruviana** (Lehm. & Lindenb) Trevis. Mem. Ist. Lomb. 13: 414. 1877.

Jungermannia peruviana Lehman & Lindenberg, in Lehman, Pug Pl. 5: 18. 1833
Mastigobryum peruvianum Nees in G L. & N , Syn. Hep. 220 1845
Mastigobryum peruvianum var. *β minimum* Gottsche & Schiffner, in Schiffner, Lebermoose. Forschungsreise S.M.S. "Gazelle" IV, 17. pl. 4, fig. 17-18. 1888
Mastigobryum Lechleri Stephani, Hedwigia 25: 134. pl. 6, fig 10-14. 1886

Plants medium size, in deep tufts or mats, dark green, becoming pigmented with brown in the older portions: stems 5 cm or more in length, with leaves to 3 5 mm. broad, prostrate; stem cells in longitudinal section to 0.17 mm. long, the cortical shorter, averaging 20μ in diameter, the vertical walls uniformly thickened and containing frequent pits, the end walls thin; lateral branches frequent, mostly 5 mm. apart, diverging at an acute angle · flagelliform branches frequent; rhizoids rare, colorless, on the bases of the leaves of the flagelliform branches; the line of leaf insertion little curved in the upper part, the leaves imbricated, plane, becoming a little deflexed on drying, unsymmetrically ovate, straight, 1.5 mm. - 2 mm. long, 1 mm. broad at the base, narrowed a little to the transversely truncate, sharply tridentate apex; the dorsal margin arched from a curved base, covering up to one-half the stem, the ventral margin somewhat concave, often conspicuously dilated, entire, the apex three-toothed, the teeth variable, mostly sharply acute, three to eight cells long, two to four cells broad, the sinuses mostly deeply lunulate, the margins serrulate to dentate; leaf cells thin-walled, the cell lumina rounded, trigones small, the cuticle verruculose; cells of the apical region averaging 20μ - 24μ, of the median portion larger, and of the base to $56\mu \times 24\mu$, a vitta not differentiated: underleaves imbricated, subquadrate in outline, 6 mm. - 8 mm. long and broad, broader than the stem, attached in a straight line, conspicuously connate with a pair of leaves, becoming squarrose and strongly recurved in the upper half, the apex more or less lobed, the lobes serrulate to spinose-dentate, the lateral margins convex, entire; the hyaline border four to eight cells broad, thin-walled, the chlorophyllose cells with thicker walls

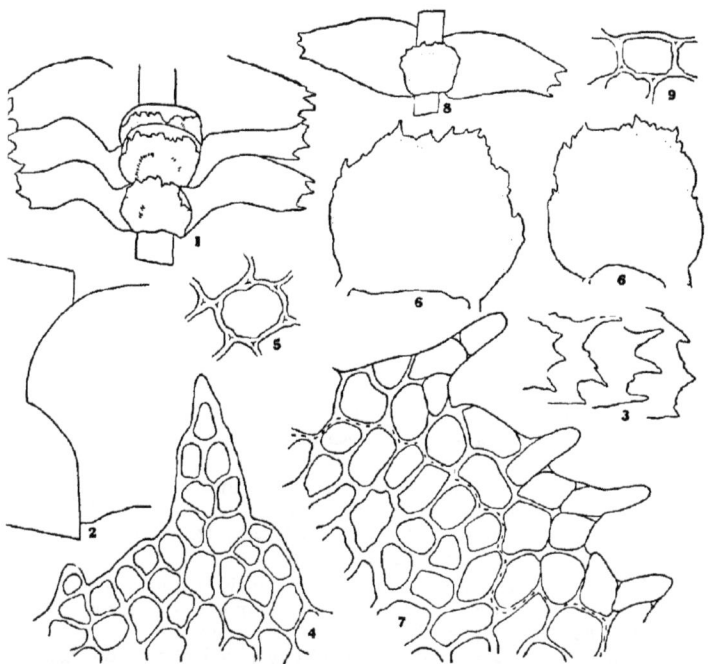

FIG 43 — *Bazzania peruviana* (Lehm & Lindenb) Trevis — 1 Portion
of a plant, ventral view, × 15. 2. Portion of a stem and leaf, dorsal view,
× 30 3. Apices of leaves, × 30. 4. Apical tooth of a leaf, × 310 5. A cell
from the apical portion of a leaf, × 400. 6. Underleaves, × 30. 7. A portion
of an underleaf to show hyaline border, × 310 8. Portion of a stem, ventral
view, × 15. 9. A cell from the apical portion of a leaf, × 400. Nos 1-7
drawn from the type of *J. peruviana;* 8-9 from the type of *M. Lechleri* from
Chile.

and small trigones: leaves of the flagelliform branches scale-like, ovate, the margins serrulate to dentate: sexual branches and perianths not seen.

HABITAT: In depressed mats or ascending tufts on soil, rocks, and tree bases.

The distinguishing characteristics of the species are its medium size, the dark green or yellowish color; the sharply three-toothed leaves which are entire or serrate along the apical margin; and the connate (with a pair of leaves) underleaves which are squarrose-recurved in the upper half, and have hyaline borders two to eight cells broad, with serrate to spinose-dentate apical margins. (FIG. 43, nos. 1-9).

The species exhibits much variation in its leaves and underleaves. On most well developed plants the teeth are long, narrowly acute to acuminate, and usually end in a point of several cells. On less well developed plants this characteristic is less often observed, for most of the teeth are short, acute, with only an occasional tooth long-pointed. The margins of the teeth also vary considerably. In the well developed plants with long teeth the margins are crenulate to serrate, often strongly so. However, the amount and degree of serration is not constant on all the leaves of a single plant, nor on the leaves of the various plants of a mat (see FIG. 43, nos. 1, 3 and 4). The serrations tend to become fewer and smaller on the less well developed plants and are often entirely absent on many of the leaves (see FIG. 43, no. 8). The thickness of the cell walls, the size of the trigones, and the roughness of the cuticle show the usual range of variation.

The underleaves are always conspicuously connate with a pair of leaves as seen in FIG. 43, no. 1. The connecting bands are broad and can easily be determined. The upper portions of the underleaves are strongly recurved on well developed plants, but tend to become less so in the poorer forms as is seen when comparing FIG. 43, nos. 1 and 8. The hyaline margin is usually very conspicuous and may be as much as ten cells broad in the apical part, but here again one finds much variation, for on some plants only two or three rows of cells are hyaline (see FIG. 43, nos. 1, 6, 7 and 8). On plants with underleaves having this narrow border the underleaf just below a flagelliform branch usually is more typical, i.e. the hyaline border is very wide. The apical portion is more or less four-lobed and the margin is serrate and dentate.

Plants having leaves with very rough cuticle, short teeth with distantly serrate margins, and underleaves with narrow hyaline borders, occur more frequently in the southern part of Chile than does the form described above, although there is no complete geographical segregation of the forms. The plants collected by SKOTTSBERG on the Swedish Pacific Expedition, 1916-1917, were for the most part robust, the teeth of the leaves were long on some plants, short on others, the hyaline border of the underleaves varied in width as described above, and the cuticle was always more verruculose than that of the type specimen, often becoming very roughly warty.

The var. *minimum* of GOTTSCHE and SCHIFFNER has the characteristics of the species except for its smaller size and much smaller underleaves. I believe that it should be considered as a habitat variation rather than a variety. It appears to be a plant which grew in a very moist, perhaps densely shaded habitat.

STEPHANI originally described the underleaves of his *M. Lechleri* as being free, but in the *Icones, Mastigobryum* no. 167, has shown several of the underleaves as connate with single leaves — some on the left and some on the right side of the stem. Since plants with underleaves connate with one leaf always show this characteristic restricted to the same side of the stem for all of the leaves on a branch, it is obvious that the underleaves of STEPHANI's plant were connate with pairs of leaves. *M. Lechleri* is a rather small form of *B. peruviana*. The portion of the type studied had the underleaves connate with pairs of leaves but the line of attachment was broader for one leaf than for the other of a pair as indicated in FIG. 43, no. 8.

The species is closely related to *B. Skottsbergii* which follows.

DISTRIBUTION. P e r u : without locality or collector's name, Hb. Gottsche, the type (H), without locality, Jameson (NY). — C h i l e : Valdivia, Hahn (H), Valdivia, Lechler, the type of *M. Lechleri* (H); Corral, Thaxter 142, 149 (Y, H); Curico, Wollemeyer 279a (H); without locality, H C Lorenz (NY); Port Montt, Bro Claude-Joseph 3216 (Y); Chiloé Island, Anderson (NY), also Cunningham 1445 (NY), Chonos Archipellago, Darwin Bay, without collector's name 442 (NY); Panguipulli, Padre Hollermeyer 279 (Y); also Bro. Claude-Joseph 2322, 2322a (Y); *Str. Magellan*, Port Otway, Cunningham 235 (NY); Gray Harbor, Cunningham 147 (NY), Hall Bay, Cunningham 212 (NY); South Channel, without collector's name (as *M. cernum*) (H), Tuesday Bay, Naumaun, the type of the var. *β minimum* (H), also nos 68, 133 p.p. (H); Desolation Island, Dusén cited by Stephani (1901, 22). — P a t a g o n i a : "occidentalis in insula Newton in Terra", cited by Stephani (1900, 51); without locality, Hatcher, cited by Evans (1903, 42). — J u a n F e r n á n d e z I s l a n d s . Skottsberg (Swedish Pac. Exp. 1916-1917), *Bazzania* nos. 1, 2, 7, 10, 14 (S).

REFERENCES· Evans (1903, 42); G L. & N. (1844-1847, 215); Lindenberg & Gottsche (1851, 25 pl 6 fig. 1-6); Stephani (1900, 51; 1901, 22; 1908, 457, 469, 1911, *Icones, Mastigobryum* nos. 114, 167)

33. Bazzania Skottsbergii (Steph.) comb. nov.

Mastigobryum Skottsbergii Stephani, in Skottsberg, K. Svensk. Handl. 46: no. 9. 60. fig. 22, i, k. 1911.

This species is very similar to *B. peruviana* in color, size, growth habit, etc. It is distinct, however, in that the underleaves are chlorophyllose throughout or have only a single row or only scattered hyaline cells along the margins. The margin is usually distantly or obscurely serrate or may even be entire. The underleaves of *B. peruviana* are bordered by three to six rows of hyaline cells and the margin is conspicuously serrate and may be dentate.

The apices of the leaves are usually less serrate than those of *B. peruviana.* The cells are slightly larger and the trigones more pronounced. The cuticle is faintly to strongly verruculose.

HABITAT: Over rocks and on bases of trees.

DISTRIBUTION: J u a n F e r n á n d e z : Masatierra, Skottsberg (Exp. Suec. 1907-09), the type (L); various localities (Exp. Suec. Pac. 1916-17), Skottsberg 3, 5, 6, 8, 9, 12, 13 (S).

Chiloé, western Patagonia, southern Patagonia and the Falkland Islands are also cited by Stephani

REFERENCE. Stephani (1924, 480, *Icones, Mastigobryum* no. 445).

The species seems to be very close to or identical with *M. cernuum* St. collected by DUSÉN in western Patagonia. The type material of this latter species has not been available for study so that detailed statements concerning the species cannot be made at this time. However, there are plants in the herbaria of the New York Botanical Garden and Yale and Harvard Universities which were collected in Patagonia by DUSÉN and determined by STEPHANI as *M. cernuum.*

These plants also are similar to *B. peruviana* except for several details. The leaf cells are slightly larger, the walls thicker, the trigones more pronounced and the cuticle more often is conspicuously warty. The principle distinction is in the underleaves   They are as large as the underleaves of *B. peruviana* but the number of hyaline cells is limited to a marginal row, or scattered individuals across the top of the underleaf. The cell walls are similar to those of the leaf, the trigones are conspicuous, and the cuticle is strongly verruculose. The apical portion is more or less four-lobed and the margins are serrate to dentate, but a little less so than in *B. peruviana.* These plants are very similar to (if not identical with) the type material of *B. Skottsbergii.*

The following specimens have been examined. Patagonia, San Pedro Island, Dusén (H); Desolation Island, Tierra del Fuego, Dusén 143 (Y, NY).

34. **Bazzania novae-zelandiae** (Mitten) Bescherelle & Massalonga, in Mission Sci. du Cap Horn 1882-1883. V. Bot. 233. 1889, by P. HARIOT and others.

Mastigobryum novae-zelandiae Mitten, in Hooker, Bot Ant Voy. 2¹: Fl N. Zel 148. pl. C, fig. 6 1854.

The plants of the type material collected on North Island, New Zealand, are robust, to 8 cm. long and with leaves to 5 cm. broad. The teeth are long, acute, and sometimes acuminate but the margins are only rarely faintly serrulate. The underleaves are very large, with broad hyaline borders. The margins are undulate and entire or nearly so. They differ from *B. peruviana* in that in the latter the underleaves are serrulate-dentate, particularly along the more or less four-lobed apices.

B. novae-zelandiae has been recorded from Patagonia and the Straits of Magellan by BESCHERELLE and MASSALONGA, and from western Patagonia, (collected by DUSÉN) by Stephani. None of these specimens has been examined.

Section 3. Fissistipulae

The Section is characterized by having the three-toothed leaves not serrate along the margins, and without appendages or conspicuous auricles at the ventral bases; the underleaves are deeply incised (approximately one-half or more) or long-toothed.

Unfortunately none of the American species which STEPHANI included in this Section actually possess a combination of characters which would include them in this subdivision. None of the species have deeply incised or long-toothed underleaves.

With the exception of *M. heterophyllum* and *M. Burchellii* the species have been transferred to sections with which they are more closely related and are discussed under those sections.

It has not been possible to examine authentic material of either *M. Burchellii* or *M. heterophyllum*. The figures in the *Icones, Mastigobryum* nos. 340, 346 and 442 indicate that these species also should be transferred, possibly to the *Grandistipulae* Section.

Section 4. Appendiculatae

Plants with leaves subentire to sharply three-toothed; attached in a hook-formed line; the ventral bases dilated to a greater or lesser degree to form entire, serrulate, or appendiculate auricles; leaf cells thin-walled, the trigones large; the underleaves large, cordate, attached in a recurved line.

Key to the Species

1. Plants very large, the leaves subentire . . .   42. B. canelensis (p 152)
1. Plants medium to large, the leaves three-toothed.
   2   Ventral auricles large, undulate, the margins serrate to dentate, the margins of the underleaves similar; cuticle very rough,
          35 B. asperistipula (p. 125)
   2. Ventral auricles and margins of the underleaves not as above.
      3. Plants very large; underleaves with one or more very long, sharp teeth at right angles to the lateral margins,
          41. B. acanthostipa (p. 151)
      3. Plants medium size to large, underleaves with shorter teeth, lobed or with entire margins.
         4. Underleaves deeply four-toothed or -lobed, often with teeth several cells long on the margins; ventral auricles of the leaves well developed . . . . . 40. B. teretiuscula (p. 144)
        4   Underleaves never *deeply* four-lobed, the ventral auricles of the leaves large or small
           5. Margins of the underleaves often angular and incised; cell cavities stellate, trigones very large, rounded; leaflets of the flagelliform branches large,
              36 B. falcata (p. 129)
           5   Margins of the underleaves usually entire, undulate; cell cavities angular-rounded to stellate, trigones large to medium size, often rounded.
              6. Leaves not conspicuously narrowed at the apex; ventral appendages absent or poorly developed; the teeth broad, equilateral, the cells averaging 16μ - 20μ, thin-walled, the cuticle verruculose; leaflets of the flagelliform branches large,
                 37 B. Hookeri (p 135)
              6   Leaves narrowed at the apex, the teeth narrow, sharply pointed, the ventral auricles conspicuous, undulate, entire or with appendages.
                7. Leaves spreading, the cells averaging 18μ - 20μ in diameter; leaflets of the flagelliform branches scale-like . . . 39 B. Liebmanniana (p. 142)
                7   Leaves falcate, the cells averaging 24μ in diameter; leaflets of the flagelliform branches large . . . . . . 38. B. robusta (p 140)

35. Bazzania asperistipula (Steph.) comb. nov.

Mastigobryum asperistipulum Stephani, Spec. Hep. 6. 453. 1924.

Plants in deep erect tufts, very large, light yellow-green, becoming light brown in the older portions: stems stout, 10 cm. or

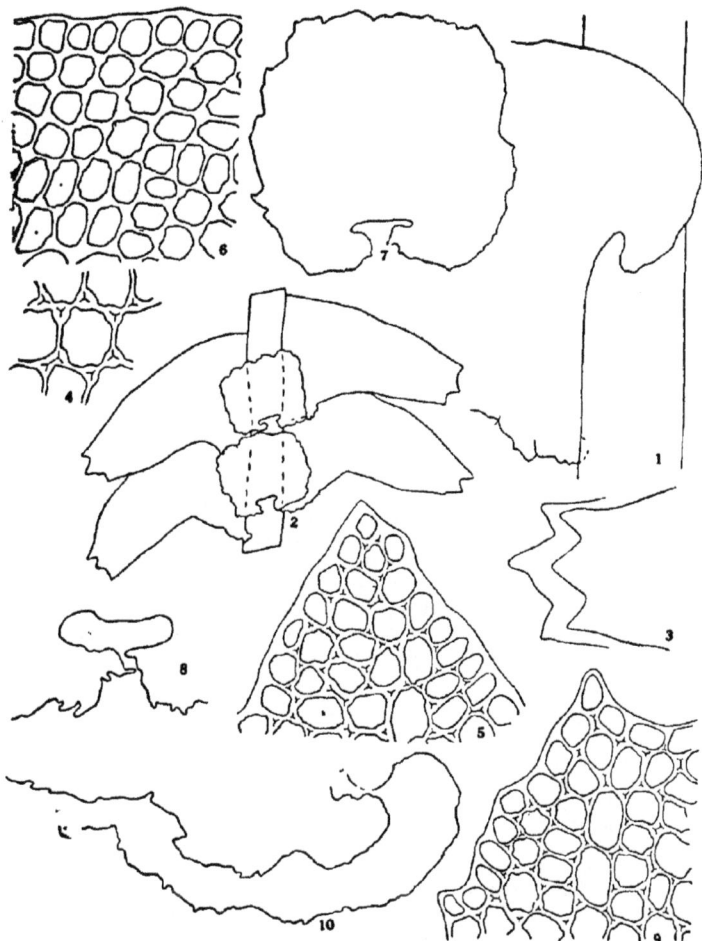

Fig. 44. — *Bazzania asperistipula* (Steph.) Fulford. — 1. Portion of a plant, dorsal view, × 30. 2. Portion of a plant, ventral view, × 10. 3. Leaf apices, × 30. 4. A cell from the apical portion of a leaf, × 350. 5. Cells of an apical tooth, × 260. 6. Cells from the dorsal base of a leaf, × 260. 7. Underleaf, × 30 8. Basal portion of an underleaf, × 30. 9 Cells from the apical portion of an underleaf, × 260. 10. Ventral appendages of two leaves, × 60. Nos. 1-10 drawn from a portion of the type material.

more long, with leaves to 6 mm. broad, erect; stem cells in longitudinal section elongate, averaging 0.18 mm. long, the cortical shorter, both averaging 18μ in diameter, the vertical walls strongly thickened and containing frequent pits, the end walls thin, the walls of the cortical and subcortical layers strongly pigmented with brown, the medulla hyaline: lateral branches infrequent, 1 cm. or more apart, diverging at a wide angle; flagelliform branches frequent, long; rhizoids colorless present on some of the leaves of the flagelliform branches: the leaf insertion curved in its upper part, the dorsal end turned downward forming a hook; leaves always spreading, subimbricated to imbricated, unsymmetrically long-ovate, a little falcate, to 4 mm. long, 2 mm. broad at the base, narrowing to the rather broad, transversely truncate, tridentate apex; the dorsal margin strongly curved from a deeply cordate base, extending across the stem and somewhat beyond, the ventral margin concave, the base conspicuously auricled, the dilation oblong, undulate and lobed, crenulate and serrate; the apex strongly three-toothed, the teeth broadly triangular, acute, five to ten cells long and five to ten cells broad at the base, the sinuses deep, broadly acute, the margins straight to repand; the leaf cells thin-walled, the cell lumina angular-rounded, the trigones small, conspicuous, often becoming confluent, the cuticle strongly verruculose; cells of the apical region and dorsal lobe quadrate in outline, averaging $22\mu \times 22\mu$, those of the marginal row and ventral auricle somewhat smaller, cells of the median portion longer, $36\mu \times 22\mu$, and those of the basal portion $45\mu \times 27\mu$, a vitta not differentiated: underleaves imbricated, twice as broad as the stem, subquadrate in outline, attached in a recurved line, somewhat squarrose, the margin repand, 0 8 mm. - 1.4 mm. long and wide, the base strongly cordate, the auricles large, undulate, the margins lobed, serrate and often short ciliate, the apex and lateral margins lobed and toothed, the lobes broad and shallow, the sinuses lunulate, shallow, the margin crenulate to serrate, often dentate or short ciliate, the cells similar to those of the leaf, those of the marginal row averaging $22\mu \times 22\mu$, those of the basal portion larger, the trigones as in the leaf; leaves of the flagelliform branches to 0.35 mm. long, ovate, the apex acute or bifid with long, one-celled teeth: female branches occasional, solitary, one to several on a stem, the bracts and bracteoles similar, little pigmented with brown; the outermost series ovate, bifid to trifid; the intermediate series long, broadly ovate, the margins entire to crenulate or dentate, one-third to one-fourth divided into two to four crenulate laciniae, the cells uniform throughout, $90\mu \times 20\mu$, thin-walled; the innermost series broadly ovate (immature), one-third to one-fourth divided into usually three, long, dentate to ciliate laciniae, the cells uniform, elongate, 72μ - $90\mu \times 20\mu$, the cell wall thin· perianth (immature) mouth long laciniate, the laciniae crenulate to ciliate, mostly twelve or more cells long: male branches and sporophytes not seen.

HABITAT: In deep tufts on stumps and logs.

The species is best characterized by its very large size, the long, seldom branched stems, the light yellow-green color; the subimbricated, elongate, tridentate leaves with large, serrate to dentate, lobed auricles, and thin-walled leaf cells with conspicuous trigones

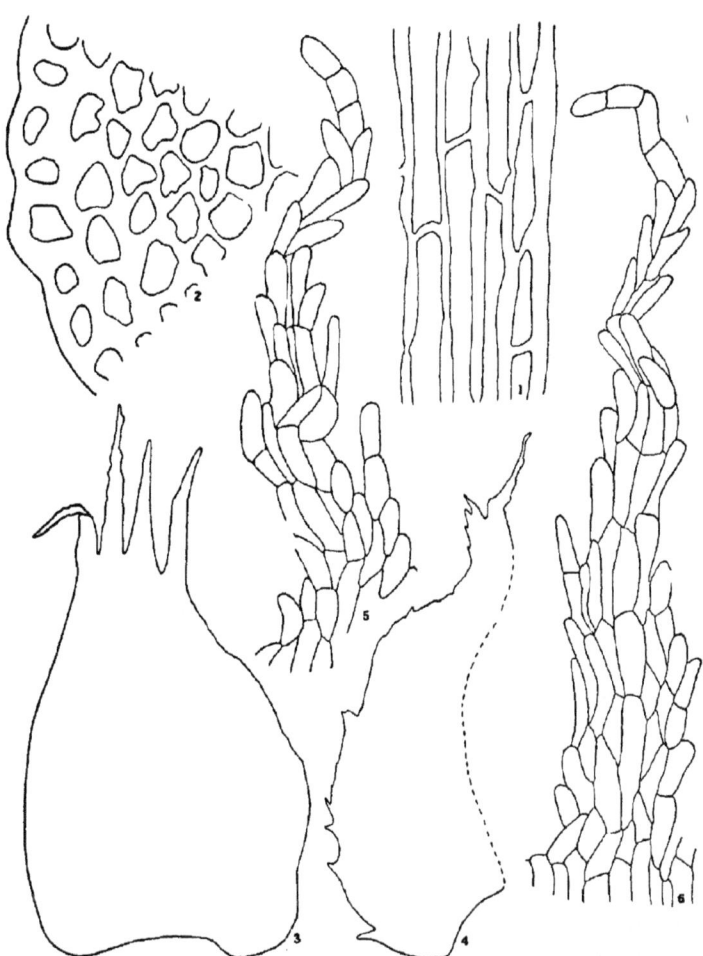

FIG. 45 — *Bazzania asperistipula* (Steph) Fulford. — 1. Portion of the
stem, longitudinal section, × 260. 2. Portion of stem, transverse section,
× 260   3 Female bract of intermediate series, × 30   4 Female bract of
innermost series (immature), × 30. 5. Portion of one of the laciniae of a
bract of this series, × 100. 6. One of the laciniae of the mouth of the perianth,
× 100   Drawn from the type material

and verruculose cuticle; and the subquadrate underleaves with strongly cordate bases, and undulate, lobed, crenulate to dentate, short ciliate margins. (FIGURES 44, nos. 1-10; 45, nos. 1-6).

The material available for study did not show much variation in the plants. The leaves are always light green in color, strongly three-toothed, and have the ventral appendages well developed. The appendage is fairly large, oblong, and is not sharply delimited from the rest of the leaf. The margin is lobed, crenulate and distantly serrate to dentate as shown in FIG. 44, no. 10. The underleaves also show little variation They are all strongly cordate and have a variously lobed or sometimes toothed margin. These lobes and teeth are usually crenulate to serrate or occasionally short ciliate. The cilia are usually found on the basal portion. The basal auricles are large and may overlap (see FIG. 44, nos. 2, 7 and 8).

STEPHANI's unpublished drawings (*Icones, Mastigobryum* nos. 307 and 373), made from plants of the type material collected by TURCKHEIM in Guatemala show two sorts of underleaves. The one has a uniformly serrate margin, while the other is broadly lobed or has broad, shallow teeth.

DISTRIBUTION: G u a t e m a l a · Alta Verapaz, Cobán, 1600 m., Turckheim 5817, the type (NY); the same, 5503 as *M. teretiusculum* (NY); the same, 5582 (H) — C o s t a R i c a: Coliblanco, 1950 m., Maxon 237 (NY); Cerro de La Carpintera, Standley 35632 (W), Orosi, Standley 39650 (W), Alto de La Estrella, Standley 39106, 39403 (W); El Muñeco, Standley 51338 (W). — C o l o m b i a : without locality, Wallace (NY). — V e n e z u e l a . Caracas, without collector's name (H).

REFERENCES. Stephani (*Icones, Mastigobryum* nos. 307, 373), Herzog (1938, 19).

36. **Bazzania falcata** (Lindenb.) Trevis. Mem. Ist. Lomb. 13: 415. 1877.

Mastigobryum falcatum Lindenberg, in G. L. & N., Syn Hep 231 1845.
Mastigobryum tocutianum Gottsche, in Stephani, Hedwigia 25 236. pl. 2. fig. 18-20. 1886.
Bazzania ancistrodes Spruce, Trans & Proc. Bot. Soc. [Edinburgh] 15· 380. 1885.
Mastigobryum ancistrodes Stephani, Spec. Hep 3: 501 1908.
Mastigobryum armatum Stephani, Spec Hep. 3. 528. 1909.

Plants large, ochraceous yellow to dark brown, greenish in the younger portions· stems robust, to 10 cm. long, with leaves to 6 mm broad, depressed to ascending; in cross section the cells thick-walled, averaging 25μ in diameter; lateral branches frequent, diverging at a wide angle; flagelliform branches frequent, short: rhizoids colorless, in tufts, from the bases of the leaves of flagelliform branches: the line of leaf insertion curved in its upper half, the dorsal end turned downward forming a hook; leaves densely imbricated, convex, deflexed, connivent when dry, unsymmetrically long-ovate, somewhat falcate, to 3.5 mm. long, 2 mm. broad at the base, narrowing to the mostly 0.65 mm. broad, truncate, tridentate apex; the dorsal edge strongly convex from a deeply cordate base, extending across the stem and somewhat beyond, the ventral edge concave, the base conspicuously auricled, the dilation large, oblong to rounded, undulate, entire to toothed; the apex three-toothed, the teeth broadly triangular, acute, five to eight cells broad at the base, to six cells high, widely spreading, the sinuses broad, lunulate, the margins straight to repand; the cell lumina stellate, the trigones very large, with convex sides, mostly confluent; cells of the apical portion 18μ in diameter, of the median portion $30\mu \times 20\mu$, and of the base $54\mu \times 25\mu$, a vitta not differentiated; cuticle faintly verruculose: underleaves imbricated, attached in a recurved line, subquadrate, 0.8 mm. to 1 mm. long from the line of attachment, the base cordate, the auricles large, undulate, rounded or toothed, the lateral margins sinuate, often with short teeth, the apex undulate to definitely two- to four-lobed, occasionally toothed, with lunulate to acute sinuses, the cells as in the leaf: leaves of the flagelliform branches large, plane, 0.25 mm. - 0.33 mm. long $\times$ 0.24 mm. broad at the base, ovate, the apex acute to shortly two- to three-toothed, the cells thick-walled as in the leaf: female branches occasional, solitary, one to several on a stem; the bracts and bracteoles similar; the outermost series short, ovate, 0.64 mm. long $\times$ 0.43 mm. wide, the apex entire; the intermediate series long-ovate, 1 mm. - 1.6 mm. long $\times$ 0.6 mm. - 0.8 mm. wide, the apex bifid or trifid with short teeth, the cells of the internal portion rectangular in outline, 45μ - $72\mu \times 22\mu$, those of the margin smaller, the trigones conspicuous, the walls unequally thickened; the innermost series similar, larger, one-fifth to one-sixth divided into two or three crenulate teeth, six to ten cells long, four to six cells broad at the base, the lateral margins crenulate, the cells 45μ - $72\mu \times 22\mu$, trigones conspicuous, walls unequally thickened: perianth (immature) mouth ciliate, laciniate, the cilia and laciniae six to twelve cells long: male branches and sporophyte not seen.

HABITAT: In tufts or scattered among mosses on logs and rocks in forests.

The species is best characterized by its large size, and the deep yellow-brown to dark brown color; the long stems with densely imbricated, tridentate leaves with undulate to toothed auricles and leaf cells with stellate cell lumina and very large, rounded trigones; and the large, subquadrate underleaves with strongly cordate bases, undulate, entire or toothed lateral margins and undulate to two- to four-lobed apices; and the flagelliform branches with large leaflets. (FIGURES 46, nos. 1-10; 47, nos. 1-20).

STEPHANI included this species in his *Cordistipula* subdivision (1886, 247), but later (1908, 500) transferred it to the *Appendiculata* group. The leaves are large and often somewhat falcate.

FIG. 46. — *Bazzania falcata* (Lindenb.) Trevis. — 1. Portion of leaf attached to stem, $\times$ 20. 2. Leaves, $\times$ 30. 3. Dorsal lobes of leaves, $\times$ 30. 4. Apices of leaves, $\times$ 30. 5. A cell from the apical portion of a leaf, $\times$ 350. 6. Cells from the apical tooth of a leaf, $\times$ 260. 7. Cells from the dorsal margin of a leaf, $\times$ 260. 8. Cells from the ventral margin of a leaf, $\times$ 260. 9. Cells from the basal portion of a leaf, $\times$ 260. 10. Portion of a cross section of a stem, $\times$ 260. Nos. 1 and 2 drawn from plants collected by Bro. CLÉMENT in Cuba; 3-10 from a portion of the type material.

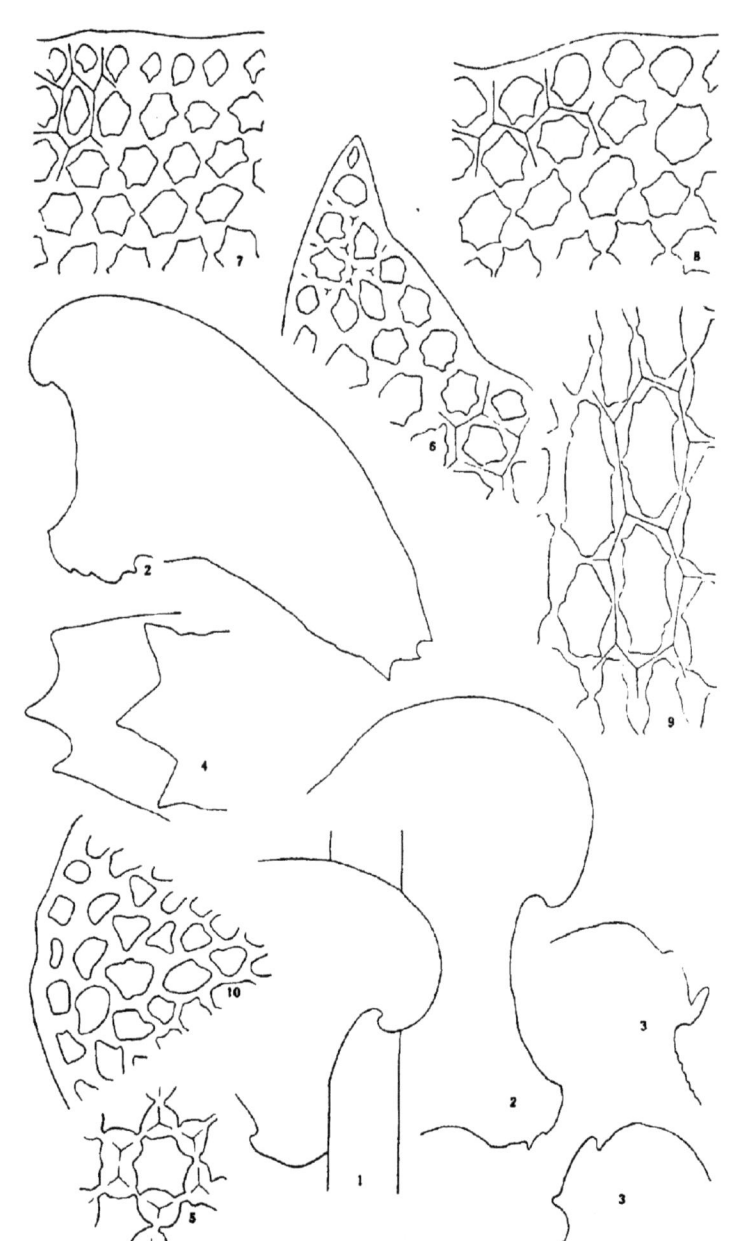

The ventral auricle or appendage (FIG. 46, nos. 1-2 and FIG. 47, no. 1) was quite distinct on all of the specimens examined. Although it varies in size on different leaves, even on the same plant, it is nevertheless conspicuous. The cells are similar to those of the ventral edge of the leaf and the margin is undulate and usually set with one or more teeth. These teeth are short, broadly triangular and one to three cells high, acute or in some instances acuminate by the projection of a two-celled point. The leaves sometimes have the dorsal margins incised as indicated by LINDENBERG and GOTTSCHE (1851, pl. 17, fig. 4) and FIG. 46, no. 3; 47, no. 11.

The leaf cells are relatively small. The trigones are very large, with convex sides, and appear rounded. They often become coalesced or are separated only by narrow pits so that the cell lumina are usually stellate. In some leaves, especially on plants from very mesophytic situations or in the youngest leaves of the stem, the trigones are not quite so large and are rarely coalesced, so that the thin cell walls may be conspicuous.

The underleaves are especially distinctive. They are more or less subquadrate, often longer than broad, deeply cordate, and attached in a recurved line. The recurved line of attachment is short and the base of the underleaf large and strongly cordate, so much so, that the basal auricles often overlap. The lateral margins are undulate, sometimes angled or shortly toothed, and the apex is rounded, undulate to two-, three-, or four-lobed or -toothed. STEPHANI's drawing (*Icones, Mastigobryum* no. 309) of a part of a plant of the type, from Guadeloupe, shows an underleaf with undulate lateral margins and a shallow-lobed apex. There is a blunt tooth on one of the auricles. In another drawing, no. 415, also from the plants collected in Guadeloupe, the several underleaves are undulate to lobed along the margins and apex.

The flagelliform branches differ from those of the species of the preceding Sections in that the leaflets are much longer and always broader than the stem. This condition is also found in several other species of the *Appendiculatae*.

FIG 47. — *Bazzania falcata* (Lindenb.) Trevis — 1. Ventral view of stem and underleaf, × 30. 2 Underleaf, × 30. 3. Cells from the apical portion of an underleaf, × 260 4. Female bract of the outermost series, × 30. 5. Female bract of an intermediate series, × 30 6. Cells of an apical tooth of this bract, × 30. 7. Apical tooth of a bract of the innermost series, × 100 8 Cells from the central portion of a bract of this series, × 350 9 One of the laciniae of the perianth mouth, × 100. 10. Underleaf, × 30. 11 Basal portion of a leaf to show dorsal and ventral lobes, × 30 12 Ventral appendage of a leaf, × 30 13 A cell from the apical portion of a leaf, × 400 14 A leaf, × 15 15. Ventral appendage of a leaf, × 15. 16. A cell from the apical portion of a leaf, × 400 17 Underleaves, × 15. 18. Ventral auricles of leaves on stem, × 15 19 A cell from the apical portion of a leaf, × 400 20 Underleaves, × 15 No 1 from a plant collected by Bro CLÉMENT in Cuba, 2-9 from a portion of the type, from Guadeloupe, 10-13 from a portion of the type of *M. tocutianum*, from Trinidad; 14-17 from a portion of the type of *B. ancistrodes*, from Peru; 18-20 from a portion of the type of *M. armatum* from Brazil.

The female branches were old, poorly developed and eroded. The bracts of the intermediate and innermost series are characterized by being one-fifth or less divided into two or three rather broad, crenulate teeth (see FIG. 47, nos. 4-8). The perianths were immature and so poorly preserved that the details of the mouth were the only characteristic observable. The mouth is divided into cilia and narrow laciniae, six to twelve cells long as is seen in FIG. 47, no. 9.

LINDENBERG, in the *Synopsis Hepaticarum* (G. L. & N., 1844-47, 231), records the plant from Guadeloupe and also from Nepal. STEPHANI (1908, 500) listed the Guadeloupe specimen and added that the plant from Nepal naturally does not belong here. The type from Guadeloupe (Hb. HOOKER) and a specimen from Nepal (LEHMANN) have been examined and seem to be identical, but more material should be studied before recording the species definitely from India.

B. ancistrodes from the mountains of Peru should also be included under *B. falcata* (see FIG. 47, nos. 14-17). The plants are not so robust but the leaf shape, ventral auricles, and the underleaves show no characteristics different from this species. Most of the trigones of the leaf cells are not quite so large, so that the thin cell wall is often conspicuous, and the brown pigmentation is not quite so deep. The presence of both smaller trigones and lighter color on one plant lead one to suspect that they are the results of the effect of the local environment and should not, therefore, be considered of specific importance. The leaves of the flagelliform branches are large.

M. armatum from Brazil (see FIG. 47, nos. 18-20) is of the color and size of *B. ancistrodes* from Peru. However, the trigones are larger, and are intermediate in size between those of the leaves of *B. ancistrodes* and *M. falcatum*. The leaves of the flagelliform branches are large.

Plants collected by CRÜGER in Trinidad and described by STEPHANI under the manuscript name of *M. tocutianum* of GOTTSCHE are identical with this species (see FIG. 47, nos. 10-13). STEPHANI suggested (1886, 236) that the species was identical with *M. falcatum* of Guadeloupe and St. Vincent but he later (1908, 500) recognized its validity. BESCHERELLE (1893, 186) recognized *M. tocutianum* and included *M. falcatum* as a synonym.

The species can readily be distinguished from *B. asperistipula*. Plants of *B. falcata* are strongly pigmented with brown, even in the younger portions, and most of the leaves are connivent, while plants of *B. asperistipula* are light yellow-green and the leaves are plane and subimbricated; the appendages of the leaves of *B. falcata* are rounded to oblong and the margins are entire, undulate, and set with one or more short teeth, while the appendages of the leaves of *B. asperistipula* are usually large, oblong, and the margins are undulate, lobed, and the lobes are crenulate to shortly dentate; the leaf-cell pattern of the two species is entirely different, the cell lumina of the former are stellate and the trigones are large, with bulging sides, and confluent, or separated by narrow pits, while those of the latter are angular-rounded, the walls are thin and the trigones are small but conspicuous and very rarely are coalesced. The underleaves of both species are approximately the same size and shape and have the same mode of attachment to the stem. The principal difference is in the configuration of the margins. In *B. falcata* the lateral margins are entire or rarely short-toothed and the apex is rounded-undulate to two-, three-, or four-lobed or -toothed; in *B. asperistipula* the whole margin is undulate to lobed, and crenulate to serrate, and has occasional short cilia. The female bracts and the mouths of the perianths of the two species are also different. The cell walls are thin and the laciniae long with ciliate or dentate margins in *B. asperistipula*, while in *B. falcata* the cell walls are unequally thickened, and the divisions of the apex are in the form of rather short, crenulate teeth. The laciniae of the perianth are also shorter in *B. falcata*.

DISTRIBUTION· C u b a : Top of Gato Hill, 100 m., Bro. Clément 1908 (Y, NY) — G u a d e l o u p e : without locality, Hooker Hb., the type (NY). — P u e r t o R i c o : Sierra de Naguabo 465-700 m , Shafer 3774, 3781 (NY). — St. V i n c e n t . Soufrière, Elliott 226, cited by Spruce (1895, 356), without locality or collector's name, Hooker Hb. (NY). — T r i n i d a d : Toccuche, Crüger, the type of *M. tocutianum* (G) — B r a z i l : subtropics, Ule, the type of *M. armatum* (H). — P e r u : Mt. Campana, Spruce, Hepat. Spruc , the type of *B ancistrodes* (H, NY) — E c u a d o r : Cayambe, Jameson (NY); Quito, Jameson (NY)

REFERENCES. Lindenberg & Gottsche (1851, 107. pl. 17); Spruce (1895, 356); Mitten (1861, 105); Bescherelle (1893, 186); Cook (1904, 13); Stephani (1908, 500; *Icones, Mastigobryum* nos. 306, 309, 313, 372, 415).

37. Bazzania Hookeri (Lindenb.) Trevis. Mem. Ist. Lomb. 13: 414. 1877.

Mastigobryum Hookeri Lindenberg, in G. L. & N., Syn. Hep. 226. 1845.
Mastigobryum superbum Montagne, Ann. Sci. Nat. Ser. IV. Bot. 5: 349. 1856
Bazzania superba Trevis. loc. cit.
Bazzania vincentina var. *subrectifolia* Spruce ms p p , Hep. Spruc.
Bazzania flavicans Spruce, Trans & Proc. Bot Soc. [Edinburgh] 15: 377 1885.
Mastigobryum flavicans Stephani, Spec. Hep 3. 529. 1909.
Mastigobryum Braunianum Stephani, *op. cit.* p. 521.
Mastigobryum guadaloupense Stephani, *op. cit.* p. 518.
Mastigobryum verrucosum Stephani, *op. cit.* p. 524.
Mastigobryum Douini Stephani, in Herzog, Biblioth. Bot 87: 224. Fig. 164, a-c. 1916.

Plants medium size to robust, in deep tufts, olive-green to brown, becoming deeply pigmented in the older portions: stems to 10 cm. long, with leaves to 4.5 mm. in width, prostrate to suberect; lateral branches infrequent, diverging at a wide angle; flagelliform branches frequent, long; rhizoids colorless, present on the bases of the leaves of flagelliform branches: the line of leaf insertion curved in its upper part, the dorsal end curved downward forming a hook; leaves approximate to imbricated, mostly plane, unsymmetrically ovate, becoming falcate, 2 mm. - 2.5 mm. long, 1 mm. -

FIG. 48. — *Bazzania Hookeri* (Lindenb) Trevis. — 1. Portion of a plant, ventral view, × 15. 2. Portion of a leaf and stem, dorsal view, × 30. 3. Leaves, × 15 4. A tooth of a leaf, × 310. 5. A cell from the apical portion of a leaf, × 400. 6 Underleaves, × 15. 7 Leaves, × 15. 8. A tooth of a leaf, × 310. 9. A cell from the apical portion of a leaf, × 400. 10. Under-leaf, × 15. Nos. 1-6 drawn from a portion of the type material; 7-10 from a portion of the type of *M. superbum.*

1.5 mm broad at the base, narrowed a little to the transversely truncate, tridentate apex; the dorsal margin strongly arched from a cordate base, extending the width of the stem and often beyond, the ventral margin straight to a little concave, the base dilated, forming an inconspicuous, entire auricle, the apex more or less equally three-toothed, the teeth broad, eight to ten cells long and broad, the sinus lunulate, the margins entire; leaf cells thin-walled, the cell lumina angular-rounded, the trigones large, with convex sides, often coalesced, the cuticle verruculose; cells of the apical portion 16μ - 20μ in diameter, those of the median portion longer, those of the base 52μ - $64\mu \times 24\mu$, a vitta not differentiated · underleaves approximate to imbricated, round-quadrate in outline, broader than the stem, attached in a recurved line, to 1.2 mm. long and broad, the base deeply cordate, the auricles large, not overlapping, entire, the lateral margins and apex entire, repand or irregularly and bluntly toothed or lobed, the cells as in the leaf: leaves of the flagelliform branches broader than the stem, spreading, to 0 3 mm. long, broadly ovate, the apex acute to shortly bifid: sexual branches not seen.

HABITAT· On soil and tree bases.

The distinguishing characteristics of the species are its medium to large size and brownish green color; the hooked line of leaf insertion; the broad leaves with broad teeth and broad shallow sinuses, and only slightly expanded ventral auricles; thin-walled cells with conspicuous trigones; and the large, round-quadrate underleaves with entire, repand margins and strongly cordate bases. (FIGURES 48, nos. 1-10; 49, nos. 1-16).

The original material is made up of large plants which are strongly pigmented with brown. The leaves are large, spreading, and are broad and transversely truncate at the apex. The teeth are always broad, more or less equal, equilateral, and are separated by broad, shallow, acute sinuses, as seen in FIG. 48, nos. 1, 3 and 4. The cells are thin-walled and have large trigones with convex sides which often become coalesced (FIG. 48, nos. 4 and 5). The cuticle is faintly to strongly verruculose and often is extremely warty on the basal portions of the leaves and underleaves where the individual deposits sometimes tend to be oblong. The ventral appendage or auricle of the leaf, which is one of the distinguishing characteristics of the Section *Appendiculatae*, is never conspicuously developed in *B. Hookeri*. While many of the leaves show scarcely any dilation or indication of appendages, others have it developed to the extent that it is readily recognizable (contrast nos. 1, 2 and 3, FIG. 48).

The underleaves are very large, round-quadrate, with well developed basal auricles which sometimes overlap. The margins are repand, entire, with occasional slime papillae in the depressions. The line of attachment is recurved.

The presence of occasional appendages, together with the pattern of the trigones of the leaf cells, the hook-formed line of leaf insertion, and the large, round-quadrate, auricled underleaves

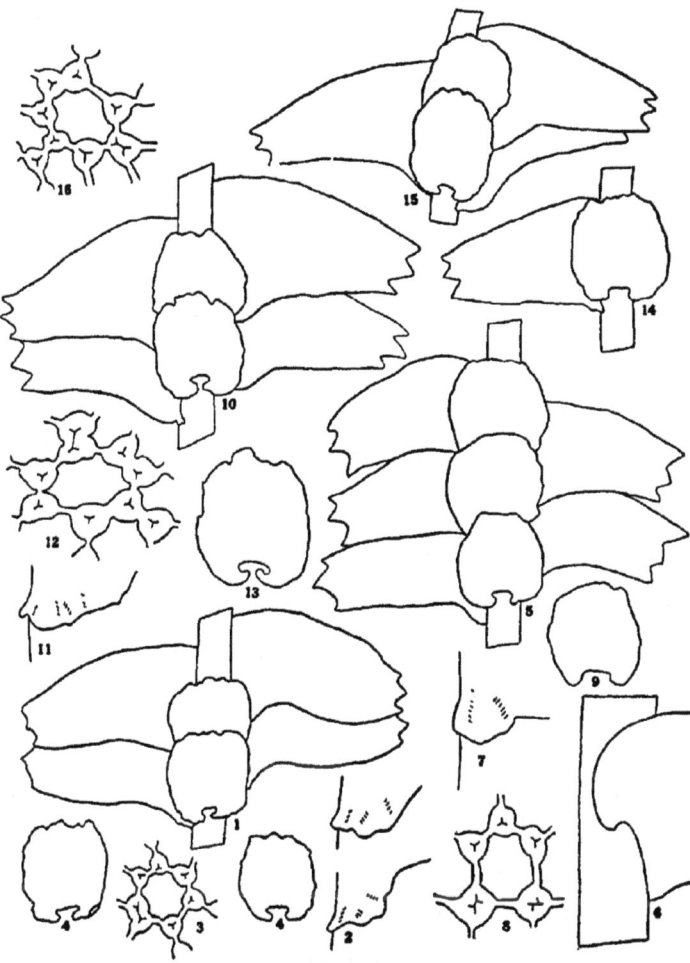

Fig. 49 — *Bazzania Hookeri* (Lindenb) Trevis — 1. Portion of a plant, ventral view, × 15   2. Ventral auricles of leaves on stem, × 30. 3. A cell from the apical portion of a leaf, × 400   4 Underleaves, × 15. 5. Portion of a plant, ventral view, × 15.   6 Portion of a leaf and stem, dorsal view, × 30   7 Ventral auricle of leaf on stem, × 30. 8 A cell from the apical portion of a leaf, × 400   9. Underleaf, × 15. 10 Portion of a stem, ventral view, × 15. 11 Ventral auricle of a leaf, × 30   12. A cell from the apical portion of a leaf, × 400. 13. Underleaf, × 15. 14. Portion of a plant, ventral view, × 15   15 Portion of a plant, ventral view, × 15. 16 A cell from the apical portion of a leaf, × 400   Nos 1-4 drawn from a portion of the type of *M. Braunianum*, from Venezuela; 5-9 from a portion of the type of *M. verrucosum*, from Ecuador; 10-13 from a portion of the type of *M. guadaloupense*, from Guadeloupe; 14 from a portion of the type of *B. vincentina* var. *subrectifolia*, from Ecuador; 15-16 from a portion of the type of *B. flavicans*, from Ecuador.

which are attached in a recurved line, furnish sufficient proof of the close relationship of this species with the other American members of the Section. STEPHANI included the species and several of its synonyms among the Section *Cordistipula*.

Plants collected by UNDERWOOD, no. 1485, in Jamaica are smaller than the type, are light brown in color, and the underleaves are longer than broad and entire along the margins. The other characteristics are typical of the species, including the large leaves of the flagelliform branches.

Mastigobryum superbum (FIG. 48, nos 7-10), from Peru, and *M. Braunianum* (FIG. 49, nos. 1-4), from Venezuela, are identical with the type, *M. Hookeri*. *B. flavicans* (FIG. 49, nos. 15-16), from Ecuador, is not so deeply pigmented and the teeth of the leaves are more acute and tend to be a bit longer than broad and more irregular, but these variations are neither constant nor of sufficient degree to characterize a distinct species.

M. guadaloupense (FIG. 49, nos. 10-13), from Guadeloupe, is slightly more robust than *M. Hookeri*. Some of the teeth of the leaves are sharply pointed, but leaves with the shorter, broader teeth are not rare. The trigones are large and most of the thin cell walls have been obliterated by the deposition of secondary thickenings, so that the trigones have become coalesced. The ventral auricles of most of the leaves are much enlarged but they do not possess teeth or appendages. The cuticle is very strongly verruculose with large, often oblong warts.

M. verrucosum (FIG. 49, nos. 5-9), from Ecuador, is very similar to *M. guadaloupense* in that the cuticle is very strongly verruculose, with oblong, wart-like protuberances, particularly in the older leaves and underleaves of the stem. The leaves are, for the most part, strongly three-toothed, but they are broad at the apex, as are those of the species mentioned above. *M. Douini* from Bolivia has these same characteristics The only conspicuous difference between *M. guadaloupense*, *M. verrucosum*, *M. Douini* and the type specimen of *M. Hookeri* is this distinctly warty cuticle. Since these protuberances are present, but in lesser degree, in *M. Hookeri* it seems justifiable to conclude that this variation represents another of the expressions of a single species.

Plants distributed by SPRUCE, from Ecuador, under the manuscript name *B. vincentina* var. *subrectifolia* in the *Hepaticae Spruceana* are also identical with *M. Hookeri*.

The species is quite similar to *B. falcata*. However, in *B. falcata* the teeth of the leaves while broad, are not so large, the trigones are larger and more rounded, the ventral auricles are more pronounced and usually exhibit ventral appendages, and the underleaves usually have teeth or appendages on the basal auricles.

DISTRIBUTION: C u b a : Sierra Maestra, Bro. Clément 351 (NY). — G a u d e l o u p e : without locality, Parker 26, the type (NY); without locality, l'Herminier (NY); without locality, Marie, the type of *M. guadaloupense* (H); Soufrière, Duss 320, as *M. portoricense* (NY). — J a m a i c a : Blue Mountain Peak, Underwood 1485 (NY). — T r i n i d a d : Mt. Tocouche,

Birch (NY). — B r a z i l : Caldas, G. A Lindberg (NY). — B o l i v i a : Yungas, Rusby 3023 (NY); Tablas, Herzog, the type of *M. Doumi* (L). — E c u a d o r . Mt. Tunguragua, Spruce, Hepat. Spruc., the type of *M verrucosum* (H); Mt. Tunguragua, Spruce, Hepat Spruc , the type of *B. flavicans* (H), the same, *as B. vincentina* var. *subrectifolia* p p. (NY); without locality, Fraser, cited by Stephani (1908, 499). — G u i a n a : Batava, Suringar, cited by Stephani (1909, 524) — P e r u . Curzco, without collector's name, Steph. Herb. as *M. Schlimianum* (H).

REFERENCES Lindenberg & Gottsche (1851, 77. pl. 14); Gottsche (1864, 140), Stephani (1908, 499; 1909, 523; *Icones, Mastigobryum* nos 158, 312, 377, 384, 385, 405).

38.   **Bazzania robusta** Spruce, Trans. & Proc. Bot. Soc. [Edinburgh] 15: 378. 1885.

Mastigobryum robustum Stephani, Spec Hep. 3: 501. 1908.
Mastigobryum bolivianum Stephani, in Herzog, Biblioth. Bot 87: 223. fig. 164, f-h 1916.

Plants large, in deep tufts, yellow-brown, becoming deeply pigmented in the older portions: stems robust, 10 cm. or more in length, with leaves to 5 mm. broad; in longitudinal section the cells mostly 0.17 mm. long, the cortical shorter, both averaging 20μ in diameter, the vertical walls strongly thickened and containing frequent pits, the end walls thin; lateral branches frequent, 1 cm. or more apart, diverging at a wide angle; flagelliform branches frequent, long; rhizoids colorless, present on the leaves of the flagelliform branches . the line of leaf insertion curved in its upper half, the dorsal end recurved forming a hook; leaves densely imbricated, strongly deflexed when dry, unsymmetrically ovate, falcate, 2.5 mm. - 3.5 mm. long, 1.5 mm. broad at the base, narrowed to the mostly transversely truncate, tridentate apex; the dorsal margin arched from a cordate base, extending across the stem and beyond, the ventral margin strongly concave, the base conspicuously auricled, the dilation large, undulate, lobed, entire or with an occasional tooth; the apex deeply three-toothed, the teeth spreading, long, acute, to acuminate, eight to ten cells long, four to six cells broad at the base, the sinuses deep, lunulate to acute, the margins entire, undulate; the cell lumina stellate, the trigones very large, with concave sides, the cell walls thin, often obliterated by the enlarging trigones, the cuticle faintly verruculose; cells of the apical portion and dorsal base averaging 24μ in diameter, those of the basal portion 32μ - 60μ long $\times$ 24μ wide, a vitta not differentiated: underleaves imbricated, subquadrate-rounded, attached in a recurved line, broader than the stem, averaging 0.6 mm. long and broad, the base cordate, the auricles mostly rounded, the margins entire, undulate, lobed or faintly toothed, the lateral and apical margins mostly undulate, lobed or faintly toothed, obscurely toothed to entire, the cells as in the leaves: leaves of the flagelliform branches large, broader than the stem, ovate, acute or shortly bifid: female branches occasional, solitary, one to several on a stem, the bracts and bracteoles ovate; the outermost series short, bifid; the intermediate and innermost series progressively longer, one-fourth to one-sixth divided into two or three slender, serrate to ciliate laciniae, the cells to 64μ long, thin-walled, the lateral margins serrate, ciliate

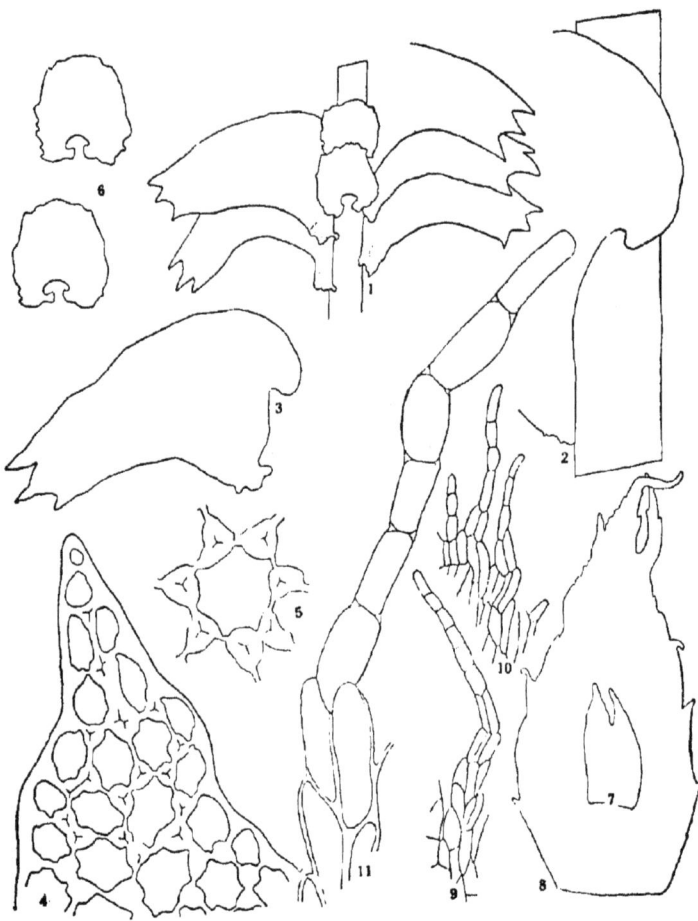

FIG. 50. — *Bazzania robusta* Spruce — 1 Portion of a plant, ventral view, × 15   2 Portion of a leaf and stem, dorsal view, × 30.   3 Leaf, × 15   4 Tooth of a leaf, × 310   5 A cell from the apical portion of a leaf, × 400. 6 Underleaves, × 15.   7. Female bract of the outermost series, × 30 8. Female bract of the innermost series, × 30.   9 A lacinia of this series, × 90.   10. Portion of the mouth of the perianth, × 90   11 A lacinia of the mouth of the perianth, × 310   Nos 1-11 drawn from a portion of the type

or even shortly laciniate; perianth to 6 cm. long, the mouth ciliate laciniate, the cells to 64μ long, thin-walled: male branches not seen.

HABITAT: In deep ascending tufts, on decaying logs and rocks and also on branches of living trees in humid forests.

The distinguishing characteristics of the species are its large size and deep brown color; the falcate leaves with large, undulate, entire ventral auricles, large spreading teeth, and large, angular-rounded to stellate cell cavities with large, rounded trigones; and the large, subquadrate-rounded underleaves with auriculate bases, and undulate, faintly lobed to obscurely toothed margins. (FIG. 50, nos. 1-11).

The species is distinguished from B. falcata because of the smaller, less rounded trigones and larger cell lumina of its leaves and underleaves; from B. Hookeri by its larger leaf cells and falcate leaves with sharp teeth; and from B. Liebmanniana by its larger, more acute teeth and the larger leaf cells.

DISTRIBUTION: B r a z i l   Panuré along the Rio Negro, Spruce, Hepat. Spruc., the type (NY); Prov. São Paulo, Hj. Mosén (H). — B o l i v i a · Santa Anna, Williams 2161 (Y, NY); Corani, Herzog 5072, the type of M. Bolivianum (L). — B r i t i s h   G u i a n a : near Baitica Grove, Jenman (NY) REFERENCES: Stephani (1924, 466); Icones, Mastigobryum nos 308, 311).

39. Bazzania Liebmanniana (Lindenb. & Gottsche) Trevis. Mem. Ist. Lomb. 13: 414. 1877.

Mastigobryum Liebmannianum Lindenberg & Gottsche, in G L & N, Syn. Hep. 719 1847.

Plants medium size, light brownish green becoming darker in the older portions: stems slender, 5 cm. or more in length, with leaves to 4 mm. broad; lateral branches diverging at a wide angle; flagelliform branches frequent; rhizoids colorless, present on the leaves of the flagelliform branches: the line of leaf insertion curved in its upper part, the dorsal end recurved forming a short hook; leaves imbricated, strongly deflexed when dry, unsymmetrically ovate, ascendent, 1.5 mm. - 2.5 mm. long, 1 mm. - 1.5 mm. broad at the base, narrowed to the transversely to obliquely truncate, tridentate apex; the dorsal margin strongly arched from a cordate base, extending across the stem and beyond, the ventral margin straight to concave, the base conspicuously auricled, the dilation undulate, lobed, or occasionally toothed, the apex three-toothed, the teeth variable, four to six cells long, four to six cells broad at the base, the sinus lunulate, the margins entire; the cell lumina angular-rounded, the cell walls thin, the trigones large, with convex sides, often becoming coalesced, the cuticle faintly verruculose; cells of the apical portion and dorsal base averaging 20μ, those of the median portion larger, those of the basal portion 40μ - 56μ × 24μ, a vitta not differentiated: underleaves imbricated, subquadrate, attached in a recurved line, broader than the stem, 0.6 mm. - 0.85 mm. long and broad, the base cordate, the lateral margins repand, sometimes with a large tooth, the apex variously lobed or toothed, the cells as in the leaf: leaves of the flagelliform branches scale-like, to 0.2 mm. long, ovate, the apex acute to shortly bifid: sexual branches and sporophyte not seen.

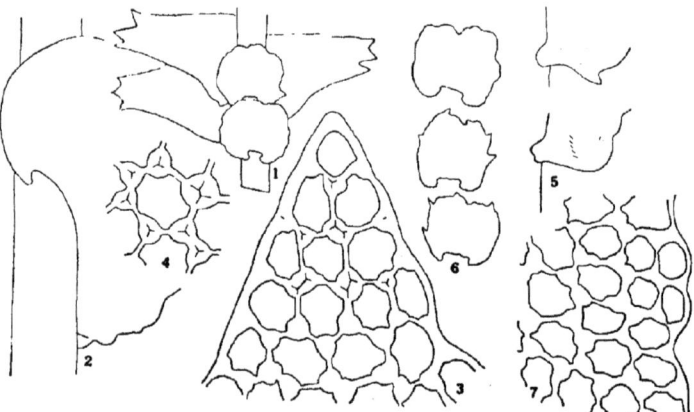

Fig 51 — *Bazzania Liebmanniana* (Lindenb. & Gottsche) Trevis
1. Portion of a plant, ventral view, × 15. 2 Portion of a leaf and stem, × 30
3 A tooth of a leaf, × 312   4 A cell from the apical portion of a leaf, × 400.
5 Ventral bases of leaf on stem, × 30. 6 Underleaves, × 15   7 Cells from
the lateral margin of an underleaf, × 310. Nos 1-7 drawn from a portion
of the type.

HABITAT. Not given.

The distinguishing characteristics of the species seem to be its size and color; the ascendent, often falcate leaves conspicuously narrowed toward the apex; the short teeth, the thin-walled cells with conspicuous trigones and angular-rounded lumina; the sub-quadrate underleaves, cordate at the base, with repand margins which are occasionally toothed; and the flagelliform branches with the typical scale-like leaves. (FIG. 51, nos. 1-7)

I believe that this species is a variation belonging to one of the other species included in this Section, but the portion of the type in the STEPHANI Collections in the Farlow Herbarium is so fragmentary that it has been impossible to get an adequate concept of the range of variability of the LINDENBERG and GOTTSCHE species.

It can be distinguished from the preceding species by its spreading leaves which tend to be narrowed in the apical region, the small, undulate ventral auricles with entire margins, and by the thin cell walls and conspicuous trigones.

DISTRIBUTION M e x i c o · Oaxaca, Liebmann, the type (H), Vera Cruz, Purpus 5548 (Y) — G u a t e m a l a · Coban, Standley 69119 (W)

REFERENCES: Gottsche (1863, 133, 136), Lindenberg & Gottsche (1851, 74, 81), Stephani (1909, 523, *Icones, Mastigobryum* no. 392), Herzog (1938, 19).

40. Bazzania teretiuscula (Lindenb & Gottsche) Trevis. Mem. Ist. Lomb. 13: 414. 1877.

Mastigobryum teretiusculum Lindenberg & Gottsche, in G L. & N., Syn. Hep. 720. 1847.

Bazzania heteroclada Spruce, Trans & Proc. Bot Soc. [Edinburgh] 15. 379. 1885.

Mastigobryum heterocladum Stephani, Spec Hep. 3: 502. 1908.

Bazzania spinigera Spruce, op. cit. p. 380.

Mastigobryum spinigerum Stephani, op cit p 500.

Bazzania humifusa Spruce, op cit. p. 379.

Mastigobryum humifusum Stephani, Hedwigia 44. 225 1905.

Bazzania conchophylla Herzog, Rev Bryol et Lichén 11 20 1938.

Mastigobryum incisostipulum Stephani, in Herzog, Biblioth. Bot 87 225 Fig. 165, c-d. 1916.

Plants medium size, in tufts or mats, greenish brown, deeply pigmented with brown in the older portions: stems to 8 cm. long, with leaves to 3 2 mm. broad, suberect; stem cells in longitudinal section elongate, averaging 0.17 mm. long, the cortical shorter, both averaging 20μ in diameter, the vertical walls uniformly thickened, containing frequent pits, the end walls thin: lateral branches 5 mm. or more apart, diverging at a wide angle; flagelliform branches frequent; rhizoids colorless, few, on the bases of the leaves of the flagelliform branches: the line of leaf insertion curved in the upper half, the dorsal end recurved forming a hook; leaves approximate to imbricated, deflexed, strongly so when dry, unsymmetrically ovate, straight to subfalcate, 1.2 mm. - 2.2 mm. long, to 1 mm. broad at the base, narrowed to the more or less obliquely truncate, tridentate apex; the dorsal margin strongly arched from a cordate base, extending the width of the stem and beyond, the ventral margin concave, the base dilated, the auricle

FIG 52 — *Bazzania teretiuscula* (Lindenberg & Gottsche) Trevis. — 1 Portion of a plant, ventral view, × 15   2 Portion of leaves and stem, dorsal view, × 30.   3. Leaves, × 15   4. Cells from the apical portions of leaves, × 400   5 Underleaves, × 15.   6. Portion of stem, showing auricles of leaves, × 15   7 Leaf, × 15   8 A cell from the apical portion of a leaf, × 400   9 Underleaves, × 15.   10. Portion of a stem, ventral view, × 15. 11 Underleaf, × 15   12 A cell from the apical portion of a leaf, × 400 13. Underleaves, × 15   Nos 1-5 drawn from a portion of the type, from Mexico; 6-9 from a portion of the type of *B humifusa*, from Peru, 10-11 from a portion of the type of *B. otites*, from Peru; 12-13 from a portion of the type of *B conchophylla*, from Costa Rica.

undulate, entire, appendiculate, toothed, or ciliate, the apex irregularly three-toothed, the teeth mostly spreading, acute, five to eight cells long, four to six cells broad at the base, the sinuses deep, lunulate, the margins entire, repand; leaf cells thin-walled, the cell lumina angular-rounded, the trigones conspicuous, with convex sides, often confluent, the cuticle faintly verruculose; cells of the apical region and dorsal base averaging $20\mu \times 20\mu$, those of the interior larger, those of the base to $36\mu \times 20\mu$, a vitta not differentiated; underleaves approximate to imbricated, subquadrate in outline, averaging 0.7 mm. long and broad, attached in a recurved line, broader than the stem, the base cordate, the auricles not overlapping, rounded, the margins entire, or dentate with one or two broad teeth, or ciliate by a row of two or three cells, the lateral margins convex, entire or rarely with one or two teeth, the apex deeply four-lobed or -toothed, the sinuses narrow, acute, the cells and trigones as in the leaf: leaves of the flagelliform branches scale-like, ovate, acute to shortly bifid: female branches occasional, solitary, one to several on a stem, the bracts and bracteoles similar, ovate (immature), the outermost series small, shortly bifid, the intermediate series larger, to one-sixth divided into three laciniae, the cells mostly $20\mu \times 16\mu$, with thick walls, the lateral margins serrate to short ciliate; the apical portion of the innermost series divided into three, serrate, ciliate laciniae, the cells mostly $36\mu \times 16\mu$, the cell walls thin: male branches and perianth not seen.

HABITAT: On rocks and bases of trees on shaded slopes in moist forests.

The distinguishing characteristics of the species are its medium size and greenish brown color; the subfalcate, tridentate leaves with thin cell walls and distinct trigones; the enlarged ventral auricles with wavy, entire, toothed or appendiculate margins; and the subquadrate, cordate, underleaves with definitely four-lobed or -toothed apices, and approximate, rounded, basal auricles, having entire or occasionally toothed or ciliate margins. (FIGURES 52, nos. 1-13; 53, nos. 1-20).

The plants show much variation both as to size and to configuration of the parts. On some areas of a stem the leaves and underleaves may be densely imbricated while on others they may be approximate or even distant. Many of the leaves tend to be narrow-elongate in the upper part, but shorter leaves are not

FIG 53 — *Bazzania teretiuscula* (Lindenb. & Gottsche) Trevis. — 1 Portion of plant, ventral view, $\times$ 15. 2. Portion of a leaf and stem, dorsal view, $\times$ 30. 3. Tooth of a leaf, $\times$ 310. 4. A cell from the apical portion of a leaf, $\times$ 400 5 Cells from the basal portion of a leaf, $\times$ 312. 6 Outline of basal auricles of leaves, $\times$ 30 7. Underleaves, $\times$ 15. 8 Female bract of an outer series, $\times$ 30. 9 Female bract of the intermediate series, $\times$ 30 10 A lacinia of a bract of the innermost series, $\times$ 100. 11. The tip of the same lacinia, $\times$ 310 12 Portion of a plant, ventral view, $\times$ 15. 13 A cell from the apical portion of a leaf, $\times$ 400. 14. Auricles of ventral bases of leaves, $\times$ 30. 15. Underleaves, $\times$ 15 16. Female bract of outer series, $\times$ 30. 17. Female bract of intermediate series, $\times$ 30 18 A lacinia of a bract of this series, $\times$ 310 19. A lacinia of a bract of the innermost series, $\times$ 100. 20 Cells of this same lacinia, $\times$ 310. Nos. 1-11 drawn from plants of the type of *B. heteroclada*, from Peru; 12-20 from plants of the type of *B. spinigera*, from Brazil.

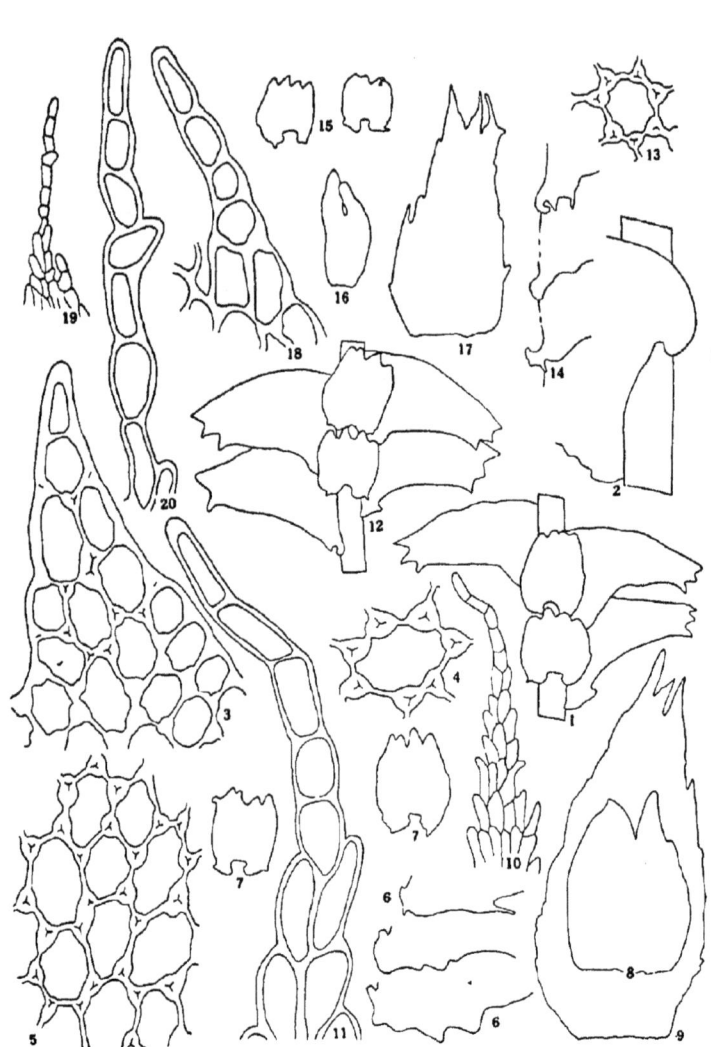

uncommon. The cell walls are thin, and in some leaves they are very conspicuous together with the small trigones, but in others (different plants of the same tuft), the trigones are much larger and many of them have become coalesced. There is so much variation in the ventral auricles of the leaves on any stem that no typical form can be distinguished. The ventral base is always dilated, but the dilation may be large or small, straight or undulate, with an entire margin or with one or two teeth, or several cilia of two or three cells

The underleaves also show a high degree of variation. They are always four-lobed or -toothed on the apical margins and are more or less auricled at the bases. The underleaves of well developed plants have auricles which are large but do not overlap. Some sort of tooth or appendage is usually developed near the base. On stems where the leaves and underleaves are only approximate or are distant, the basal auricles of the underleaves are smaller and are rounded-entire and show no indication of projections on the margins. They are usually four-lobed but may be only four-toothed.

The plants of the type material, from Mexico (FIG. 52, nos. 1-5), are robust, well developed, and show a wide range of variation both in the leaves and underleaves. The plants of *B. heteroclada,* collected by SPRUCE in Peru (FIG. 53, nos. 1-11), are very similar. Some of the teeth of the leaves are narrower and more acute, and there is more variation in the margins of the ventral auricles of the leaf (see FIG. 53, nos. 1 and 6), but these two characteristics are not constant, even on adjacent leaves.

SPRUCE has also described plants with similar characteristics from Brazil as *B. spinigera* (see FIG. 53, nos 12-20) The shape of the leaves is similar to that of the well developed forms of *M. teretiusculum;* the leaf cells are of approximately the same size and the cell walls are thin, but the trigones often tend to be somewhat larger in most plants. Here too, the ventral auricles exhibit a wide variety of forms on a single stem, but those with one or two cilia, two or three cells long, are more abundant, although auricles with blunt teeth or with rounded-entire margins are not uncommon. The underleaves also show much variation in the cordate bases. One or two teeth or cilia are usually well developed and occur on most of the auricles, although auricles with entire margins are frequent. The apical margins more often are divided into four teeth rather than four lobes as is the more usual condition in *B. heteroclada.*

Female branches were present in both *B. heteroclada* and *B.*

FIG. 54. — *Bazzania acanthostipa* Spruce — 1. Portion of a plant, ventral view, $\times$ 15 2 Portion of a leaf and stem, dorsal view, $\times$ 30 3 Ventral auricle of leaf on stem, $\times$ 30. 4. Tooth of a leaf, $\times$ 312. 5. A cell from the apical portion of a leaf, $\times$ 400. 6. Underleaf, $\times$ 30. 7 Female bract of the innermost series, $\times$ 30 8. A part of the perianth mouth, $\times$ 90 9. A portion of a lacinia of the perianth mouth, $\times$ 312. 10. Portion of a transverse section of a stem, $\times$ 312. Nos. 1-10 drawn from a portion of the type.

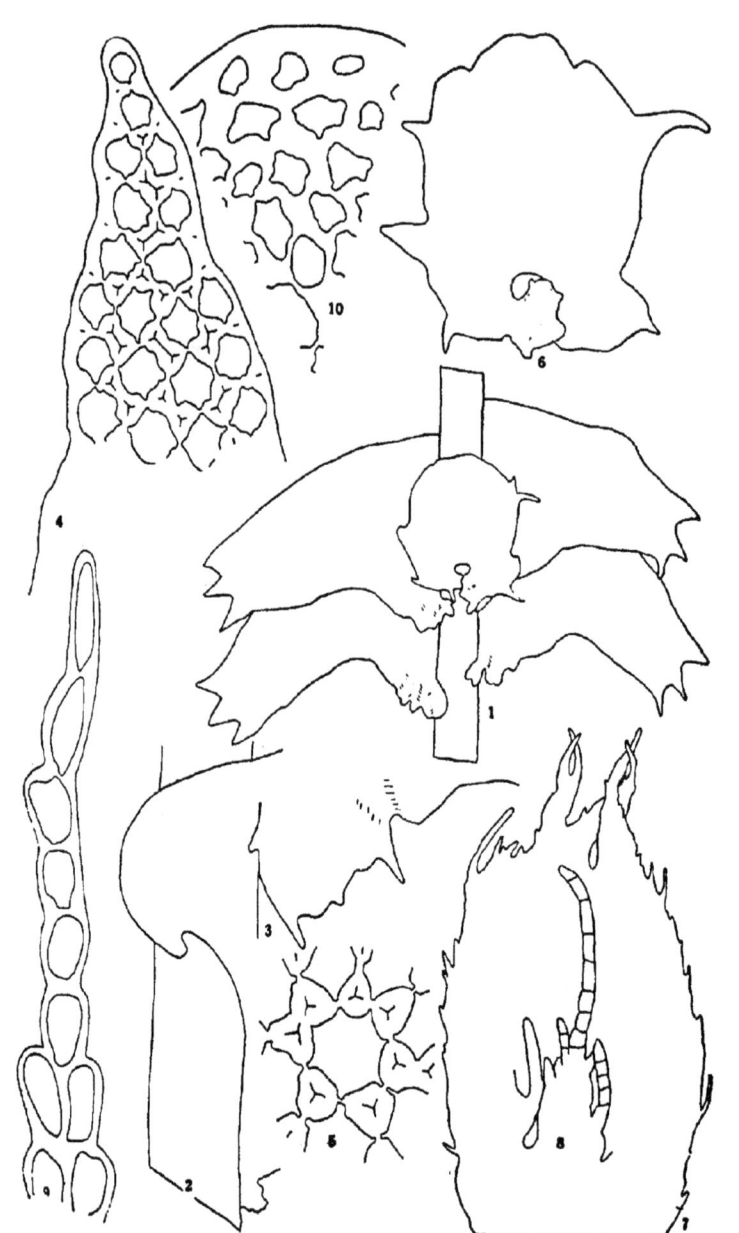

spinigera. The bracts were immature and the archegonia unfertilized. While a comparison of the two (FIG. 53, nos. 8-11 and 16-20), shows that there are minor variations, in general the two are very similar as to form, margin, type of laciniae and shape of the cells.

SPRUCE collected plants with similar characteristics on Mt. Campana, Peru, among Sphagnum, and distributed them as *B. humifusa* (see FIG. 52, nos. 6-9), in the *Hepaticae Spruceana.* Although the leaves exhibit a wide variation in outline, with the ventral auricles less well developed, and with only occasional short teeth on the basal auricles of the underleaves, the plants possess no distinctive characteristics not present in the forms described above. The four lobes of the underleaves are always well developed. The cell walls are thin but the trigones are conspicuous. All of the features of the plants indicate that they grew under very moist or wet conditions of habitat.

In the Herbier Boissier at Geneva there is a collection made by SPRUCE in 1885 on Mt. Campana, Peru, filed under *M. teretiusculum,* but on the packet in SPRUCE's handwriting is the name *B. otites* R. S. n. sp. The plants are large, green and well developed but sterile, and exhibit on one part or another, all of the characteristics of *M. teretiusculum* (see FIG 52, nos. 10-11). Most of the underleaves are definitely four-lobed and some of them have in addition, a large lateral tooth. The basal auricles are well developed and occasionally appendages in the form of cilia occur.

B. teretiuscula of SPRUCE (1885, 375), is *B. longistipula.*

The plants collected by STANDLEY in Costa Rica and distributed as *B. conchophylla* Herzog, also belong to this species (see FIG. 52, nos. 12-13). They are lighter in color than many of the South American plants, but the leaves and underleaves have all of the characteristics of *M. teretiusculum.*

M. incisostipulum Stephani collected by HERZOG in Bolivia also belongs here. The plants are robust, greenish or yellow-brown, and the underleaves are typically conspicuously four-lobed.

The species can be distinguished from those preceding by the deeply four-lobed or -toothed apical portions of the underleaves and the well developed ventral auricles of the leaves.

DISTRIBUTION: M e x i c o : Vera Cruz, Hacienda de Mirador, Liebmann, the type (G). — C o s t a R i c a : La Estrella, Standley 39426 (W); San José, Standley 41629 (W); Cartago, Standley 50, 884 (W) — B r a z i l : Rio Taruma at the Rio Negro, Spruce, Hepat Spruc , the type of *B spinigera* (NY). — B o l i v i a : Comarapa, Herzog, the type of *M. incisostipulum* (L). — C o l o m b i a : Bogotá, Apollinaire, cited by Stephani (1909, 520). — E c u a d o r · Quito, Cuming, cited by Stephani (1909, 520). — P e r u : Mt. Guayrapurina, Spruce, Hepat. Spruc., the type of *B heteroclada* (NY); Mt. Campana, Spruce, Hepat Spruc., the type of *B. humifusa* (NY); Mt Campana, Spruce, under *M. teretiusculum* and *B. otites* Sp. (G); Rio Huallaga, Ule, cited by Stephani (1904, 225).

REFERENCES: Lindenberg & Gottsche (1851, 85. pl. 20); Gottsche (1863, 182); Stephani (1909, 522, 520; *Icones, Mastigobryum* nos. 166, 310, 387, 402); Herzog (1938, 11).

41. **Bazzania acanthostipa** Spruce, Trans. & Proc. Bot. Soc. [Edinburgh] 15: 381. 1885.

Mastigobryum acanthostipum Stephani, Spec. Hep. 8: 499. 1908.

Plants large, in deep tufts, light brown, greenish in the younger portions: stems robust, to 14 cm. in length, with leaves to 5 mm. broad; in longitudinal section the cells mostly 0.17 mm. long, the cortical shorter, both averaging 18μ in diameter, the vertical walls strongly thickened and containing frequent pits, the end walls thin, walls of the cortical layer deeply pigmented; lateral branches occasional, diverging at a wide angle; flagelliform branches frequent, long: rhizoids colorless, present on the leaves of the flagelliform branches: the line of leaf insertion curved in its upper half, the dorsal end recurved forming a hook; leaves densely imbricated, deflexed when dry, unsymmetrically ovate, falcate, 2.5 mm. - 3.5 mm. long, 2 mm. broad at the base, narrowed to the mostly transversely truncate, more or less equally tridentate apex; the dorsal margin arched from a cordate base, extending across the stem and beyond, the ventral margin strongly concave, the base conspicuously auricled, the dilation very large, undulate, lobed, toothed, often appendiculate; the apex deeply three-toothed, the teeth spreading, long, broadly triangular, acute, eight to fifteen cells long, four to six cells broad at the base, the sinuses deep, lunulate, the margins entire, repand; the cell lumina stellate, the trigones very large, with convex sides, the cell walls thin but obscured by the enlarged trigones, the cuticle faintly verruculose; cells of the apical portion and dorsal base averaging 20μ × 20μ, those of the basal portion 48μ - 64μ × 24μ, a vitta not differentiated: underleaves imbricated, subquadrate, attached in a recurved line, broader than the stem, averaging 1.2 mm. long and broad, the base cordate, auriculate, the auricles very large, overlapping, undulate, serrate, lobed, toothed, or appendiculate, the lateral margins coarsely toothed or lobed, and with one or more broad to narrow, apiculate, widely spreading teeth, the apical margin convex, undulate, sometimes four-lobed, the cells and trigones as in the leaf; leaves of the flagelliform branches plane, ovate, to 0.22 mm. long, acute to shortly bifid: female branches occasional, solitary, one to several on a stem; the bracts and bracteoles similar, ovate; the outermost series short, bifid; the intermediate series larger, to one-third divided into usually three, ciliate laciniae, the lateral margins ciliate; the innermost series to 2.2 mm. long, one-fourth divided into three ciliate and serrate laciniae, the cells to 64μ long, with thickened walls, the lateral margins serrate to long-ciliate · perianth to 6 mm. long, the mouth ciliate laciniate, the cells averaging 32μ long, thick-walled: male branches not seen.

HABITAT: In deep ascending tufts, on rocks in moist places in the mountains.

The distinguishing characteristics of the species are its large size and light brown color; the falcate leaves, with large, spreading teeth, stellate cell cavities, with very large, nearly round trigones, and very large, undulate, lobed, often appendiculate, ventral auricles; and the very large, subquadrate, cordate underleaves, with large basal auricles similar to those of the leaves, and one or more large, widely spreading, usually long apiculate, lateral teeth. (FIG. 54, nos. 1-10).

The species is distinct from all other members of the *Appendiculatae* because of its size, the very large teeth of the leaves, and the long, pointed teeth of the lateral margins of the underleaves.

DISTRIBUTION. C o l o m b i a · without locality, A Wallace (NY). — B o l i v i a · Mapiri, Rusby 3027 p.p. (NY). — P e r u : Mt. Campana, Spruce, Hepat. Spruc., the type (NY)

REFERENCES. Stephani (*Icones, Mastigobryum* no. 305)

42. Bazzania canelensis (Steph.) comb nov.

Mastigobryum canelense Stephani, Spec. Hep. 3· 518 1909.
Bazzania vincentina var *submutica* Spruce, Trans. & Proc. Bot. Soc. [Edinburgh] 15. 378 1885
Bazzania vincentina var. *subedentata* Spruce ms , Hepat Spruc.

Plants large, in deep tufts, olive-green to yellow-brown, becoming more deeply pigmented in the older portions: stems large, to 10 cm. or more in length, with leaves to 5 mm broad, ascending to erect; stem cells in longitudinal section to 0.25 mm. long, the cortical shorter, both averaging 18μ in diameter, the vertical walls uniformly thickened and containing frequent pits, the end walls thin; lateral branches rare, diverging at a wide angle; flagelliform branches frequent, short; rhizoids very abundant, on the leaves of the flagelliform branches: the line of leaf insertion curved in its upper part, the dorsal end recurved forming a prominent hook; leaves approximate to imbricated, plane, becoming a little deflexed when dry, unsymmetrically ovate to oblong, straight, 2.5 mm. - 3 mm. long, 1.5 mm. broad at the base, narrowed a little to the broadly rounded to faintly tridentate apex; the dorsal margin strongly arched from a cordate base, extending across the stem and somewhat beyond, the ventral margin straight, the base dilated, the auricle large, undulate, sometimes lobed, the margin entire to serrulate, the apex broad, rounded or undulate to three-lobed or -toothed, the lobes or teeth broad, short, the sinuses broad, lunulate, the margins entire; leaf cells thin-walled, the cell lumina angular-rounded, the trigones conspicuous, sometimes becoming coalesced, the cuticle smooth to faintly verruculose; cells of the apical region and dorsal lobe averaging 16μ - 20μ, those of the interior larger, those of the base to 60μ × 20μ, a vitta not differentiated; underleaves approximate to imbricated, subquadrate in outline, attached in a recurved line, broader than the stem, 1.5 mm. - 2 mm. long, 1.5 mm. broad, the base strongly cordate, the auricles large, overlapping or nearly so, the margins entire, undulate, the lateral margins convex, the apical margins rounded, undulate, slime papillae present in the depressions, the cells as in the apical portion of the leaves: leaves of the flagelliform branches scale-like, ovate, acute to shortly bifid: sexual branches and perianths not seen.

HABITAT: On tree trunks and branches, forests.

The distinguishing characteristics of the species are its large

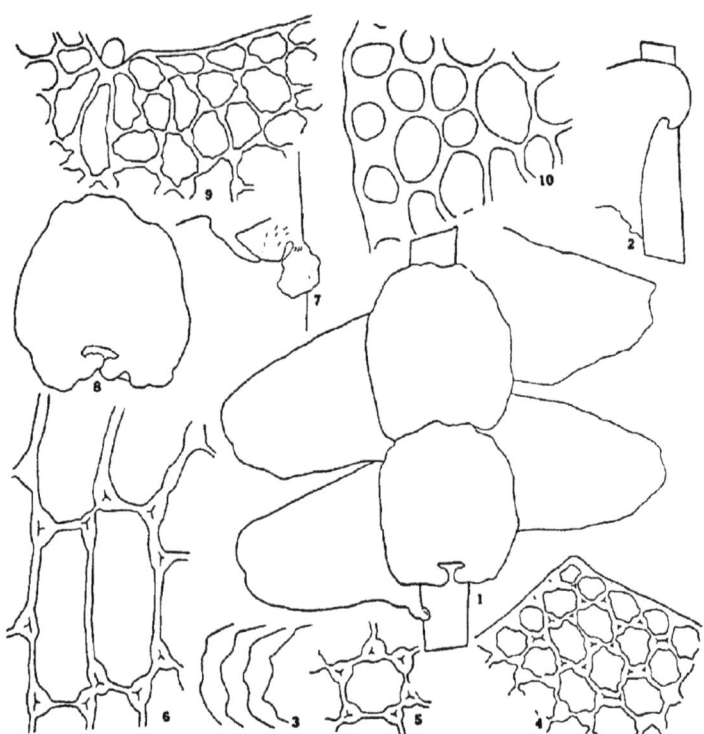

FIG 55 — *Bazzania canelensis* (Steph.) Fulford — 1 Portion of a plant,
ventral view, × 15 2 Portion of a leaf and stem, dorsal view, × 15. 3 Leaf
apices, × 15   4 Tooth of a leaf, × 310. 5. A cell from the apical portion of
a leaf, × 400. 6. Cells from the basal portion of a leaf, × 310 7. Ventral
base of a leaf with appendage, × 30. 8. Underleaf, × 15. 9. Portion of the
apical margin of an underleaf, × 310. 10. Portion of a cross section of a
stem, × 310. Nos 1-10 drawn from plants of the type of *B. subedentata*
Spruce, from Canelos, Ecuador.

size and pale brownish green color; the large leaves with rounded-entire to faintly three-lobed or -toothed apices, large, undulate, entire to crenulate ventral auricles, and thin-walled cells with angular-rounded cell lumina and conspicuous trigones; and the large, subquadrate, auriculate underleaves with entire, repand to undulate margins. (FIG. 55, nos. 1-10).

While the type plants of *B. vincentina* var. *submutica* Spruce, collected by SPRUCE at Canelos have not been available for study, his description of the variety agrees in detail with the plants which he distributed under the manuscript name *B. vincentina* var. *subedentata* in the *Hepaticae Spruceana*. In addition, STEPHANI described the species *M. canelense* from material collected by SPRUCE from the same locality and lists *B. vincentina* var. *submutica* as a synonym. The plants of *M. canelense* in the STEPHANI Collection at Harvard are identical with those distributed by SPRUCE as *B. vincentina* var. *subedentata*. It would seem that the two varieties and the species named above are all based on plants from the same collection.

The species is distinct from all other members of the *Appendiculatae* because of its large size, the entire or obscurely three-toothed leaf apices, and the large underleaves with more or less entire margins.

DISTRIBUTION. E c u a d o r : Canelos, Spruce, Hepat. Spruc., the type of *B. vincentina* var. *subedentata* (NY); the same, the type of *M. canelense* (H); the same, the type of *B. vincentina* var. *submutica*, cited by Spruce.

REFERENCES Stephani (*Icones, Mastigobryum* no. 379).

Section 5. Vittatae

The species of this Section have three-toothed leaves in which a vitta is conspicuously developed. The vitta is made up of several rows of cells which are elongate in outline, thin-walled, and with conspicuous trigones, and it extends from the base of the leaf to beyond the middle.

Key to the Species

1 Plants with underleaves chlorophyllose throughout; the margins variously lobed or toothed . . . . 43 **B. Spruceana** (p. 155)
1. Plants with the underleaves hyaline at least in the upper part; more or less regularly four-toothed, the lateral margins entire.
 2 Cuticle of the leaves and underleaves abundantly minutely punctuate; underleaves hyaline throughout . . . . 44. **B. Tayloriana** (p 157)
 2 Cuticle of the leaves and underleaves smooth to verruculose; underleaves chlorophyllose in the lower part.
  3 Underleaves to one-half divided into four, equal, narrow teeth or lobes; medium size . . . . 45. **B. convexa** (p. 159)
  3 Underleaves very large, often four-toothed or -lobed in the upper part . . . . 46. **B. Stephani** (p. 162)

43. Bazzania Spruceana Stephani, Hedwigia 32: 213. 1893.

Mastigobryum Spruceanum Stephani, Spec Hep. 3: 469. 1908.

Plants small, brownish green becoming deeply pigmented with brown in the older portions: stems slender, 3 cm. or more long, with leaves to 2 mm. broad: lateral branches frequent, 2 mm. or more apart, diverging at a wide angle; flagelliform branches occasional; rhizoids colorless, present on the bases of some of the underleaves: the line of leaf insertion curved in the upper part; the leaves vittate, imbricated, plane, unsymmetrically ovate, ascendent, 0.7 mm. - 0.9 mm. long, 0.4 mm. broad at the base, narrowed a little to the mostly transversely truncate, tridentate apex; the dorsal margin convex from a straight base, covering one-half the stem, the ventral margin straight, the base scarcely dilated, the apex mostly equally three-toothed, the teeth small, acute, spreading, two to five cells long, two to six cells broad at the base; the sinuses shallow, lunulate, the margins entire: the leaf cells round-quadrate in outline, the walls uniformly thickened, the cell lumina rounded, trigones inconspicuous or absent, the cuticle very strongly verruculose; the cells of the apical region 16µ - 22µ in diameter, those of the median portion larger, and those of the base to 48µ × 24µ, forming a distinct vitta of three or four rows of cells extending beyond the middle of the leaf: underleaves distant to imbricated, subquadrate in outline, attached in a straight line, a little broader than the stem, mostly 0.35µ long and broad, the lateral margins slightly convex, entire or occasionally with a tooth, the apex entire, crenate, undulate or two- to four-lobed, the cells

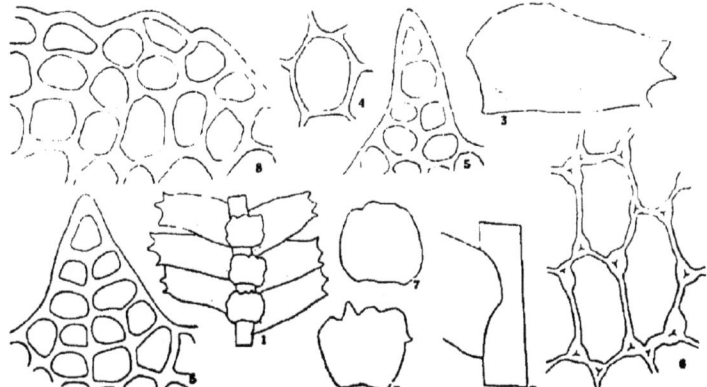

Fɪɢ. 56 — *Bazzania Spruceana* Stephani. — 1 Portion of a plant, ventral view, × 15. 2. Portion of a leaf and stem, dorsal view, × 30 3 A leaf, × 30. 4 A cell from the apical portion of a leaf, × 400 5. Teeth from a leaf, × 310. 6. Cells of the vitta near the base of a leaf, × 310. 7. Underleaves 8 Cells from the apical portion of an underleaf, × 400. Nos. 1-8 drawn from a portion of the type material.

as in the leaf: leaves of the flagelliform branches scale-like, ovate: sexual branches not seen.

HABITAT: Not given.

The distinguishing characteristics of the species are its small size; the plane, ascendent leaves with three small, sharp teeth at the apex, cells with equally thickened walls, and a distinct vitta; and the small, subquadrate underleaves with variously lobed margins. The cuticle is coarsely verruculose. (FIG. 56, nos. 1-8).

DISTRIBUTION· P e r u · Mt Guayrapurina, Spruce, the type (H).

REFERENCE. Stephani (Icones, Mastigobryum no. 177)

44. Bazzania Tayloriana (Mitten) comb. nov.

Mastigobryum Taylorianum Mitten, in Hooker, Bot. Ant Voy. 2¹. Fl. N. Zel. 147. pl. C, fig. 5. 1854

Plants small, growing in depressed mats, pale, glaucous green, becoming deeply pigmented with brown in the older portions: stems slender, delicate, to 3 cm. or more in length, with leaves mostly 1.5 mm broad, prostrate; stems cells in longitudinal section elongate, the vertical walls uniformly thickened and containing frequent pits, the end walls thin; lateral branches occasional, diverging at a wide angle, the ventral branches frequent, usually leafy; rhizoids not seen: the line of leaf insertion little curved in its upper part; the leaves approximate to subimbricated, vittate, spreading, plane, becoming somewhat deflexed beyond the middle, unsymmetrically oblong-ovate, 0.7 mm. - 1.0 mm. long, mostly 0.5 mm. broad at the base, little narrowed to the transversely truncate, conspicuously tridentate apex; the dorsal margin convex from a straight base which covers less than one-third the stem, the ventral margin nearly straight, the base scarcely dilated, the apex tridentate, the teeth large, spreading, eight to ten cells long, four to six cells broad at the base, the sinuses deep, acute to rounded, the margins entire; the leaf cells quadrate in outline, uniformly thick-walled, the cell lumina rounded, a vitta of three or four rows of enlarged cells with conspicuous trigones clearly differentiated, the cuticle very abundantly minutely punctate; cells of the apical portion and dorsal base mostly $16\mu \times 16\mu$, of the vitta, to $32\mu \times 24\mu$, the walls thin, trigones conspicuous: underleaves distant, hyaline throughout, attached in a straight line, subrectangular in outline, broader than the stem above, 0 22 mm - 0 35 mm. long, to 0.28 mm. broad above, the lateral margins nearly straight from a straight base, one-fourth to one-half divided into usually four equal, blunt teeth four to ten cells long, two to four cells broad, the sinuses acute, the margins entire; the cells quadrate to rectangular in outline, hyaline, the walls uniform, the cuticle abundantly minutely punctate as in the leaves sexual branches not seen.

HABITAT: On soil among other bryophytes.

The distinguishing characteristics of the species are its small size and glaucous to brownish green color; the strongly three-toothed leaves with small, quadrate leaf cells, and a well marked

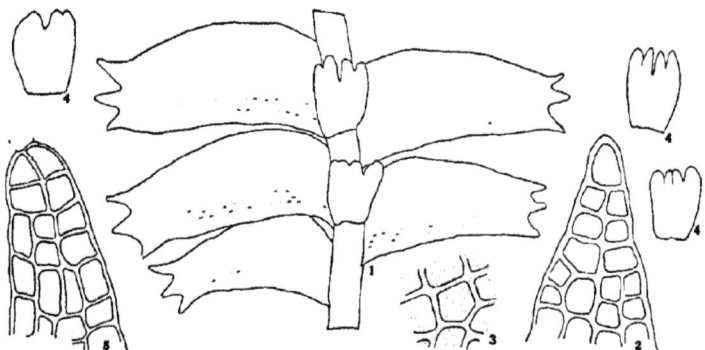

FIG 57. — *Bazzania Tayloriana* (Mitten) Fulford — 1. Portion of plant, ventral view, × 30. 2. A tooth of a leaf, × 310. 3. A cell from the apical portion of a leaf, × 400. 4. Underleaves, × 30 5. A tooth of an underleaf, × 310 The drawings are from the type material.

vitta; the hyaline, two- or four-parted elongate underleaves; and a very abundantly and minutely punctate cuticle. (FIG. 57, nos. 1-5).

B. Tayloraniana can readily be separated from all of the other South American species because of the abundantly minutely punctate cuticle of the leaves and underleaves.

DISTRIBUTION: C o l o m b i a : Bogotá, 4000', Weir (NY). — N e w Z e a l a n d : North Island, Zotov (NY); North Island, Colenso, the type (NY); also Colenso 223, 1218 (NY); North Island, Sinclair (NY); Kaipara ?, Mossman 760d (NY); without locality, Hooker, Knight, Kirk, cited by Stephani. — S a m o a : without locality, Rechinger, cited by Stephani.

REFERENCES: Hooker (1867, 524); Stephani (1909, 533; *Icones, Masti-gobryum* no. 465).

45. **Bazzania convexa** (Thunb.) Trevis. Mem. Ist. Lomb. 13: 414. 1877.

Jungermannia convexa Thunberg, Prod. Pl. Cap. 173. 1794.
Jungermannia nitida Weber, Prodromus 43. 1815.
Mastigobryum convexum Lindenberg, in G L. & N., Syn. Hep. 215. 1845.
Mastigobryum Richardianum Mitten, in Hooker, Bot. Ant. Voy. 2³. Fl N. Zel. 147. 1854.
Mastigobryum heterostipum Stephani, Spec. Hep. 3: 532. 1909.

Plants scattered, or growing in depressed mats, pale, yellow-green · stems very slender, to 3 cm. or more in length, with leaves to 1.5 mm. broad, prostrate; lateral branches few, diverging at a wide angle, ventral branches frequent, usually leafy, sometimes flagelliform: rhizoids frequent on the bases of the leaves of the flagelliform branches: the line of leaf insertion little curved in its upper part; the leaves vittate, spreading, approximate to subimbricated, nearly straight, the teeth and a little of the apical portion deflexed, unsymmetrically oblong-ovate, 0.7 mm. - 0.9 mm. long, mostly 0.35 mm. broad at the base, narrowed a little to the transversely truncate, mostly obscurely tridentate, decurved apex; the dorsal margin convex from a straight base which covers less than one-half the stem, the ventral margin nearly straight, the base scarcely dilated, the apex obscurely tridentate, the teeth triangular, one or two cells long and wide, the sinuses lunulate, the margins entire; the leaf cells quadrate to rectangular in outline with uniformly thickened walls, the cell lumina rounded, the vitta of three or four rows of enlarged cells clearly differentiated; the cuticle verruculose; cells of the apical portion, margins and dorsal base averaging $16\mu \times 16\mu$, those of the vitta to $32\mu \times 24\mu$, the walls thin, the trigones conspicuous: underleaves distant, hyaline above, attached in a straight line, subquadrate in outline, averaging 0.28 mm. $\times$ 0.28 mm., mostly one-third divided into four equal, acute teeth, the teeth mostly five cells long, to four cells broad at the base, the sinuses acute, the margins entire; cells of two sorts, the chlorophyllose cells restricted to a small, interior, basal area, similar to those of the margins of the leaf, the hyaline cells larger, more or less rectangular in outline, averaging 18μ - 22μ long and wide, the walls uniformly thickened: leaves of the flagelliform branches, ovate, scale-like: sexual branches not seen.

HABITAT: On soil, among rocks, mixed with other bryophytes. The distinguishing characteristics of the species are its small size and yellowish green color, the straight, obscurely tridentate leaves with slightly decurved tips and distinct vittas; and the equally four-toothed underleaves which are hyaline except for a small area at the base. (FIG. 58, nos. 1-17)

The plants are always small and on well developed stems the leaf apices are shortly three-toothed (FIG 58, no. 6), with the teeth and a portion of the leaf decurved. This characteristic is not always present however, for in many examples the leaves may be entirely plane and rounded-entire, or very slightly three-lobed. Some leaves of the more typical form can usually be found on any stem more than 1 cm. in length.

Very often stems with normally developed leaves suddenly become flagelliform for a distance and then produce ordinary leaves again The ventral branches are usually flagelliform but leafy branches are not uncommon.

The underleaves are extremely variable. Usually they are one-third to one-half divided into four acute teeth but very often the teeth do not develop in the ordinary way or the cells of the upper part soon disappear, for many of the underleaves are only bluntly four-lobed. The cells of the chlorophyllose area, in the basal part of the underleaf, are similar to the cells of the apical portion of the leaf. The hyaline cells are usually rectangular in outline, more or less regularly arranged in rows, and have uniformly thickened walls (see FIG. 58, nos. 4, 5 and 17). This is particularly true of the plants of South Africa and Australia. However, one often finds, growing in the same patches with the plants bearing underleaves of the sort described, similar plants in which the cells of the underleaves are more irregularly arranged, are slightly larger, and for the most part, have thin walls, although some of the walls may be thick (see FIG. 58, no. 14). Most of the plants of the type of *M. Richardianum* have this latter sort of underleaves. FIG. 58, no. 5 shows a tooth with large cells but with thick walls. Plants with underleaves which have the larger, irregularly arranged, thin-walled cells can likewise be found in the African material. Since this combination of characters is not entirely constant in any mat of plants they do not seem of sufficient significance to serve as a

---

FIG. 58 — *Bazzania convexa* (Thunb) Trevis. — 1 Portion of plant, ventral view, × 30. 2 A cell from the apical portion of a leaf, × 400 3. An underleaf, showing the hyaline part, × 30 4-5 A tooth of an underleaf, × 310 6 Portion of a plant, ventral view, × 30 7. Portion of a stem and leaf, dorsal view, × 30 8. Apices of leaves, × 30 9. A leaf, × 30 10. A cell from the apical portion of a leaf, × 400 11. An apical tooth, × 310. 12. Cells of the vitta, × 310. 13. Underleaf, showing the hyaline portion, × 30. 14 Two teeth of an underleaf, × 310 15 Portion of a plant, ventral view, × 30. 16 Underleaf showing the hyaline part, × 30 17. A tooth of an underleaf, × 310 Nos. 1-4 drawn from the type of *J. convexa* from the Cape of Good Hope, 5 from *J convexa* of Lindenberg from Peru, 6-14 from the type of *M. Richardianum* from the Straits of Magellan, 15-17 from the type (?) of *M heterostipum* from Brazil.

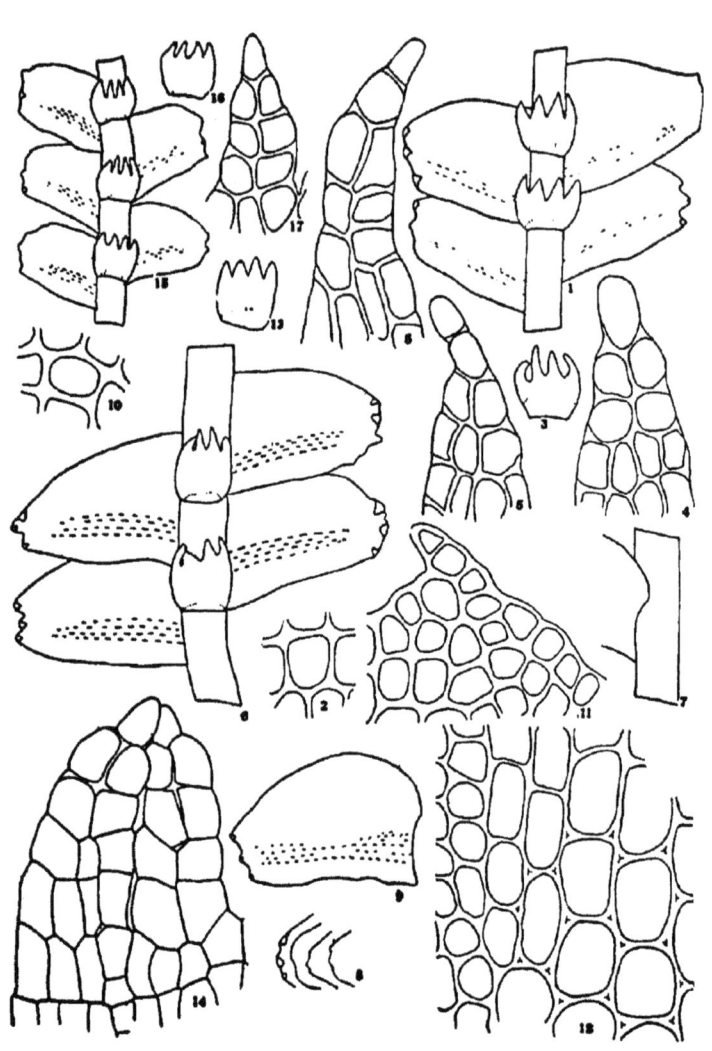

basis on which to establish a separate species. Although the type plants of *M. Richardianum* collected in the Straits of Magellan had underleaves with the hyaline cells larger and more or less irregularly arranged, the other South American material showed a whole series of variation in size and the arrangement of these cells.

Plants collected by ULE in Brazil, in the STEPHANI Herbarium at Harvard University under the name of *M. heterostipum* (FIG. 58, nos. 15-17), have been taken as the type of that species. STEPHANI (1909, 532) gives as the habitat "America tropica et subtropica, haud rara", and does not mention a collector's name. The underleaves of most of these plants have the teeth well developed, the cells mostly of the smaller size and with thickened walls. The other variation can also be found.

DISTRIBUTION. B r a z i l : without locality, Ule, the type (?) of *M. heterostipum* (H); Organ Mountains, Gardner (NY). — P e r u : without locality, "Hb. Dr. Gottsche", a part of the material referred to by Lindenberg (G. L. & N. p. 215), (NY, H); Tatanara, Lechler (NY); without locality, Jameson (NY). — C h i l e : Chiloé Island, Captain King (NY). — P a t a g o n i a : Albert Bay, Dr. Coppinger (NY); Straits of Magellan, Richard, the type of *M. Richardianum* (NY). — Also Central Africa, South Africa and Australia. The original material of *J convexa* was collected at the Cape of Good Hope by C. P. THUNBERG.

REFERENCES: Hooker (1867, 524); Lehmann (1829, 364); Mitten (1855, 147); Schwaegrichen (1814, 22); Sprengel (1827, 225); Stephani (1909, 532, 534; *Icones, Mastigobryum* nos. 439, 443, 444).

46. Bazzania Stephani (Jack) comb. nov.

Mastigobryum Stephani Jack, in Stephani, Hedw. 25: 235. pl. 1, fig. 10-12. 1886.

Plants scattered among mosses, pale yellow-green to brownish: stems very slender, to 3 cm. in length, with leaves to 1.5 mm. broad, prostrate; the lateral branches occasional, diverging at a wide angle, ventral branches frequent, usually leafy: rhizoids occasional from the bases of the underleaves of ventral branches: the line of leaf insertion little curved in its upper part; the leaves vittate, approximate to subimbricated, spreading, plane, the teeth and a little of the apical portion often deflexed, unsymmetrically oblong-ovate, 0.7 mm. - 0.9 mm. long, mostly 0.35 mm. broad at the base, narrowed a little to the transversely truncate, obscurely tridentate apex; the dorsal margin convex from a straight base, covering one-third the stem, the ventral margin nearly straight, the base scarcely dilated, the apex obscurely three-toothed or -lobed, the teeth one or two cells high, two to four cells broad at the base, the sinuses lunulate, the margins entire; the leaf cells quadrate to rectangular in outline, with uniformly thickened walls, the cell lumina rounded, the vitta of three or four rows of enlarged cells clearly differentiated, the cuticle verruculose; cells of the apical portions and dorsal base averaging $16\mu \times 16\mu$, those of the vitta to $32\mu \times 24\mu$, the walls thin, the trigones conspicuous: the underleaves large, approximate to imbricated, hyaline above, attached in a straight line, rectangular in outline, averaging 0.35 mm. - 0.42

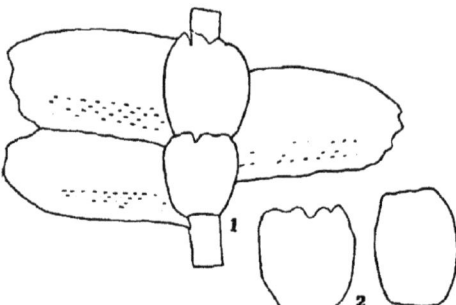

Fig. 59 — *Bazzania Stephani* (Jack) Fulford. — 1. Portion of plant, ventral view, × 30   2. Underleaves.   Nos. 1-2 drawn from plants of Burchell, Cat. Geog. Pl. Brasil. Trop. No. 3847.

mm. long × 0.28 mm. wide, the apex undulate, two- to four-lobed or -toothed, the lateral margins entire, the chlorophyllose cells restricted to a small, interior, basal area, the cells all quadrate to rectangular in outline, the walls uniformly thickened: sexual branches not seen.

HABITAT: Over rocks and soil with other bryophytes.

The distinguishing characteristics of the species are its small size, the yellow-green color, the plane, obscurely tridentate, vittate leaves, and the large, elongate underleaves, often two- or four-lobed or -toothed at the apex, and hyaline to near the base. The cuticle is verruculose. (FIG. 59, nos. 1-2).

The plants are very similar to *B. convexa*. The leaves of the two species are identical. However, the underleaves of *B. convexa* are medium size and to one-half divided into four slender teeth, while those of *B. Stephani* are very large and divided to one-fifth or less into two or four lobes which are often obscure. Both species have the chlorophyllose cells of the underleaves restricted to a small basal area.

DISTRIBUTION: B r a z i l : without locality, Burchell, Cat. Geog. Pl. Brasil. Trop. 3847 (NY) The original material was collected on Johanna Island of the Comoro group in the Indian Ocean.

REFERENCES: Stephani (1909, 535; *Icones, Mastigobryum* no. 441).

EXCLUDED SPECIES

Mastigobryum mutans Herzog, n. sp. Repert Spec. Novarum Regni Veg. 21. 26. pl. XI, fig. 2, 1925, Brazil, belongs to some other genus (*Isotachis ?*).

SPECIES NOT AVAILABLE FOR THIS STUDY

Because of the unsettled world conditions and the war, it has been impossible to borrow some of the type material of South American species from the European Herbaria. A study of these species and varieties will no doubt reveal many synonyms among them. The species and varieties not included are as follows:-

Bazzania adnexa (L et L.) Trevis. reported from Chile by HERZOG. Arch. Esc. Farm. Fac Cien. Méd. Córdoba 1938. No. 7. p. 26. 1938.

Mastigobryum arcuatum Lindenberg & Gottsche, in G. L. & N., Syn. Hep. 718. 1847 Mexico.

Mastigobryum azuayense Stephani, Spec Hep. 6: 454. 1924. Ecuador.

Bazzania bidens var. heterodonta Spruce, Trans. & Proc. Bot. Soc. [Edinburgh] 15: 372. 1885. Peru.

Mastigobryum bogotense Stephani, Hedwigia 24· 246. 1885. Colombia.

Mastigobryum brasiliense Gottsche & Lindenberg, in G. L. & N., Syn. Hep. 227. 1845. Brazil.

Mastigobryum Breutelianum var. guadeloupense Bescherelle, Jour Bot. 7. 187. 1893. Guadeloupe. (nomen nudum).

Mastigobryum Burchellii Stephani, Spec. Hep. 3. 509. 1908. Magellan Straits.

Mastigobryum cerinum Stephani, Spec. Hep. 3: 457. 1908.

Mastigobryum columbicum Stephani, Spec. Hep. 6. 458 1924. Colombia.

Mastigobryum creberrimum Stephani, K Svenska Vetensk. Handl. 46: no. 9. 60. 1911.

Mastigobryum decurrens Stephani, Bibliotheca Bot. 87· 223. 1916. Bolivia.

Mastigobryum ecuadorense Stephani, Spec. Hep 6: 461. 1924.

Mastigobryum heterophyllum Stephani, Spec Hep. 6: 466. 1924. Ecuador.

Bazzania humifusa var. olivacea Spruce, Trans. & Proc. Bot. Soc. [Edinburgh] 15 380 1885. Peru.

Mastigobryum portoricense var. laxa Bescherelle, Jour. Bot. 7: 186. 1893. Guadeloupe (nomen nudum).

Mastigobryum Schlimianum Gottsche, Ann. Sci. Nat. V. Bot. 1. 140. 1864. Colombia. (The portion of the type in the Farlow Herbarium is too fragmentary for determination.)

Herpetium scutigerum Montagne, Ann. Sci. Nat. II. Bot. 9: 44. 1838. Peru.

Mastigobryum venezuelanum Molkb ms. in Sande Lacoste, Syn. Hep. Javan. 104. 1857 Venezuela.

Mastigobryum venezuelanum Stephani, Spec. Hep. 3: 530. 1909. Venezuela. (Fendler.)

Bazzania vincentina var macrophylla Spruce, Trans. & Proc. Bot. Soc. [Edinburgh] 15: 378. 1885. Ecuador.

DISTRIBUTION

Few accurate statements concerning the distribution of the species of *Bazzania* can be made at this time, since our present knowledge of the occurrence of the plants represents a "distribution of collectors", and unfortunately few adequate collections have been made in most areas.

The *Bidentatae* group seems to be restricted to the West Indies and northern South America. *Bazzania Herminieri* and perhaps *B. platystipula* may be endemic to the West Indies, and *B. roraimensis* seems to be limited to Mt. Roraima in British Guiana. The other species are rather widely distributed within the area, with *B. gracilis* most abundant.

Most of the members of the *Grandistipulae* Section occur throughout the West Indies, often in Mexico and Central America, and are abundant in tropical South America. Among the most frequently collected species may be mentioned *B. stolonifera, B. Breuteliana, B. jamaicensis* and *B. longistipula.* At the present time *B. pallide-virens, B. Glaziovii* and *B. tricuspidata* are known only from restricted areas in South America and may be localized endemics. *B. longa* is very abundant throughout the West Indies but no specimens from Mexico, Central, or South America have come to light.

The *Connatae* Section contains three distinct geographic segregates; the one, made up of *B. Schwaneckiana, B. pycnophylla, B. Eggersiana, B. armatistipula* and *B. cubensis,* in which the leaf apices are serrate and the underleaf is connate with one leaf by only a few cells, is restricted to the West Indies, with some of the species further limited in their distribution to one or two of the islands; another, *B. Fendleri,* in which the underleaf is also connate with only one leaf but differing from the above group in habit, color, cells, etc., occurs in Brazil, Ecuador, and Venezuela; and the third, including *B. peruviana, B. Skottsbergii* and related species, in which the underleaf is connate with a pair of leaves, occurs south of the equator from Peru south to the Straits of Magellan. The species of this latter group show close relationships with species from South Africa and New Zealand, and in some instances may even be identical.

The *Appendiculatae* Section is made up of a group of closely related species which are most abundant in tropical and subtropical South America. *B. teretiuscula* is also abundant in Central America and Mexico; *B. asperistipula* seems to be restricted to northern South America and Central America; *B. falcata* and *B. Hookeri* in addition to a widespread distribution in South America occur also in the West Indies; *B. robusta* and *B. acanthostipa* are fairly abundant but restricted to South America; and *B. canelensis* seems to be an endemic of the mountains of Ecuador.

Three of the four members of the *Vittatae* Section are known to occur also in Africa, New Zealand or Australia. *B. Tayloriana* occurs in Colombia and New Zealand; *B. Stephani* in Brazil and Johanna Island of the Comoro group off the coast of Africa; and *B. convexa,* from Brazil, Peru, Chile and Patagonia, is also abundant in central and southern Africa, New Zealand and Australia. *B. Spruceana* seems to occur only in Peru.

LITERATURE

BESCHERELLE, E. et MASSALONGO, C. 1889 1. Hépatiques. Mission Scientifique du Cap Horn. 1882-1883. V. Botanique. 201-252. pl. 1-5. *Paris.*

BESCHERELLE, E. 1893 Énumération des Hépatiques connues jusqu'ici aux Antilles françaises (Guadeloupe et Martinique). *Journal de Botanique* 7: 174-180; 183-194.

BOSWELL, HENRY. 1887 Jamaica Mosses and Hepaticae. *Journal of Botany* 25: 45-50.

BUCH, H. 1928. Die Scapanien Nordeuropas und Sibериens, 2. *Soc. Sci. Fenn. Commentationes Biol.* 3: 5. 1928.

—— ——. 1929. Eine neue moossystematische Methodik nebst einigen ihrer Resultate und ein neues Nomenklatursystem. *Skand. Naturforskermode* 18. 225-229.

COOKE, C M. Jr. 1904. The Hawaiian Hepaticae of the tribe *Trigonantheae.* *Transactions of the Connecticut Academy of Arts and Sciences* 12: 1-44. 15 pl.

DUMORTIER, B. C 1831. Sylloge Jungermannidearum Europae indigenarum, earum genera et species systematice complectens. 1-100. pl. 1, 2. *fig* 1-24 *Tournay.*

DUSS, R. P. 1903, 1904 *See* STEPHANI, F. 1903, 1904.

EVANS, A. W. 1903. Hepaticae collected in southern Patagonia. 1896-1899. *In* SCOTT, W. B. *Reports of the Princeton University Expeditions to Patagonia, Botany* 8¹· 35-62. pl 4-6

—— ——. 1933. Some representative species of *Bazzania* from Sumatra. *Papers of the Michigan Acad of Sci. Arts and Letters* 17· 69-118. 6 pl.

—— —— 1934 A revision of the genus *Acromastigum.* *Annales Bryologica,* Supplement 3. i-viii, 1-178 fig. 1-40

FULFORD, M. 1936 The genus *Bazzania* in the United States and Canada. *American Midland Naturalist* 17: 385-424. 12 fig.

GOTTSCHE, C. M. 1863 De Mexikanske Levermooser 1-284 20 pl. *Copenhagen.*

—— ——. 1864 Hepaticae *In* TRIANA, J. et PLANCHON, J. E. Prodromus Florae Novo-Granatensis *Annales des Sciences Naturelles, Botanique* V, 1: 95-198 pl. 17-20.

GOTTSCHE, C M., LINDENBERG, J. B. G. & NEES AB ESENBECK, C. G. 1844-1847. Synopsis Hepaticarum i-xxvi, 1-834. *Hamburg.*

GRAY, S. F. 1821 A Natural Arrangement of British Plants 1: i-xxviii, 1-824. pl 1-21 *London.*

HAMPE, E 1847. Bericht uber die Hepaticae, welche Hr. MORITZ in Columbien sammelte und dem koniglichen Herbarium in Schoneberg uberlieferte, nach der *Synopsis Hepaticarum* und den MORITZschen Nummern aufgeführt. *Linnaea* 20: 321-336.

—— ——. 1851 Hepaticae Oerstedianae. *Linnaea* 24. 300-304, 640-641.

HAMPE, E and GOTTSCHE, C. M. 1852. Expositio Hepaticarum Portoricensium, quas collegit SCHWANECKE *Linnaea* 25: 337-358.

HERZOG, TH. 1926. Geographie der Moose. i-xi, 1-439. 151 fig. 8 pl. *Jena.*

—— —— 1938. Hepaticae Standleyanae Costaricenses et Hondurenses. *Revue Bryologique et Lichénologique* 11· 5-30. fig. 1-6.

HOOKER, J. D. 1867. Handbook of the New Zealand Flora. Hepaticae. p. 497-549 *London.*

HUSNOT, T. 1875. Catalogue des Muscinées récoltées aux Antilles françaises par T. HUSNOT. *Rev. Bryologique* 2: 1-5.

JACK, J. B. and STEPHANI, F. 1892. Hepaticae Wallisianae. *Hedwigia* 31: 11-27. pl. 1-4.

LEHMANN, J G C. 1829. Hepaticarum Capensium a C. F. ECKLON collectarum Brevem Recensionem cum schlechtendalio suo communicavit J. G. C. LEHMANN. *Linnaea* 4: 357-371.

LINDENBERG, J. B. G. and GOTTSCHE, C. M. 1851. Species Hepaticarum. *Mastigobryum.* i-xii, 1-118. pl. 1-22. *Bonn.*

LUNAN, J. 1814. Hortus Jamaicensis. 1: i-viii. 1-538. *Jamaica.*

MARTIUS, C. F. PH. VON. 1833. See NEES AB ESENBECK.

MITTEN, W. 1855. Hepaticae. *In* HOOKER, J. D. Botany Antarctic Voyage 2³ Flora of New Zealand. p. 125-172. pl. 94-104. *London.*

——. 1861. Hepaticae Indiae Orientalis· an Enumeration of the Hepaticae of the East Indies. *Journal of the Linnean Society, Botany.* 5: 89-128.

MONTAGNE, C. 1838. Centurie de plantes cellulaires exotiques nouvelles, Hepaticae. *Annales des Sciences Naturelles, Botanique* II, 9: 37-49.

——. 1839. Hepaticae. Florulae Boliviensis, *in* D'ORBIGNY, Voyage dans l'Amérique Méridionale 7³: 49-86. pl. 1-2. *Paris.*

—— —— 1840. Plantes cellulaires exotiques nouvelles, Hepaticae. *Annales des Sciences Naturelles, Botanique* II, 14: 332-337.

——. 1843. Plantes cellulaires exotiques nouvelles, Hepaticae, *Annales des Sciences Naturelles, Botanique* II, 19: 243-266.

—— ——. 1844-1846. Hepaticae. *In Gaudichaud-Beaupré,* C. Voyage autour du Monde . . . La Bonite, Botanique p. 205-266.

—— ——. 1855 Cryptogamia Guyanensis, Hepaticae. *Annales des Sciences Naturelles, Botanique* IV, 3· 313-320.

—— —— 1856. Sylloge generum specierumque plantarum cryptogamarum. I-XXIV, 1-498 *Paris.*

—— ——. 1856 Plantes cellulaires Nouvelles VII. Plantae Weddellianae, Hepaticae. *Annales des Sciences Naturelles, Botanique* IV, 5: 348-374.

NEES AB ESENBECK, C G 1830 Hepaticae Javanicae. Enumeratio Plantarum cryptogamicarum Javae et Insularum Adjacentium. i-viii, 1-86. *Breslau.*

—— —— 1831. Berichtigungen zur Enumeratio plantarum cryptogamicarum Javae *Linnaea* 6. 602-623.

—— ——. 1833a. Naturgeschichte europaischen Lebermoose 1: i-lxxii 1-539. *Berlin*

—— —— 1833b Hepaticae. *In* MARTIUS, C F. PH. VON, Flora Brasiliensis. 1. 294-390 *Stuttgart* and *Tubingen.*

PAGÁN, F M. 1939. A preliminary list of the Hepaticae of Puerto Rico including Vieques and Mona Island. *Bryologist* 42· 1-12; 37-50; 71-82

PEARSON, W. H. 1931. Notes on a collection of Hepaticae from Jamaica. (Posthumous paper) *Annales Bryologici* 4: 95-112. pl. 1-2.

SCHIFFNER, V 1893. Lebermoose *In* ENGLER-PRANTL, Die Natürlichen Pflanzenfamilien 1¹: 3-141. fig. 1-73. *Leipzig.*

SCHWAEGRICHEN, C. F. 1814. Historiae Muscorum Hepaticorum Prodromus. 1-39. 1 pl. *Leipzig.*

SPRENGEL, C. 1827 C. LINNAEI, Systema Vegetabilium 4¹. 1-592. *Gottingen.*

SPRUCE, R 1885. Hepaticae Amazonicae et Andinae *Transactions and Proceedings of the Botanical Society [Edinburgh]* 15: i-xi, 1-588. pl. 1-22.

—— 1890. Hepaticae Bolivianae. *Memoirs Torrey Botanical Club* 1: 113-140.

—— ——. 1895 Hepaticae Elliottianae, insulis Antillanis St. Vincentii et Dominica a clar W. R. ELLIOTT, annis 1891-92, lectae, RICARDO SPRUCE determinatae. *Journal of the Linnean Society* 30: 331-372. pl. 20-30.

STEPHANI, FR. 1885. Hepaticarum species novae vel minus cognitae, III-IV. *Hedwigia* 24: 214-218. pl. 1, 2; 246-250. pl. 1-3

—— ——. 1886 Hepaticarum species novae vel minus cognitae, V-VIII. *Hedwigia* 25: 5-9. pl 2-4; 133-134 pl. 3-6; 202-208. pl. 1-3; 233-249. pl 1-2.

—— ——. 1888a. Westindische Hepaticae. I, Hepaticae portoricenses. *Hedwigia* 27: 276-299. pl. 11-14.

—— ——. 1888*b*. Westindische Hepaticae. II, Hepaticae ex insulis St. Domingo et Dominica, quas collegit EGGERS. *Hedwigia* 27. 299-302. pl. 11-14

—— —— 1894. Hepaticae. *In* LEHMANN, F. Cryptogamae Centrali-Americanae in Guatemala, Costa Rica, Colombia and Ecuador. *Bull. Herb Boissier* 2· 402-403.

——————. 1900. Beiträge zur Lebermoos-Flora Westpatagoniens und des Sudlichen Chile. *Bihang K. Svenska Vetensk. Akad. Handl.* 26 (6) : 1-69

—— ——. 1901. Lebermoose der Magellanslander. *Bihang K. Svenska Vetensk. Akad. Handl.* 26 (17) : 1-36.

—— ——. 1901-05. Hepaticae. In Report of two Botanical Collections made by Messrs. F. V. McCONNELL and J. J. QUELCH at Mount Roraima in British Guiana. *Trans. Linnean Society, Botany* II. 6: 93-100

—— ——. 1903. Hepaticae. *In* DUSS, Muscinées des Antilles françaises. 1-41. *Lons-le Saunier*. (Published also in 1904 with lichen section, supplement, and index added, as Flore cryptogamique des Antilles françaises, Hepaticae p. 131-167.)

—— ——. 1905. Hepaticae amazonicae ab ERNESTO ULE collectae *Hedwigia* 44: 223-229.

—— ——. 1908-09. Species Hepaticarum *Mastigobryum* 3 413-540. Pages 413-522 were reprinted from the *Bull. Herb. Boissier* II, 8 681-696, 745-776, 837-866, 941-972 1908.

—— ——. 1911 Die Lebermoose. *In* SKOTTSBERG, Botanische Ergebnisse der Schwedischen Expedition nach Patagonien und dem Feuerlande 1907-1909. *Svenska Vetensk. Akad. Handl.* 46, no 9.

—— —— 1916 Hepaticae. *In* HERZOG TH Die Bryophyten meiner zweiten Reise durch Bolivia, II *Bibliotheca Botanica* 87²: 169-347 fig 82-234

—— ——. 1924. Species Hepaticarum. *Mastigobryum.* 6· 452-489

—— ——. Icones Hepaticarum *Mastigobryum* Nos. 1-465. Unpublished drawings made by FR STEPHANI, recently several sets of tracings of these have been made and distributed by MISS JOHANNA STEPHANI of Leipzig

SWARTZ, O. 1806. Flora Indiae occidentalis. Hepaticae. 3: 1842-1885 *Erlangen.*

TAYLOR, TH 1846. New Hepaticae *London Journal of Botany* 5. 258-284; 365-417

WALLROTH, C F. G 1831 Flora Cryptogamica Germaniae. Pars Prior. i-xxvi, 1-654 *Nürnberg.*

WEBER, FR. 1815. Historiae Muscorum hepaticorum prodromus 1-160 *Kiel.*

WEBER, FR. und MOHR, D. M. H. 1807 Handbuch der Einleitung in das studium der kryptogamischen Gewachse. i-xlvi, 1-509. 12 pl. *Kiel.*

INDEX

Synonyms are listed in italics, descriptions of the species in bold face type, and figures in italics.